Praise for the authors' other bestselling books

QuarkXPress Visual QuickStart Guide:

"Elaine Weinmann's book is truly visual! Every page is filled with QuarkXPress screen shots combined with precise, step-by-step instructions for how to perform specific tasks in QuarkXPress. The documentation for QuarkXPress is comprehensive, as it must be. The *Visual QuickStart* complements the documentation as an ideal desktop reference for new users — when you want to brush up on a specific skill, you can quickly turn to the appropriate page, walk through the steps, and accomplish your goal."

Becky Reed Petersen
Training Manager
Quark Inc.

"The terse, 1-2-3 instructions are to-the-point. No foot-dragging here."

Computer Book Review

"The text is direct and concise, and the book is organized as a reference volume so readers can go straight to the task at hand."

Art & Design News

"...shows rather than tells how to use the page layout software. Text supports the illustrations and moves the reader from one illustration to the next. The book is well-designed, with thumb tabs at the outer edges listing chapter heads and subheads."

Communications Manager

"This comprehensive 'how-to' on QuarkXPress serves as a great learning tool to this popular, but somewhat difficult, program. Since QuarkXPress is becoming the program of choice for many DTP users, this handy guide should prove to be an essential guide for Macintosh artists."

Carl Calvert
MacArtist

"This book's method of teaching you is so simple, it eliminates the fear factor.... I especially enjoyed the look of the *Visual QuickStart Guide QuarkXPress 3.1* because of the variety of the visual examples.... For the beginning Quark user, I recommend buying this book. It will ease you into Quark, giving you the basics you need to function in the program."

Kathleen Blavatt
Macintouch

Photoshop Visual QuickStart Guide:

"Excellent — a way to learn all the basics of Photoshop without freaking out. Elaine Weinmann and Peter Lourekas' *Photoshop 2.5 for Macintosh: Visual QuickStart Guide* is what every Photoshop beginner wants: step-by-step explanation and illustration of how to do things in Photoshop. Think of it as 'Intro to Photoshop' in a box."

Design Tools Monthly

"*Visual QuickStart Guide: Photoshop 2.5 for the Macintosh* is a great choice for someone just starting out with Photoshop. In under 250 pages, it covers all of Photoshop's fundamental techniques. The book is heavy on illustrations and diagrams, and each technique is covered in a straightforward 1-2-3 manner."

Mac Monitor
Savannah Macintosh Users Group

"This book provides a no-nonsense, step-by-step guide to get readers up and running in hours rather than days....The *Visual QuickStart* format allows you to pick up new skills without wading through endless pages of text....With a heavy emphasis on graphics, the book includes hundreds of tips to steer beginners out of harm's way."

It's News 2 Me

"The authors describe each command's function clearly and simply, and pictures accompany throughout to help you understand effects achieved. If you've been asked to start using Photoshop right now, this book may be your best bet for getting something done fast."

Washington Apple Pi

VISUAL QUICKSTART GUIDE

Illustrator 5.5

FOR MACINTOSH

Elaine Weinmann
Peter Lourekas

 **Peachpit Press**

Visual QuickStart Guide
Illustrator 5.0/5.5 for Macintosh
Elaine Weinmann and Peter Lourekas

Copyright © 1995 by Elaine Weinmann and Peter Lourekas

Peachpit Press
2414 Sixth Street
Berkeley, CA 94710
510/548-4393
510/548-5991 (fax)

Peachpit Press is a division of Addison-Wesley Publishing Company.

Cover design: The Visual Group
Interior design and production: Elaine Weinmann and Peter Lourekas
Illustrations: Elaine Weinmann and Peter Lourekas, except as noted in the text

ISBN 1-56609-160-8

9 8 7 6 5 4

Printed and bound in the United States of America

This book is dedicated to

Martine

and

Danielle

Special Thanks

to

Ted Nace and all the Peachpitters —
always a pleasure to work with.

and

Miriam Schaer, New York City artist
and designer, for her illustrations on
pages 79, 203, and the *Teacup* on
this page.

and

Peter Fahrni, New York City designer, for his illustrations on pages 73,
104, 128 and 143, and for contribut-
ing the content and illustrations on
manual tracing, pages 77-78.

and

LinoGraphics Corporation, for their
output services.

Table of Contents

Table of Contents

Table of Contents

Table of Contents

Table of Contents

APPLE & PEAR

the button company

WORST WINTER IN MEMORY

NORTH AMERICAN
T S
TERRASYSTEMS
TRAIL & SITE

Gratuitous Violence Productions

NEW YORK HARBOR

THE BASICS

W E WERE DELIGHTED to have the opportunity to write a book about Adobe Illustrator because it's such a well-designed program. Illustrator has a complete set of tools for creating many different kinds of drawings, from corporate logos, symbols and labels to children's book illustrations. It has power, precision, loads of features, and a well-designed interface. It is sophisticated, yet easy to use.

Using this book, you will learn how to create, select, modify, and arrange objects. You will learn how to draw objects "from scratch" or create standard geometric objects and then reshape them. You can reshape objects "by hand" or by using commands and dialog boxes. With Illustrator you can Fill or Stroke objects with flat colors, gradients, or patterns. You can create and style type, or you can create your own letterforms by converting type into outlines and then reshaping the outlines. You can create simple illustrations or you can use features like masks, compounds, or filters to create complex illustrations composed of multiple shapes on multiple layers. Once your illustration is completed, you can print it or color separate it.

This book contains hundreds of screen captures of program features. We also created hundreds of our own illustrations to illuminate key concepts and to entertain you. We've even thrown in a few tutorial-type exercises to help you practice using various features. As in our other *QuickStart Guides*, the absolute, read-me-first essentials are concentrated in the early chapters. The later chapters are like a smorgasbord that you can sample in an orderly or haphazard fashion — as you wish.

If you are new to Illustrator, you'll quickly see that its features are extensive. It's not difficult to make simple drawings, though. Some of the newest features, like the filters and palettes, are actually very easy to use. We hope you have fun using this book. ■

Introduction

The Illustrator screen

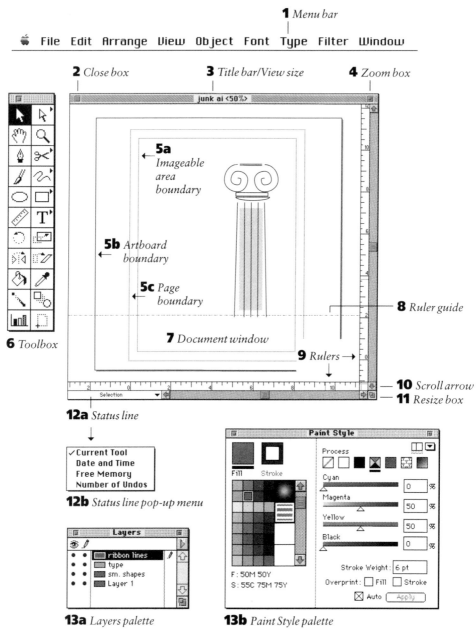

1 *Menu bar*

É File Edit Arrange View Object Font Type Filter Window

2 *Close box*   **3** *Title bar/View size*   **4** *Zoom box*

junk ai <50%>

5a
*Imageable
area
boundary*

5b *Artboard
boundary*

5c *Page
boundary*

8 *Ruler guide*

7 *Document window*

9 *Rulers* →

6 *Toolbox*

10 *Scroll arrow*
11 *Resize box*

Selection

12a *Status line*

✓ Current Tool
Date and Time
Free Memory
Number of Undos

12b *Status line pop-up menu*

Layers
ribbon lines
type
sm. shapes
Layer 1

13a *Layers palette*

Paint Style

Fill   Stroke

Process
Cyan   0 %
Magenta   50 %
Yellow   50 %
Black   0 %

F : 50M 50Y
S : 55C 75M 75Y

Stroke Weight : 6 pt
Overprint : ☐ Fill ☐ Stroke
☒ Auto (Apply)

13b *Paint Style palette*

Figure 1.

Key to the Illustrator screen

1 *Menu bar*
Press any menu heading to access dialog boxes, submenus, and commands.

2 *Close box*
To close a window or a palette, click its close box.

3 *Title bar/View size*
Displays the illustration's title and view size.

4 *Zoom box*
Click a document window zoom box to enlarge the window or shrink it to its previous size. Click a palette zoom box to shrink the palette or restore it to its previous size.

5a,b,c *Imageable area, Artboard, and Page boundaries*
The Imageable area — within the margin guides — is the area that will print on the currently selected printer paper size. The Artboard is the user-defined work area and the largest possible printable area. The non-printing Page boundary corresponds to the paper size for the currently selected printer.

6 *Toolbox*
The Toolbox contains 30 drawing and editing tools.

7 *Document window*
The illustration window.

8 *Ruler guide*
A non-printing guide used for aligning objects. Press and drag from either ruler to create a guide.

9 *Rulers*
The current position of the pointer is indicated by a mark on the horizontal and vertical rulers. Ruler and dialog box increments can be displayed in a choice of three units of measure.

10 *Scroll arrow*
Click the down arrow to move the illustration upward in the document window. Click the up arrow to move the illustration downward.

11 *Resize box*
To resize a window, press and drag its resize box diagonally.

12a,b *Status line*
Displays the name of the currently selected tool, the current Date & Time from the Macintosh Control Panel, the amount of Free Memory (RAM) available for the currently open file, or the Number of Undos/Redos available, depending on which category you select from the pop-up menu.

Hold down Option and press on the Status line pop-up menu to choose special information options (**try it!**).

13a,b *Palettes*
Two of six moveable palettes that open from the Window menu. The other palettes are Info, Character, Paragraph, and Gradient.

THE TOOLBOX

The Toolbox contains 30 tools used for object creation and modification. Click once on a tool to select it. Double-clicking some tools will open an Options dialog box. Press on a tool with an arrowhead to choose a related tool from a fly-out menu. Press and drag the top bar to move the Toolbox.

Toolbox

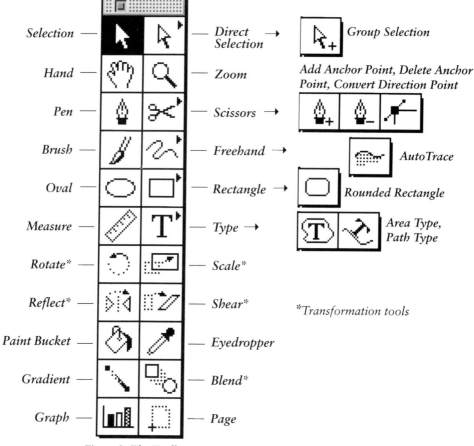

Figure 2. *The Toolbox.*

POINTER ICONS

The pointer matches the icon on the Toolbox when most tools are used. In addition, you will also see these other icons. Press Caps Lock to turn all pointers into a crosshair for precise editing.

| *Press and drag* | *Snap to point or guide* | *Drag copy* | *Close path* | *Convert Direction Point tool* | *Transform tool with Option key down* |

HOW TO USE THE MOUSE

The mouse is used in three basic ways.

Click ➤ Press and release the mouse button quickly.

Use to: Choose a tool; choose a color name, layer name, or other palette option; turn a check box or button on or off in a dialog box; close a window or a palette; select or deselect an object, path, segment, anchor point, or direction line; or create an anchor point.

Double-click ➤➤ Press and release the mouse button twice in quick succession.

Use to: Launch Illustrator, open or place a file, open a tool dialog box, or highlight an entry field.

Press and drag ⋯➤ Press and hold down the mouse button, move the mouse on the mousepad, then release the mouse button. Press and drag when you read the instruction "drag" or "move."

Use to: Choose from a menu, pop-up menu, or submenu; draw, resize, reshape, or move an object; or move a dialog box, palette, or window.

Pointer Icons; the Mouse

Mini-Glossary (sidebar)

MINI-GLOSSARY

Object   Any individual shape created in Illustrator.

Path   The edge of an object that is defined by anchor points, segments, and direction lines. These elements can be modified to reshape the object. A path can be open or closed.

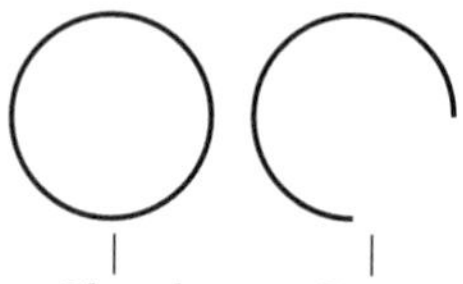

◆

Anchor Point   A corner point or a curve (smooth) point that joins two segments of a path.

Curve Segment   The segment between two curve anchor points or a corner point and a curve anchor point.

Straight Segment   The segment between two corner points.

Direction Line   The control handle that defines the shape of a curved path segment. Rotate, lengthen, or shorten a direction line to reshape a segment.

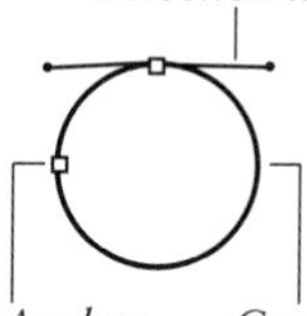

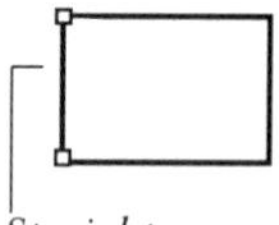

◆

Select   Click on an object or group with the Selection or Group Selection tool to select the whole object or group. All anchor points and segments will be highlighted.

Direct Select   Click on an anchor point or segment with the Direct Selection tool to select only that anchor point or segment.

Objects

Closed path   *Open path*

Direction line

Anchor point   *Curve segment*

Straight segment

Selected object

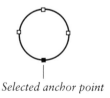

Selected anchor point

MINI-GLOSSARY

Stroke The color applied to the edge (path) of an object.

Fill A color, pattern or gradient applied to the inside of an object.

Stroke

Gradient Fill A graduated blend between two or more colors. A Gradient Fill can be linear (side to side) or radial (radiating outward from a center point of your choice).

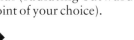

Linear   Radial

◆

Stack The positioning of objects on top of one another within a layer. The most recently created object is placed at the top of the stack.

Layer The positioning of a stack of objects relative to other stacks. An illustration can contain multiple layers, which can be reordered.

◆

Compound Path Two or more objects that are combined into a larger, single object. Areas where the original objects overlapped become transparent.

Compound Path

Mask An object that trims ("clips") away other objects that extend beyond its border. Only parts of objects that are within the confines of the mask object will show.

Group Individual objects that are combined so they can be moved or modified as a unit. When objects are grouped, they are moved to the layer of the topmost object.

Mask

UNITS OF MEASURE

You can enter numbers in dialog boxes or on palettes in any unit of measure used in Illustrator. You can choose a default unit of measure for the application *(see page 201)* or for a particular document *(see page 194)*. If you enter a number in a unit of measure other than the default unit, the number will be translated into the default unit.

SYMBOLS YOU CAN USE

UNIT	SYMBOL
Picas	**p**
Points	**pt**
Inches	**"** *or* **in**
Centimeters	**cm**

INSTRUCTION TERMS

Check/Uncheck Click a check box to turn an option on or off. An x in a box indicates that option is turned on.

Choose Click on a tool or highlight a tool on a tool fly-out menu; highlight a menu, pop-up menu, or submenu entry; or pick a color or other palette or dialog box option.

Enter Highlight an entry field (referred to as "field") in a dialog box or on a palette and replace with a new number. Press Tab to highlight the next field in succession. Press Shift-Tab to highlight the previous field.

Move Press and drag an object or a triangle slider on the Paint Style or Gradient palette.

Press Quickly press and release a key on the keyboard, usually as part of a keyboard shortcut.

Select Click on an object, path, anchor point, or segment, so it can be modified.

MENUS

Each menu heading provides access to related commands for modifying objects. The nine Illustrator menus are displayed on the following pages.

To choose from a menu, press and drag downward through the menu or to the right and downward through the submenu, then release the mouse when the desired entry is highlighted.

Keyboard equivalents are listed next to some menu entries.

Choose a menu entry that is followed by an ellipsis (...) to open a dialog box or a palette.

A line separates entry categories.

Press on a menu item with an arrowhead to open a submenu. To choose an entry, keep the mouse button held down and drag through the submenu, then release the mouse when the desired entry is highlighted.

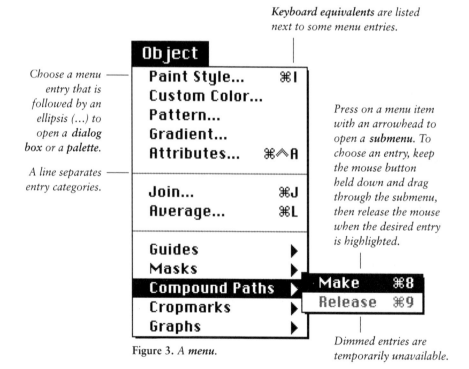

Figure 3. *A menu.*

Dimmed entries are temporarily unavailable.

File and Edit Menus

The File menu.

File menu commands are used to create, open, close, save, or print an illustration, import art from another application or paint styles from another document, choose document or printer specifications, set defaults and quit Illustrator.

The Edit menu.

Edit menu commands include Undo and Redo, the Clipboard commands Cut and Copy, and Paste, the Select commands, and the Paste In Front/Paste In Back commands, which place the Clipboard contents in front of or behind the currently selected object.

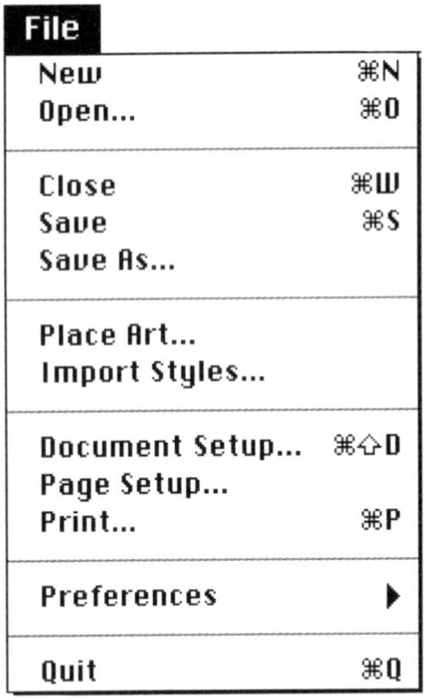

File	
New	⌘N
Open...	⌘O
Close	⌘W
Save	⌘S
Save As...	
Place Art...	
Import Styles...	
Document Setup...	⌘⇧D
Page Setup...	
Print...	⌘P
Preferences	▶
Quit	⌘Q

Figure 4. *The File menu.*

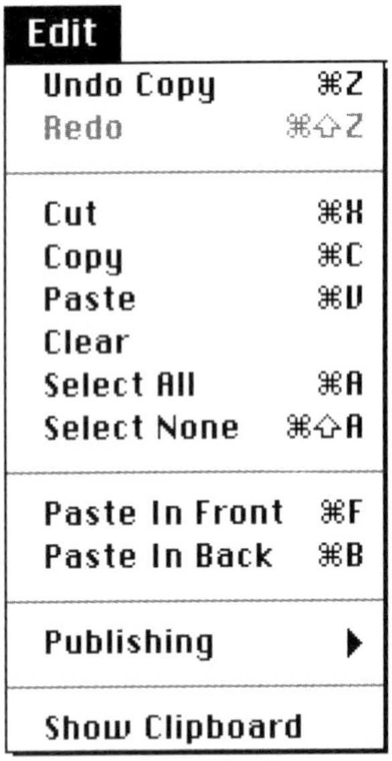

Edit	
Undo Copy	⌘Z
Redo	⌘⇧Z
Cut	⌘H
Copy	⌘C
Paste	⌘U
Clear	
Select All	⌘A
Select None	⌘⇧A
Paste In Front	⌘F
Paste In Back	⌘B
Publishing	▶
Show Clipboard	

Figure 5. *The Edit menu.*

The Arrange menu.

Arrange menu commands are used to move an object or objects, reposition an object within its stack, and group, lock, or hide objects. The Repeat Transform command repeats the last modification made with any Transformation tool.

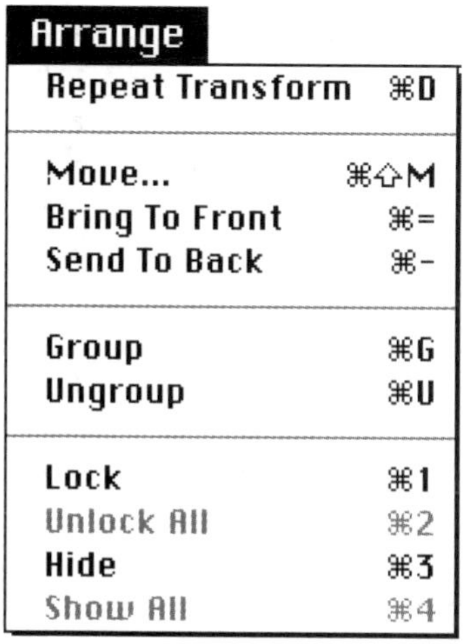

The View menu.

View menu commands affect document display. You can choose the full-color Preview view or "wireframe" Artwork view, show or hide Rulers, Tiling, Edges, and Guides, enlarge or reduce the view size, and create and choose custom view settings via the View menu.

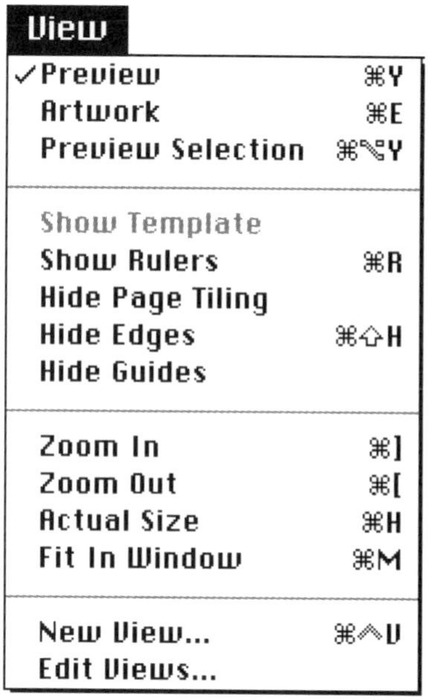

Arrange	
Repeat Transform	⌘D
Move...	⌘⇧M
Bring To Front	⌘=
Send To Back	⌘-
Group	⌘G
Ungroup	⌘U
Lock	⌘1
Unlock All	⌘2
Hide	⌘3
Show All	⌘4

Figure 6. *The Arrange menu.*

View	
✓Preview	⌘Y
Artwork	⌘E
Preview Selection	⌘⌥Y
Show Template	
Show Rulers	⌘R
Hide Page Tiling	
Hide Edges	⌘⇧H
Hide Guides	
Zoom In	⌘]
Zoom Out	⌘[
Actual Size	⌘H
Fit In Window	⌘M
New View...	⌘⌃V
Edit Views...	

Figure 7. *The View menu.*

Arrange and View Menus

Object and Font Menus

The Object menu.

Object menu commands are used to Fill and Stroke objects, Join line segments, turn objects into Guides, and create Cropmarks and Graphs. Masks and Compound Paths are special Illustrator features for merging objects.

The Font menu.

Use the Font menu to choose from fonts that are currently installed and available in your System. If Adobe Type Reunion is installed (as in this illustration), fonts are organized in families, and various weights and fonts within those families are chosen from submenus (designated by arrowheads).

Object

Paint Style...	⌘I
Custom Color...	
Pattern...	
Gradient...	
Attributes...	⌘⌥A
Join...	⌘J
Average...	⌘L
Guides	▶
Masks	▶
Compound Paths	▶
Cropmarks	▶
Graphs	▶

Figure 8. *The Object menu.*

Font

AGaramond	▶
AGaramond Alternate	▶
AGaramond Expert	▶
American Typewriter	▶
Arcadia	▶
Avant Garde	▶
Banco	
Bank Gothic BT	▶
Bauer Bodoni	▶
Bernhard	▶
Bernhard Fashion ICG	
Birch	
Blackoak	
Bodoni	▶
Bookman	▶
Brush Script	
BSymbol	▶

Figure 9. *The Font menu.*

The Type menu.

Type menu commands are used to apply character and paragraph specifications and to link type blocks. The Create Outlines command converts type characters into objects.

Type

Size	▶
Leading	▶
Alignment	▶
Tracking...	⌘⇧K
Spacing...	⌘⇧O
Character...	⌘T
Paragraph...	⌘⇧T
Link Blocks	⌘⇧G
Unlink Blocks	⌘⇧U
Make Wrap	
Release Wrap	
Fit Headline	
Create Outlines	

Figure 10. *The Type menu.*

The Filter menu.

Filters, chosen from submenus, recolor, create, distort, reposition, combine, select, and stylize objects.

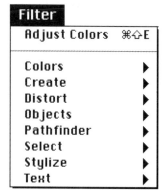

Filter

Adjust Colors	⌘⇧E
Colors	▶
Create	▶
Distort	▶
Objects	▶
Pathfinder	▶
Select	▶
Stylize	▶
Text	▶

Figure 11. *The Filter menu.*

The Window menu.

Window menu commands create new illustration windows, hide and show the Toolbox and palettes, and activate open illustrations.

Window

New Window	
Hide Toolbox	⌘⌃T
Hide Layers	⌘⌃L
Show Info	⌘⌃I
Hide Paint Style	
Show Gradient	
Hide Character	
Show Paragraph	
✓ junk ai <50%>	

Figure 12. *The Window menu.*

Type, Filter, and Window Menus

DIALOG BOXES

Dialog boxes are like fill-in forms with multiple choices. The various ways to indicate choices are shown in Figure 13.

To open a dialog box, select any menu item followed by an ellipsis (...) or use a keyboard shortcut.

Some modifications are made by entering numbers in entry fields. Press **Tab** to highlight the next field in a dialog box. Hold down **Shift** and press **Tab** to highlight the previous field.

Click **OK** or press **Return** to accept modifications and exit a dialog box.

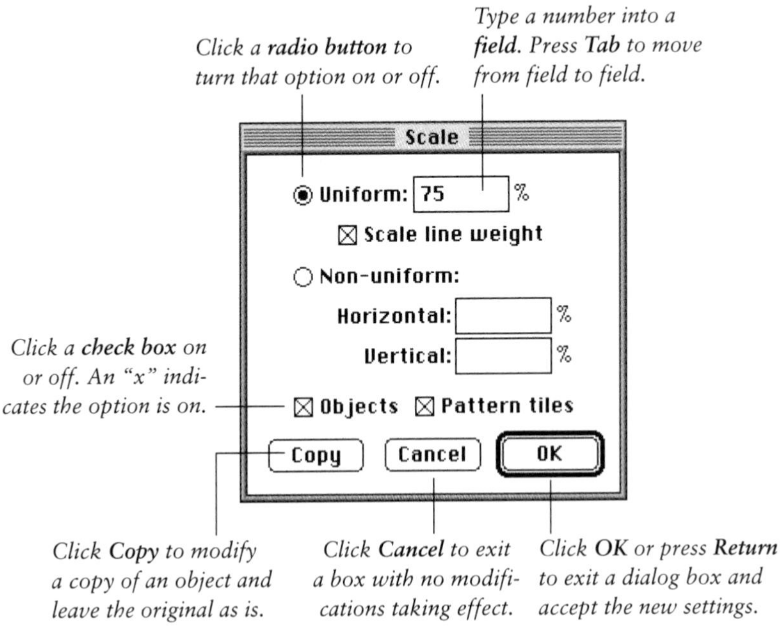

*Click a **radio button** to turn that option on or off.*

*Type a number into a field. Press **Tab** to move from field to field.*

Scale

◉ Uniform: `75` %
⊠ Scale line weight
◯ Non-uniform:
Horizontal: `    ` %
Vertical: `    ` %

⊠ Objects ⊠ Pattern tiles

[Copy] [Cancel] [**OK**]

*Click a **check box** on or off. An "x" indicates the option is on.*

*Click **Copy** to modify a copy of an object and leave the original as is.*

*Click **Cancel** to exit a box with no modifications taking effect.*

*Click **OK** or press **Return** to exit a dialog box and accept the new settings.*

Figure 13. *A dialog box.*

The Six Illustrator Palettes

(pages 15-18)

THE PAINT STYLE PALETTE

The Paint Style palette is used to mix and apply Fill and Stroke colors to objects. The palette is divided into three panels: paint swatch window *(left)*, color selection method icons and color mixing options *(right)*, and Stroke attributes *(bottom)*.

Color selection method icons.

None   Black   Custom   Gradient

White   Process   Pattern

LEFT PANEL

Fill and Stroke boxes. The currently highlighted box is underlined.

Paint swatches.

Fill and Stroke name or breakdown.

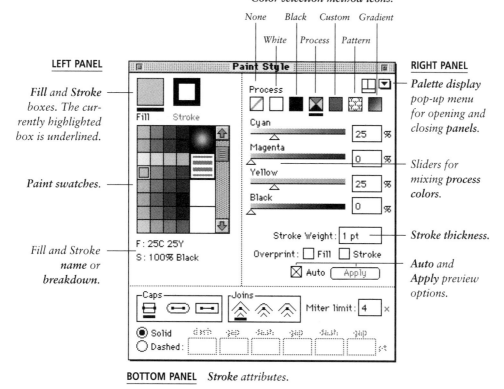

RIGHT PANEL

Palette display pop-up menu for opening and closing panels.

Sliders for mixing process colors.

Stroke thickness.

Auto and Apply preview options.

BOTTOM PANEL   *Stroke attributes.*

Figure 14. *The Paint Style palette.*

THE GRADIENT PALETTE

The Gradient palette is used to create and save Gradient Fills with two or more colors that are mixed or selected right on the palette. The currently highlighted gradient is displayed in the color bar.

*Click the **palette display lever** to open or close the bottom panel.*

Color bar.   *Midpoint diamond.*

UPPER PANEL

Starting color triangle.

Color selection method icons.

LOWER PANEL

*Sliders for mixing **process** colors.*

Ending color triangle.

Gradient Fill scroll list.

Name field.

Linear and Radial Fill buttons.

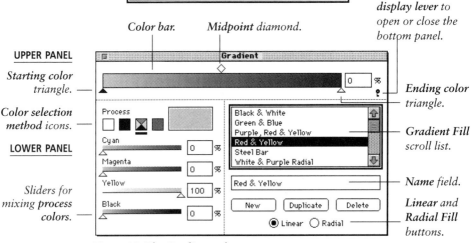

Figure 15. *The **Gradient** palette.*

THE CHARACTER PALETTE

The Character palette is used to apply type attributes: Font, Size, Leading, Baseline Shift, Horizontal Scale, Tracking, and Kerning. Press Return to apply specifications.

Font field.   *Weight or style field.*

UPPER PANEL

Size and Leading pop-up menus.

LOWER PANEL

Font pop-up menu.

Palette display lever to open or close the bottom panel.

*Check box to apply a font's **Auto kerning** settings.*

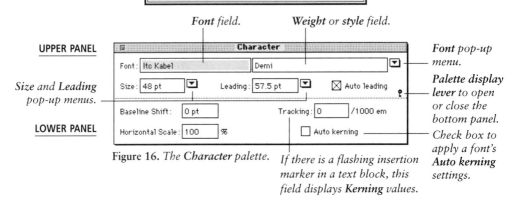

Figure 16. *The **Character** palette.*

*If there is a flashing insertion marker in a text block, this field displays **Kerning** values.*

THE PARAGRAPH PALETTE

The Paragraph palette is used to apply Horizontal Alignment, Indentation, Leading before, Hyphenation, Word spacing and Letter spacing values. Press Return to apply specifications.

Horizontal Alignment icons.

Left Center Right Justify Justify Last line

UPPER PANEL

Indentation.

Leading (space) before paragraphs.

Palette display lever.

LOWER PANEL

Hyphenation.

Spacing between words in non-justified paragraphs. 100% uses the default (built-in) word spacing for a font. The other options are available for justified paragraphs.

Spacing between characters (letters) in non-justified paragraphs. 0% uses the default (built-in) character spacing for a font.

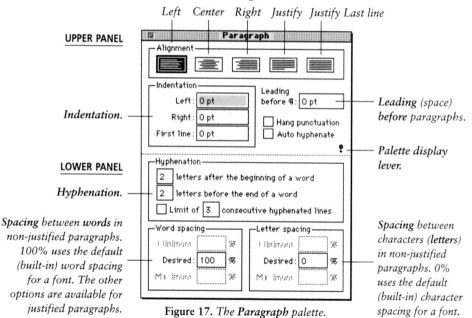

Figure 17. *The Paragraph palette.*

Paragraph Palette

THE LAYERS PALETTE

The Layers palette is used to add, delete, hide, show, and reorder layers in an illustration. You can also use this palette to control which layers are editable or move an object to a different layer.

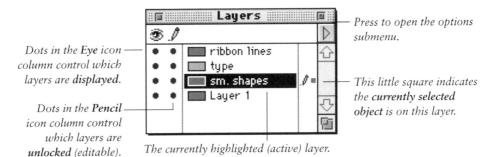

Press to open the options submenu.

*Dots in the **Eye** icon column control which layers are **displayed**.*

*Dots in the **Pencil** icon column control which layers are **unlocked** (editable).*

*This little square indicates the **currently selected object** is on this layer.*

The currently highlighted (active) layer.

Figure 18. *The Layers palette.*

THE INFO PALETTE

If no object is selected, the Info palette shows the horizontal and vertical position of the pointer on the illustration, as in Figure 19. If an object is selected, the palette displays the position of the object on the page and the width and height of the object. If a type tool and type are selected, the palette displays type specifications. The Info palette automatically opens when the Measure tool is used, and displays the distance and angle calculated by the tool.

*The **horizontal position** of the pointer.*

X: 2.194 in	W: 0 in	
Y: 5.972 in	H: 0 in	

*The **vertical position** of the pointer.*

Figure 19. *The Info palette.*

Layers and Info Palettes

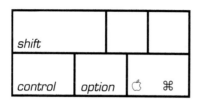

Figure 20. *The Shift, Command (⌘), and Option keys are situated on the left and right side of the keyboard, and are used in keyboard shortcuts.*

Keyboard shortcuts:

Some commands have keyboard equivalents. To perform a keyboard shortcut, hold down one or more keys, such as Command (⌘) and Shift, press and release a second key, then release the first key or combination of keys (**Figures 20-21**).

(Appendix A is a complete list of shortcuts. Some shortcuts are listed next to commands on the menus.)

To perform the Save command:

1. Hold down Command (⌘).

2. Press and release the "S" key.

3. Release Command (⌘).

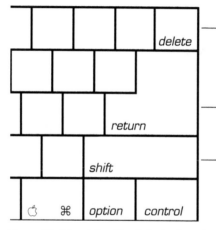

Figure 21. *The right side of the keyboard.*

Press **Delete** *to delete a selected object or path, or to delete characters to the left of the cursor in a dialog box or a type block.*

Press **Return** *to create a new paragraph of type, to apply palette specifications, or to exit a dialog box.*

Hold down **Shift** *to constrain the movement of an object, to contrain a line drawn with the Pen tool to a horizontal or a vertical axis, to create a perfect circle or square, or to add to a selection.*

The Keyboard

Other keys.

*Press **Tab** to highlight the next field in a dialog box or to create a line break within a type block.*

*Press **Del** to delete a character to the right of the flashing insertion marker in a type block or in an entry field.*

HARDWARE

Illustrator will run on a Macintosh II or Quadra with at least 3.1 megabytes of RAM (random access memory) available for the application, System 6.07 or later, and a hard disk. It will run fastest on a Quadra with at least 8 megabytes of RAM and System 7 or later, or on a PowerPC Macintosh with the PowerPC Illustrator edition.

To improve Illustrator's performance speed, the first step is to increase the processing speed of your CPU. An add-in accelerator board will speed up processing operations by increasing the computer's clock rate. Accelerator boards come with 25, 33, 40, or 50 Megahertz clock rates. For a Mac II you can purchase a "Quadra-style" 040 processor card, or upgrade a Quadra with a PowerPC logic board or PDS card to improve processing speed.

To access all the Filter commands and to handle the complex filter calculations, you should have a math co-processor in your Mac II or Quadra. If you purchase an add-in accelerator board, make sure a math co-processor is included. You may encounter a problem with certain filters if you run a non-PowerPC version of Illustrator in emulation mode on a PowerPC.

Illustrator files are usually small in storage size. However, illustrations that contain placed EPS scans will be significantly larger and you will need a large hard drive (200 Megabytes or more) to store them. You can purchase a removable storage device — such as a SyQuest or magnetic optical drive — to store files and transport large files to and from a service bureau.

Color monitors display 8-bit, 16-bit, or 24-bit color, depending on the amount of Video RAM or the video card installed. With 8-bit color, 256 colors are available for on-screen color mixing. With a 24-bit color card, 16.7 million colors are available. A 24-bit card provides optimal display, because every color can be represented exactly (and gradients will look better). On a 16" or larger monitor, you will have room to display your illustration in a workable size and also have several palettes open.

If you have the means to invest in a fast Macintosh, a large monitor, a large hard drive and adequate RAM, you will be able to work most efficiently.

DISK STORAGE

Disk Type	Capacity
Double density (DD) floppy	800KB
High density (HD) floppy	1.4MB
SyQuest removable	44MB, 88MB 105MB, 270MB
Hard drive	120MB, 230MB, 1GB...

FILE SIZE UNITS

Byte = 8 bits of digital information *(approx. one black or white pixel, or one character*

Kilobyte (KB) = 1,024 bytes

Megabyte (MB) = 1,024 kilobytes

Gigabyte (GB) = 1,024 megabytes

HOW ILLUSTRATOR WORKS

Illustrator is an object-oriented program

There are two main types of picture-making applications on the Macintosh: bitmapped and object-oriented. (The fancier terms "raster-based" and "vector-based" are sometimes also used.) It's important to know the strengths and weaknesses of bitmapped and object-oriented programs. Bitmapped programs are great for creating soft, painterly effects; object-oriented programs are great for creating sharp, smooth-edged layered images, such as logos and typographic designs.

In an **object-oriented** program like Adobe Illustrator, drawings are composed of separate, distinct objects that are positioned on **one or more layers**. Objects are drawn using free-style or precise drawing tools, and are mathematically defined. An illustrator object can be recolored, resized, and reshaped without affecting its sharpness or smoothness. It can be moved easily without affecting other objects. An object in an object-oriented drawing looks smooth and sharp regardless of the size at which it is displayed or printed.

Object-oriented files are usually relatively small in storage size, so you can save multiple versions of a file without filling up valuable hard drive space.

And object oriented drawings are **resolution independent**, which means that print quality is dependent only on the resolution of the printer. The higher the resolution, the sharper and finer the printout.

An image created in a **bitmapped** program, on the other hand, is composed of a single layer of dots, called pixels. If you "paint" on a bitmapped image, the existing layer of pixels is replaced by new ones. If you zoom in on a bitmapped image, you'll see a checkerboard of tiny squares.

Bitmapped files tend to be quite large, and the printout quality of a bitmapped image is dependent on the resolution of the image.

OBJECT-ORIENTED PROGRAMS

Adobe Illustrator

Aldus FreeHand

BITMAPPED PROGRAMS

Adobe Photoshop

Fractal Design Painter

Fractal Design Color Studio

Aldus SuperPaint

Illustrator objects

Illustrator drawings are composed of multiple, independent elements, called **objects**. Objects are composed of **anchor points** connected by **curved** or **straight segments**. The edge of an object is called its **path**. A path can be open (with two endpoints) or closed and continuous.

Some Illustrator tools produce complete, closed paths. Where and how many points are necessary to create an object is determined automatically. For example, the **Rectangle** tool produces various sized rectangles or squares, and the **Oval** tool produces various sized ovals or circles. There are also some **filters** that produce closed shapes. The **Brush** tool creates ribbon-like "brush stroke" shapes.

Other tools produce open or closed paths, such as the Freehand and Pen tools. The **Freehand** tool creates open or closed freeform lines. Using the **Pen** tool, you can create as many **corner** or **curve anchor points** as you need to form an object.

Illustrator type

Illustrator has many features for creating PostScript type. Type can be free floating, it can conform to the edge of an object, or it can fill the inside of an object. It can be repositioned, edited, restyled, and recolored. Or, you can convert type characters into graphic objects, called **outlines**. Type outlines can be reshaped or otherwise modified using any of Illustrator's drawing features.

Before an object can be modified...

An object must be selected before it can be modified. There are three selection tools: the **Selection** tool, the **Direct Selection** tool, and the **Group Selection** tool.

How objects are modified

Objects can be modified using a variety of features, including filters and other menu commands, dialog boxes, palettes, and tools.

An object's path can be reshaped by moving its anchor points or segments or by converting curve anchor points into corner anchor points (or vice versa). A curve segment can be reshaped by rotating, lengthening, or shortening its direction lines. Because a path can be reshaped easily, you can draw a simple shape first and then develop it into a more complicated form later on.

Some tools are specifically designed for modifying paths, such as the **Add Anchor Point** tool, which adds points to a path, the **Delete Anchor Point** tool, which deletes points from a path, the **Scissors** tool, which splits a path in two, and the **Convert Direction Point** tool, which converts points from corner to curved (or vice versa).

Spot colors, such as Pantone colors, and **process colors** and can be applied to any object. You can **Fill** the inside of an object or **Stroke** the edge of an object. A Fill can be a flat color, a graduated blend of several colors, called a **gradient**, or a **pattern** of repeating shapes.

Illustrator's **filters** modify objects in one or two easy steps. They randomly distort an object's shape, modify color, combine multiple, overlapping objects, divide areas where objects overlap into separate objects, or apply color to areas where objects overlap. The **Pathfinder** filters combine two or more objects into a new object.

Other modifications can be made using the **Transformation** tools. The **Scale** tool enlarges or reduces an object's size. The **Rotate** tool rotates an object. The **Reflect** tool creates a mirror image of an object. The **Shear** tool slants an object. The **Blend** tool transforms one object into another object by creating a series of transitional shapes.

Still other Illustrator commands combine individual objects into complex configurations. The **Compound Path** command, for example, "cuts" a hole through an object to reveal underlying shapes. Or you can use an object as a **mask** to hide parts of other objects that extend beyond its edges.

Working tools

You can change the **view size** of an illustration as you work to facilitate editing. You can **Zoom in** to work on a small detail or **Zoom out** to see how the drawing looks as a whole. Or you can move the illustration in the document window using the **Hand** tool.

An illustration can be displayed and edited in **Preview view**, in which colors are displayed. To speed up editing and screen redraw, you can display your illustration in **Artwork view**, in which objects are displayed as "wire frame" outlines. Or, you can selectively preview individual objects in **Preview Selection view.**

You can draw an illustration "by eye" or you can use any of Illustrator's precision tools to help you work more exactly: **rulers, guides,** the **Measure** tool, the **Move** dialog box, and the **Align Objects** filter.

The six movable palettes — **Paint Style, Gradient, Character, Paragraph, Layers,** and **Info** — are great time-saving features. Changes entered on a palette are immediately reflected in the illustration. You will probably find the Paint Style and Layers palettes to be particularly useful, and may want to leave them open while you work if your monitor is large enough. If you do a lot of typographic work, you'll also find the Character and Paragraph palettes indispensible.

When your illustration is finished

An Illustrator file can be **printed** on any PostScript output device. You can output an illustration on paper or film from Illustrator or you can produce **color separations** using the Adobe Separator utility. If you save your illustration with a preview, you can **import** it into another PostScript program, such as PageMaker or QuarkXPress. ■

• •

*I*N THIS CHAPTER you will learn how to launch Illustrator, create a new illustration with or without a template, define the working and printable areas of a document, open an existing illustration, place an EPS file from another application into Illustrator, save or close an illustration, and quit Illustrator.

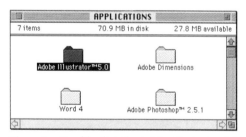

Figure 1a. *Double-click the Adobe Illustrator folder.*

Figure 1b. *Then double-click the Adobe Illustrator application icon.*

Figure 2. *Or double-click an Illustrator file icon.*

To launch Illustrator:

Double-click the Adobe Illustrator folder on the desktop (**Figure 1a**), then double-click the square Illustrator application icon (**Figure 1b**).
or
Double-click an Illustrator file icon (**Figure 2**).

Tip

■ If you launch Illustrator by clicking the application icon, a new untitled document window will appear automatically.

Launch Illustrator

A **template** is a background image that you can use to trace over. For example, you can scan a hand drawn sketch, save it in the MacPaint or PICT file format, open it as a template in Illustrator, and then trace over it with the Auto Trace tool or the Pen tool. You cannot select, preview, or print a template.
(The Auto Trace tool is discussed on page 76)

To create a new document without a template:

When you launch Illustrator, a new document window opens automatically. If Illustrator is already open and you want to create a new document, choose New from the File menu (**Figure 3**).

Figure 3. *Choose New from the* **File** *menu.*

To create a new document with a template:

1. With Option held down, choose New from the File menu (**Figure 3**).
2. Click on a MacPaint or PICT file to use as a template, then click Open (**Figure 4**).
   or
   Double-click the file name. A new document window will appear with a gray template shape in the center.

Tips

■ If you reopen the document, the template will reopen with it. To reopen the document without the template or with a new template, see the second tip on page 34.

■ If you change your mind and decide to open a new document without a template, click None.

■ Choose Hide Template from the View menu to hide the template. Choose Show Template from the View menu to display the template again.

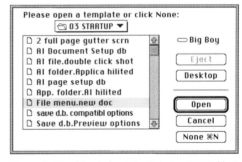

Figure 4. *Double-click a MacPaint or PICT file to use as a* **template***.*

File	
New	⌘N
Open...	⌘O
Close	⌘W
Save	⌘S
Save As...	
Place Art...	
Import Styles...	
Document Setup...	**⌘⇧D**
Page Setup...	
Print...	⌘P
Preferences	▶
Quit	⌘Q

Figure 5. *Choose* **Document Setup** *from the* **File** *menu.*

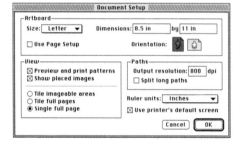

Figure 6. *In the* **Document Setup** *dialog box, choose a preset* **Artboard Size**, *or enter custom* **Dimensions**, *or check the* **Use Page Setup** *box to use the paper size currently selected in the Page Setup dialog box.*

In the center of every Illustrator document is a non-movable **Artboard** work area that represents the maximum printable size of the illustration. The default Artboard area is 8 ½ inches wide by 11 inches high. You can specify whether the Artboard will contain one printable page or facing printable pages. Or you can tile (subdivide) an oversized illustration into a grid so it can be printed in sections on standard size paper. The size of the printable page is specified in the Page Setup dialog box.

To change the Artboard dimensions:

1. Choose Document Setup from the File menu (**Figure 5**).

2. Choose from the Artboard Size pop-up menu (**Figure 6**).
or
Enter numbers in the Dimensions fields. The maximum work area is 120 by 120 inches.
or
Check the Use Page Setup box to match the Artboard dimensions with the Paper size currently selected in the Page Setup dialog box (File menu).

3. Click OK or press Return.

Tips

■ Changes made in the Page Setup dialog box cannot be undone using the Undo command. You must open the dialog box again to redo the settings. Artboard changes can be undone via the Undo command.

■ Objects positioned beyond the edges of the Artboard will be saved with the illustration but will not print.

■ If the Page Setup Reduce or Enlarge percentage is other than 100%, the illustration will print proportionately smaller or larger. If the Use Page Setup box is unchecked in the Document Setup dialog box, the Artboard will not be affected by this Page Setup percentage; if it is checked, the Artboard dimensions will match the custom printout size.

Change the Artboard Dimensions

You can switch the printable area of an illustration from a vertical (portrait) to a landscape orientation, and then make the Artboard conform to the new orientation.

To create a landscape page:

1. Choose Page Setup from the File menu (**Figure 7**).

2. Click the Landscape Orientation icon (**Figure 8**).

3. Click OK or press Return (**Figure 9**).

Tip

■ Press and drag with the Page tool if you want to reposition the printable area within the Artboard.

To create a landscape Artboard:

1. Choose Document Setup from the File menu.

2. Click the Landscape Orientation icon.

3. *Optional:* Enter new Dimensions to increase the size of the Artboard to accommodate the new orientation.

4. Click OK or press Return (**Figure 10**). *(See the Tip above).*

Figure 7. *Choose* **Page Setup** *from the* **File** *menu.*

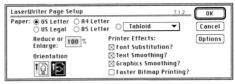

Figure 8. *Click the* **Landscape Orientation** *icon in the* **Page Setup** *dialog box.*

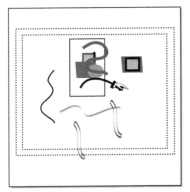

Figure 9. *The printable page in the Landscape Orientation.*

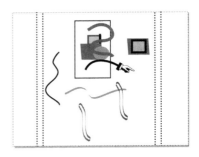

Figure 10. *The* **Artboard** *in the* **Landscape Orientation**. *The printable page does not extend beyond the Artboard.*

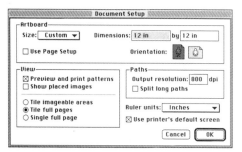

Figure 11. *Click the **Tile full pages** button in the* ***Document Setup*** *dialog box.*

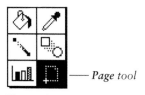

— *Page tool*

Figure 12.

By default, a new document contains a single page, but you can turn it into a multi-page document. If you turn on the Tile Full Pages option, as many full page borders as can fit in the current size of the Artboard will be drawn. Changing the Artboard size will increase or decrease the number of page borders.

To divide the Artboard into multiple pages:

1. Choose Fit in Window from the View menu.

2. Choose Document Setup from the File menu.

3. Click the View: "Tile full pages" button (**Figure 11**).

4. Click OK or press Return.

5. *Optional:* Select the Page tool (**Figure 12**), then click near the left edge of the Artboard. New page borders will be drawn (**Figure 13**). (If the tile lines are not visible, choose Show Page Tiling from the View menu.)

Tip

■ To Tile Full Pages in landscape mode, click the Landscape Orientation icon in the Page Setup dialog box, then click with the Page icon tool near the top or bottom of the Artboard to cause the new page borders to be drawn.

Parts of objects that fall within this "gutter" area will not print.

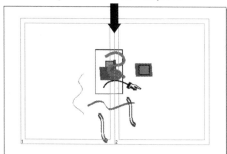

Figure 13. *The **Artboard** divided into two pages.*

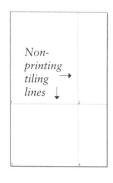

Non-printing tiling lines →

Figure 14. *An oversized illustration tiled into sections for printing (see page 206)*

Divide the Artboard

A file saved in the native Illustrator
format — None (Omit EPSF Header) —
will be smaller in file size than the same
file saved in the EPS format. However,
if you wish to open an Illustrator file
in another application, you must save it
as an EPS *(instructions are on the following
page)*.

To save a new illustration in the native Illustrator format:

1. Choose Save from the File menu
(**Figure 15**).

2. Enter a name in the "Save illustration
as" field.

3. Click Desktop (**Figure 16**).

4. Highlight a drive, then click Open.

5. *Optional:* Highlight a folder in which
to save the file, then click Open.

6. Click Save or press Return.

Figure 15. *Choose* Save *from
the* File *menu.*

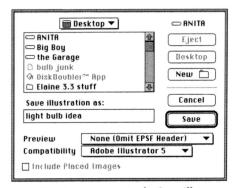

Figure 16. *Enter a name in the* Save illustration as *field, click* Desktop, *open a drive and
folder, then click* Save.

A file in the native Illustrator 5 format has a preview option of "None (Omit EPSF Header)," and can only be opened and modified in Illustrator. To import an Illustrator file in another application, such as QuarkXPress or PageMaker, save it in an EPS file format with a Preview option other than None.

Note: Regardless of the preview option you choose, color information will be saved with the file, and the illustration will print normally in Illustrator or any application you import it into.

To save a new illustration as an EPS:

1. Follow steps 1-5 on the previous page.

2. From the Preview pop-up menu (**Figure 17**):

Choose **None (Include EPSF Header)** to save the illustration without a preview. The EPS file will not display on screen in any other application, but it will print.
or
Choose **Black & White Macintosh** to save the illustration with a black-and-white preview.
or
Choose **Color Macintosh** to save the illustration with a color preview. This option will produce the largest file storage size.

3. Click Save or press Return.

Tip

■ If you save an illustration with an IBM PC Preview and then translate it from a Macintosh format into a DOS format, it can then be opened and displayed in any DOS or Windows application that reads EPS files.

■ The icon for an EPS file, when displayed in Icon View in the Finder, will contain the letters "EPS" (**Figure 18**).

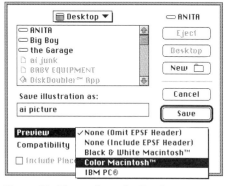

Figure 17. *Choose from the* **Preview** *pop-up menu in the* **Save** *dialog box.*

Figure 18. *An EPS file icon.*

Save an Illustration as an EPS

You can use the Save or Save As dialog box to convert a file to an earlier version of Illustrator. If the illustration was created using features that are not part of the earlier version, the illustration may be altered or information may be deleted from it to make it compatible with the earlier version. For example, a Gradient Fill may be reduced to a Black Fill or converted to a blend. The earlier the Illustrator version, the more the illustration may be altered.

To save a file so it can be opened in an earlier version of Illustrator:

1. Choose Save or Save as from the File menu.

2. Choose the appropriate Adobe Illustrator version from the Compatibility pop-up menu (**Figure 19**). (The newest version is the default compatibility option.)

3. *Optional:* To save the file in an earlier version and preserve your original illustration with all its Adobe Illustrator 5 features, modify the name in the "Save illustration as" field.

4. Click Save or press Return.

Tip

■ An Illustrator 1.1 file can be opened in Aldus Freehand version 3 on the Macintosh and in Corel Draw in Windows. Features such as Pattern Fills, masks, compounds, and placed EPS graphics will not translate into either application.

An Illustrator 3 file can be opened in Freehand version 4, and more features will be preserved.

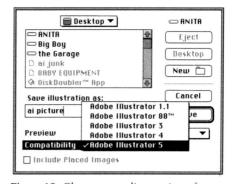

Figure 19. *Choose an earlier version of Illustrator from the* **Compability** *pop-up menu.*

Figure 20. *Choose Save As from the File menu.*

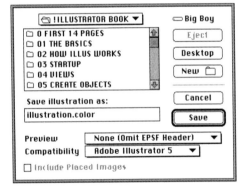

Figure 21. *Modify the name in the Save illustration as field in the Save As dialog box.*

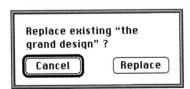

Figure 22. *The Replace warning prompt.*

The prior version of a file is overwritten when the **Save** command is executed. Don't be shy — save frequently!

To save an existing file:

Choose Save from the File menu.
or
Hold down Command (⌘) and press "S".

You can use the **Save As** dialog box to save an illustration with a different Preview or Compatibility option. Or use Save As to create a new version of an illustration if you wish to preserve the original file.

To save a new version of an illustration:

1. Open a file.

2. Choose Save As from the File menu (**Figure 20**).

3. Enter a new name in the "Save illustration as" field (**Figure 21**).
or
Modify the existing name.

4. Choose a location in which to save the new version.

5. *Optional:* Choose a different Preview or Compatibility option.

6. Click Save or press Return.

Tip

■ If you do not alter the name of the file and you click Save, a warning prompt will appear (**Figure 22**). Click Replace to save over the original file or click Cancel to return to the Save As dialog box.

Save an Existing File

You can open and edit a file in Illustrator's file formats: the native Illustrator format or the EPS Black & White or Color Macintosh format. Also, you can open an illustration from another object-oriented program, such as Adobe Dimensions or Type Styler (Macintosh and Windows platforms) if you save it in an EPS format that Illustrator recognizes (look for the word "Illustrator" among that application's EPS export options). *(To open a bitmap picture in Illustrator, follow the instructions on the next page)*

To open an illustration from within Illustrator:

1. Choose Open from the File menu (**Figure 23**).

2. Locate and highlight a file name, then click Open.
or
Double-click a file name (**Figure 24**).

Tips

■ A new untitled document opens when you launch Illustrator. It will close and be deleted automatically if you have not created anything in it and you then open an existing Illustrator document.

■ To open a document with a new template, with Option held down, choose Open from the File menu. Locate and open the document, then locate and open the template. (Click None to open the document without a template.)

To open an illustration from the Finder:

Double-click an Illustrator file icon in the Finder (**Figure 25**). Illustrator will launch if it is not aready open.

Figure 23. Choose Open from the File menu.

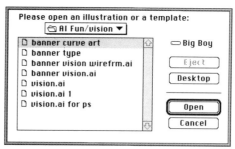

Figure 24. Double-click a file name in the Open dialog box.

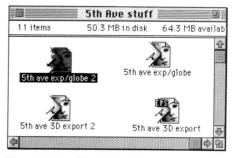

Figure 25. Double-click a file icon.

Open an Illustration

Figure 26. *Choose Place Art from the File menu.*

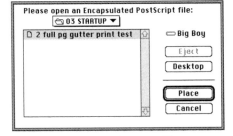

Figure 27. *Double-click an EPS file.*

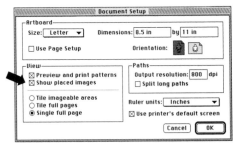

Figure 28. *Check the Show placed images box in the Document Setup dialog box.*

You can place a scanned picture, saved as an EPS (Encapsulated PostScript) file, into Adobe Illustrator, or you can place a picture in the EPS file format from a bitmap program, such as Adobe Photoshop.

An EPS image placed in Illustrator will appear in an outlined box. The image can be moved, placed on a different layer, masked, or modified using any transformation tool. It cannot be modified using other Illustrator features.

To place an EPS file from another application into an Illustrator document:

1. Choose Place Art from the File menu (**Figure 26**).

2. Locate and highlight a file name, then click Place.
   or
   Double-click a file name (**Figure 27**).

By default, a placed EPS image will display as an outlined box with an "x" through it in Artwork view. Follow these instructions to display a black-and-white version of the image in the outlined box in Artwork view.

If it was saved in its original application with an EPS preview that Illustrator recognizes, the full version of a placed EPS image will display in Preview view, regardless of the "Show placed images" setting.

To display a placed EPS in Artwork view:

1. Choose Document Setup from the File menu.

2. Check the "Show placed images" box (**Figure 28**).

3. Click OK or press Return.

Place an EPS File in Illustrator

By default, an EPS file will not be saved with the Illustrator file into which it is placed. Only a screen version of the picture will be saved, with a reference to the actual EPS file for printing. Follow these instructions to save a copy of a placed EPS file with an illustration.

To save a copy of a placed EPS file with an illustration:

1. Choose Save As from the File menu.

2. Choose Black & White Macintosh or Color Macintosh from the Preview pop-up menu.

3. Check the "Include Placed Images" box (**Figure 29**).

4. Click Save or press Return.

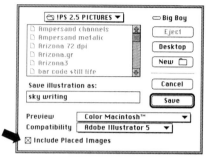

Figure 29. *In the Save As dialog box, choose **Black & White Macintosh** or **Color Macintosh** from the **Preview** pop-up menu, and check the **Include Placed Images** box.*

To see where the actual placed EPS file is located:

1. Choose a selection tool.

2. Click on the placed image.

3. Choose Attributes from the Object menu (**Figure 30**).

4. Press on the "Location of placed art" pop-up menu (**Figure 31**). The drive and folder location of the actual placed image file will be listed.

5. Click OK or Cancel.

Figure 30. *Choose Attributes from the Object menu.*

Object
Paint Style...   ⌘I
Custom Color...
Pattern...
Gradient...
Attributes...   ⌘⌃A
Join...   ⌘J
Average...   ⌘L
Guides   ▶
Masks   ▶
Compound Paths   ▶
Cropmarks   ▶
Graphs   ▶

Tips

■ Hold down Option and double-click the placed image to launch the application in which it was created, if the application is available on your system. If you then modify the original placed image and save it, the placed image in the Illustrator document will be updated automatically.

■ If you place a Photoshop EPS file with a clipping path into Illustrator, the area around the image will be transparent, and will remain so if you move or scale it. However, if you reflect, rotate or shear it, the transparent area will become opaque white.

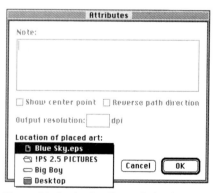

Figure 31. *In the Attributes dialog box, press and hold on the Location of placed art pop-up menu to see the file's location.*

Figure 32. *Choose* Close *from the* File *menu.*

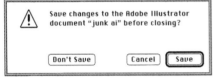

Figure 33. *If you try to close a picture that was modified since it was last saved, this prompt will appear.*

To revert to the last saved version:

1. Choose Close from the File menu (**Figure 32**).

2. Click Don't Save when the warning prompt appears.

3. Choose Open from the File menu.

4. Locate and highlight the file name again, then click Open.
or
Double-click the file name.

Tip

■ Illustrator 5.0.1 has a Revert to Saved command (File menu).

To close an illustration:

Click the Close box in the upper left corner of the document window.
or
Choose Close from the File menu (**Figure 32**).
or
Hold down Command (⌘) and press "W".

Tip

■ If you attempt to close a picture and it was modified since it was last saved, a warning prompt will appear (**Figure 33**). You can close the file without saving, save the file, or cancel the close operation.

Revert to Saved; Close an Illustration

To quit Illustrator:

Choose Quit from the File menu
(**Figure 34**).
or
Hold down Command (⌘) and press
"Q".

Tip

■ If you quit Illustrator, all open
   Illustrator files will close. If changes
   have been made to an open file
   since it was last saved, a warning
   prompt will appear. You can save
   the file before quitting or cancel the
   quit operation.

Figure 34. *Choose* **Quit**
from the **File** *menu.*

Quit Illustrator

DISPLAY  4

● ●

*I*N THIS CHAPTER you will learn how to change view sizes, change views, create custom view settings, display the same illustration in two windows, and move an illustration in its window.

The current view size.

Figure 1.

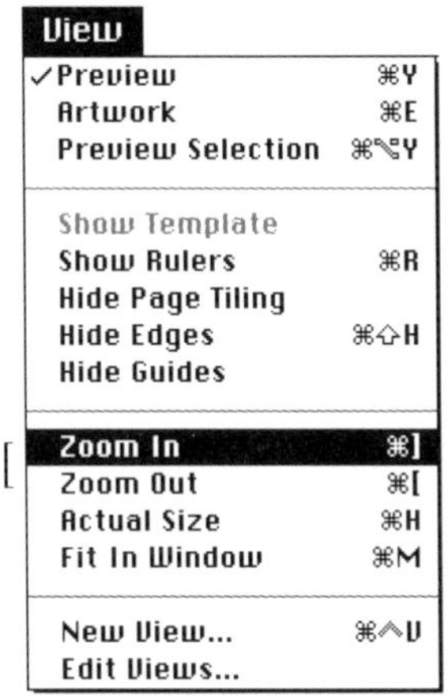

Zoom In or Zoom Out

Within the document window, you can display the entire Artboard, the illustration at actual size, an enlarged detail of an illustration, or any view size in between.

The display size is indicated as a percentage on the title bar (**Figure 1**), and can range from 6.25% to 1600%. 100% is actual size. The display size does not affect the printout size.

To magnify an illustration:

Choose Zoom In from the View menu (**Figure 2**).
or
Hold down Command (⌘) and press "]".

To reduce the view size of an illustration:

Choose Zoom Out from the View menu (**Figure 2**).
or
Hold down Command (⌘) and press "[".

Figure 2. *Choose Zoom In or Zoom Out from the View menu.*

To change the view size using the Zoom tool:

1. Choose the Zoom tool (**Figure 3**).

2. Click on the illustration or drag a marquee across an area to magnify that area (**Figure 4**).
or
Hold down Option and click to reduce the display size (**Figure 5**).
or
Drag a marquee, then, without releasing the mouse, press and hold down Space bar and continue to drag the marquee over the area you wish to magnify.

Tips

■ Double-click the Zoom tool to display an illustration at Actual Size (100%). Or, choose Actual Size from the View menu.

If you double-click the Zoom tool when your illustration is in a small display size, the white area around the Artboard may appear in the document window, instead of the center of the illustration appearing in the window. Click the left or right scroll arrow to reposition the illustration in the window, if desired.

■ To magnify the display size when another tool is selected, hold down Command (⌘) and Space bar and click in the document window. To reduce the display size, hold down Command (⌘), Option, and Space bar and click.

■ You can click to change the view size while the screen is redrawing.

■ The smaller the marquee you drag with the Zoom tool, the greater the level of magnification.

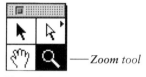

Figure 3.

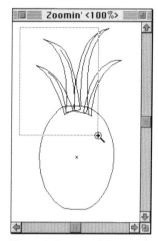

Figure 4. *Press and drag with the* **Zoom** *tool.*

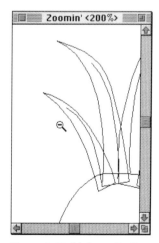

Figure 5. *Hold down* **Option** *and click to reduce the view size.*

View

Preview	⌘Y
✓ Artwork	⌘E
Preview Selection	⌘⌥Y
Show Template	
Show Rulers	⌘R
Hide Page Tiling	
Hide Edges	⌘⇧H
Hide Guides	
Zoom In	⌘]
Zoom Out	⌘[
Actual Size	⌘H
Fit In Window	⌘M
New View...	⌘⌃V
Edit Views...	

Figure 6. *Choose Preview, Artwork, or Preview Selection from the View menu.*

An illustration can be displayed and edited in three views: Preview, Artwork, or Preview Selection.

To change the view:

From the View menu, choose **Preview** to display all the objects with their Fill and Stroke colors and all printable placed images (**Figures 6-7**).
or
Choose **Artwork** to display all the objects as "wire frames" with no Fill or Stroke colors. A placed image will display as a box with an "x" in the middle or as a rough black-and-white version of the placed image (**Figure 8**).
or
Choose **Preview Selection** to display any currently selected object or objects in Preview view, and all other objects in Artwork view. To preview an object, click on it with any selection tool (**Figure 9**).

Tips

- You can use the Layers palette to select a view for an individual layer or for the entire illustration *(see page 118)*.

- In all three views, the other View options — Hide/Show Templates, Page Tiling, Edges, and Guides — are accessible, and any selection tool can be used.

Figure 7. *Preview view.*

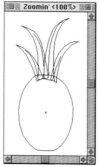

Figure 8. *Artwork view.*

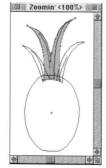

Figure 9. *Preview Selection view.*

Preview and Artwork Views

You can define and save up to 25 custom view settings that you can switch to quickly. You can specify whether your illustration will be in Preview view or Artwork view for each setting that you define.

To define a custom view setting:

1. Follow the instructions on page 39 or page 40 to display your illustration at the desired view size.

2. Choose Preview or Artwork from the View menu.

3. Choose New View from the View menu (**Figure 10**).

4. Enter a name for the New View in the Name field (**Figure 11**).

5. Click OK or press Return.

Figure 10. *Choose* **New View** *from the* **View** *menu.*

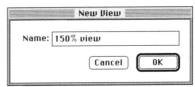

Figure 11. *Enter a* **Name** *for the view setting in the* **New View** *dialog box.*

To choose a custom view setting:

Choose the view name from the bottom of the View menu (**Figure 12**).
or
Hold down Control and Command (⌘) and press the number that was automatically assigned to the view setting. The shortcut will be listed next to the view name under the View menu.

Figure 12. *Choose a custom view setting from the* **View** *menu.*

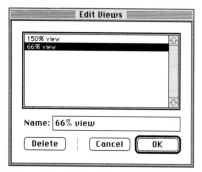

Figure 13. *In the **Edit Views** dialog box, highlight a view, then change the **Name** or click **Delete**.*

To rename or delete a custom view setting:

1. Choose Edit Views from the View menu (**Figure 12**).

2. Highlight the view you wish to alter (**Figure 13**).

3. Type a new name in the Name field.
or
Click Delete to delete the view setting.

4. Click OK or press Return. The View menu will update to reflect your changes.

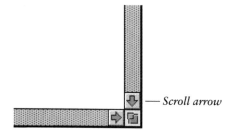

Figure 14.

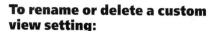

Hand tool —

Figure 15.

To move an illustration in its window:

Click the up or down scroll arrow (**Figure 14**).
or
Choose the Hand tool, then drag the illustration to the desired position (**Figure 15**).

Tips

■ Double-click the Hand tool to fit the entire Artboard in the document window.

■ Hold down Space bar to turn the currently selected tool temporarily into the Hand tool.

Move an Illustration in its Window

The number of Illustrator documents that can be open at a time is limited only by the amount of RAM (Random Access Memory) currently available to Illustrator (**Figure 16**). Open windows are listed under and can be activated via the Window menu (**Figure 17**).

You can open the same illustration in two windows: one in a large display size, such as 200%, to edit a detail, and the other in a smaller view size so you can see the whole illustration. In one window you could hide individual layers or display individual layers in Artwork view and in another window you could Preview all the layers together.

Note: The illustration in the window for which Preview view is selected will redraw each time you modify the illustration in the window for which Artwork view is selected, however, so your production speed will remain the same.

To display an illustration in two windows:

1. Open an illustration.

2. Choose New Window from the Window menu (**Figure 17**). A new window of the same size will appear on top of the first window, with the same title followed by ":2".

3. Reposition the new window by dragging its title bar so the original and new windows are side by side, and resize one or both windows (**Figure 18**).

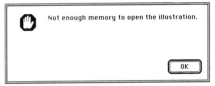

Figure 16. *This warning will appear if there is not enough RAM to open another file.*

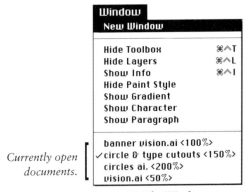

Currently open documents.

Figure 17. *The Window menu.*

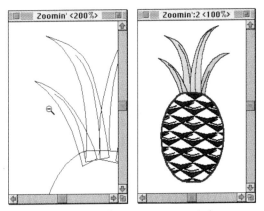

Figure 18. *The same illustration in two windows.*

One Illustration in Two Windows

CREATE OBJECTS 5

A N **OBJECT** IS a shape composed of anchor points connected by straight and/or curved line segments. An object can be open or closed. A **path** is the edge of an object that defines its shape. Rectangles and ovals are closed paths because they have no endpoints. A line is an open path.

In this chapter you will learn how to use the creation tools to draw rectangles and ovals. How to use the Brush tool to create filled shapes which look like hard-edged or calligraphic strokes. How to use the Freehand tool to create hand-drawn lines. And how to create geometric shapes using the Create filters.

(The Pen tool, which produces curved and straight line segments, is covered in Chapter 8)

To create a rectangle or oval by dragging:

1. Choose the Rectangle or Oval tool (**Figure 1**).

2. Press and drag diagonally (**Figure 2**). A wireframe representation of the rectangle or oval will appear. When you release the mouse, the rectangle or oval will be selected and colored with the current Fill and Stroke settings.

Tips

■ Hold down Option while dragging to draw a rectangle or oval from the center. Or, double-click the Rectangle or Oval tool before dragging to draw from the center (**Figure 3**), then double-click the tool again to restore its default setting.

■ Hold down Shift while dragging to create a square with the Rectangle tool or a circle with the Oval tool.

To create a rectangle or oval by specifying dimensions:

1. Select the Rectangle or Oval tool.

2. Click on the Artboard where you wish the object to appear.

3. In the Rectangle or Oval dialog box, enter dimensions in the Width and Height fields (**Figure 4**).

4. *Optional:* To create a rectangle with rounded corners, enter a value greater than 0 in the Corner radius field. If the radius is equal to or greater than the height or width, an oval or a circle will be created.

5. Click OK or press Return.

Tip

■ Values in dialog boxes are displayed in the unit of measure selected in the General Preferences dialog box, opened from the the Preferences submenu under the File menu.

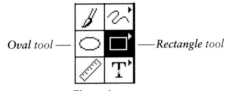

Oval tool —— Rectangle tool

Figure 1.

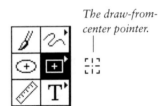

Figure 2. *Press and drag diagonally.*

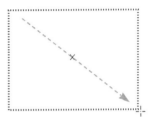

The draw-from-center pointer.

Figure 3. *Double-click the Rectangle or Oval tool to draw from the center.*

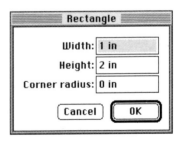

Figure 4. *Enter **Width** and **Height** dimensions in the **Rectangle** (or Oval) dialog box.*

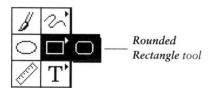

Figure 5.

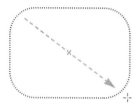

Figure 6a. *Press and drag diagonally.*

Figure 6b. *The rectangle is automatically painted with the current Fill and Stroke settings.*

Rounded Rectangle tool

To create a rounded rectangle:

1. Choose the Rounded Rectangle tool (**Figure 5**).

2. Press and drag diagonally. A wireframe representation of the rounded rectangle will appear (**Figure 6a**). When you release the mouse, the selected rounded rectangle will be painted with the current Fill and Stroke settings (**Figure 6b**).

Tips

■ You can also create a rounded rectangle using the Rounded Rectangle dialog box. Choose the Rounded Rectangle tool, click on the Artboard, then enter values in the Width, Height, and Corner radius fields.

■ The current Corner radius value in the General Preferences dialog box, which determines how rounded the corners of the rectangle will be, is entered automatically in the Corner radius field in the Rounded Rectangle dialog box, and vice versa.

HOW TO UNDO AN OPERATION

To Undo one or more operations in reverse order, choose **Undo** from the **Edit** menu (or hold down **Command** (⌘) and press "**Z**"). The number of consecutive operations that can be undone is specified in the Undo levels field in the General Preferences dialog box *(see page 201)*.

To delete an object:

1. Select the object.

2. If all the anchor points on the object are selected, press Delete once.
or
If only some points are selected, press Delete twice.

Create a Rounded Rectangle; Delete an Object

You can use the **Brush tool** with its default settings to produce hard edged brush "strokes" in a uniform thickness or you can customize the Brush tool to create calligraphic "strokes."

Note: A line is an open path with endpoints and a Stroke color. A brush "stroke" is a closed path.

To create a brush stroke:

1. Double-click the Brush tool (**Figure 7**).

2. Enter the desired stroke thickness in the Width field (**Figure 8**).

3. Click the round or square-cornered Caps button.

4. Click the smooth or square-cornered Joins (bends) button.

5. Click OK or press Return.

6. Press and drag to draw a stroke (**Figure 9**). When you release the mouse, the stroke will be painted with the current Fill and Stroke settings *(see page 89)*.

Tip

■ If you are using a pressure-sensitive drawing tablet you can specify maximum and minimum Stroke Widths in the Brush dialog box. The brush stroke width will vary between these designated limits as you increase or decrease stylus pressure on the tablet.

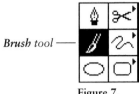

Brush tool ——

Figure 7.

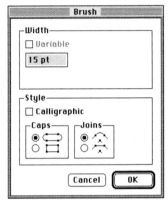

Figure 8. *Enter a Width in the Brush dialog box.*

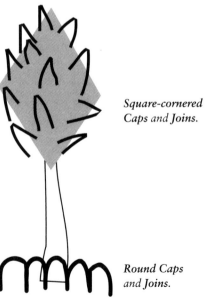

Square-cornered Caps and Joins.

Round Caps and Joins.

Figure 9.

Create a Brush Stroke

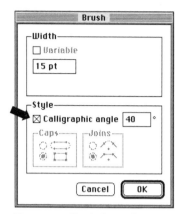

Figure 10. *Check the Calligraphic angle box.*

Figure 11.

Figure 12.   Figure 13.

The **Brush tool** can be used to create calligraphic "strokes" that vary in thickness as you draw, mimicking traditional drawing tools.

To create a calligraphic brush stroke:

1. Double-click the Brush tool (**Figure** 7).

2. Check the Calligraphic angle box (**Figure 10**).

3. Enter a number in the Calligraphic angle field.

The **Calligraphic** angle determines the thickness of the horizontal and vertical strokes relative to each other. A 0° angle will produce a thin horizontal stroke and a thick vertical stroke. A 90° angle will produce the opposite effect. Other angles will produce different effects.

4. Click OK or press Return.

5. Press and drag to draw a stroke. The stroke will preview as you drag. When you release the mouse, the stroke will be painted with the current Fill and Stroke settings (**Figures 11-15**).

Tip

■ To make a line calligraphic **after** it is created, apply the Calligraphy filter, opened from the Stylize submenu under the Filter menu.

Figure 14.   Figure 15.

Create a Calligraphic Brush Stroke

Lines drawn with the **Freehand tool** look hand drawn or quickly sketched.

Note: The Freehand tool tends to produce bumpy curves, and it doesn't produce straight lines. Use the Pen tool to create straight lines and smooth curves.

To draw a line using the Freehand tool:

1. Choose the Freehand tool (**Figure 16**).

2. *Optional:* Click the Stroke box on the Paint Style palette, then enter a new number in the Stroke Width field.

3. Press and drag to draw a line. A dotted line will appear. When you release the mouse, the line will be colored with the current Fill and Stroke settings and its anchor points will be selected (**Figures 17a-b**).

Tips

■ If the current Fill setting is other than None, curves on the line path will be filled in. To remove the Fill and leave only a Stroke along the path of the line, choose a Fill of None and a Stroke color of your choice from the Paint Style palette *(see page 89)*.

■ In Artwork view, only a wireframe representation of the line will be displayed, with its anchor points selected.

To erase part of a line while drawing with the Freehand tool:

1. Keep the mouse button down, then hold down Command (⌘) and drag with the erasure pointer over any section of the dotted line preview you wish to erase.

2. To continue to draw the line, release Command (⌘). The pencil pointer will reappear.

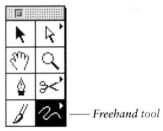

Figure 16.

— *Freehand* tool

Figure 17a. *A dotted line will appear as you draw.*

Figure 17b. *When you release the mouse, the line will be painted with the current Fill and Stroke settings.*

Draw a Line

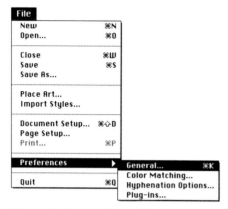

Figure 18. *Choose* **General** *from the Preferences submenu under the* **File** *menu.*

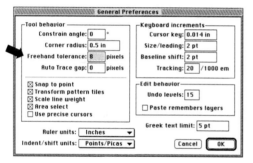

Figure 19. *Enter a number between 0 and 10 in the* **Freehand tolerance** *field.*

The number of anchor points produced with the Freehand tool is determined by the **Freehand tolerance** setting in the General Preferences dialog box. The fewer the anchor points, the smoother the line. If you change the Freehand Tolerance, only subsequently drawn lines will be affected, not existing lines.

To specify the amount of anchor points the Freehand tool produces:

1. Choose General from the Preferences submenu under the File menu (**Figure 18**).

2. Enter a number between 0 and 10 in the Freehand tolerance field (**Figure 19**). A Freehand tolerance of 0 will produce many anchor points. A Freehand tolerance of 10 will produce anchor points only at sharp line direction changes.

3. Click OK or press Return.

Tip

■ You can remove anchor points from a line using the Delete Anchor Point tool. You can reposition points on a line using the Direct Selection tool.

Figure 20. *A line drawn with a Freehand tolerance of 2.*

Figure 21. *A line drawn with a Freehand tolerance of 8.*

Freehand Tolerance

To add to a line:

1. Select the Freehand tool (**Figure 16**).

2. Position the pencil pointer directly over either end of the line. The pencil icon will change to a white point with a black eraser tip when it is positioned over an endpoint (**Figures 22-23**).

3. Press and drag the mouse to create an addition to the line. When you release the mouse, the completed line path and its anchor points will be selected and the addition will be connected to the existing line.

Tip

■ If the new and existing lines did not connect, delete the new line and try again or use the Join command to join the two lines *(see page 71)*.

Figure 22. *Continue-a-line pointer.*   Figure 23. *Start-a-new-line pointer.*

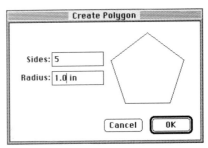

Figure 24. *Choose **Polygon** from the Create submenu under the **Filter** menu.*

Using the **Polygon**, **Spiral**, and **Star** filters, you can easily create perfect geometric objects without having to draw with the mouse. The current Fill and Stroke settings are automatically applied to objects produced using these filters.

To create a polygon:

1. Choose Polygon from the Create submenu under the Filter menu (**Figure 24**).

2. In the Sides field, enter a number between 3 and 4000 for the number of sides (**Figure 25**). The sides will be of equal length. The polygon will preview in the dialog box.

3. Enter a value in the Radius field (the distance from the center of the object to the corner points).

4. Click OK or press Return (**Figure 26**).

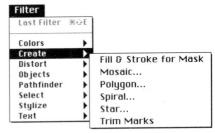

Figure 25. *In the **Create Polygon** dialog box, enter a number in the **Sides** and **Radius** fields.*

Figure 26.

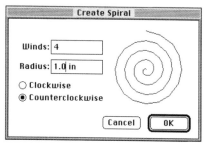

Figure 27. *In the* Create Spiral *dialog box, enter numbers in the* Winds *and* Radius *fields, and click* Clockwise *or* Counterclockwise.

To create a spiral:

1. Choose Spiral from the Create sub-menu under the Filter menu (**Figure 24**).

2. Enter a number in the Winds field (the number of revolutions around the center point) (**Figure 27**).

3. Enter a number in the Radius field (the distance from the center of the spiral to the outermost point).

4. Click Clockwise or Counterclockwise (the direction the spiral will wind from the center point).

5. Click OK or press Return (**Figures 28a-c**).

Tip

■ Be sure to apply a Stroke color to the spiral *(see page 89)*.

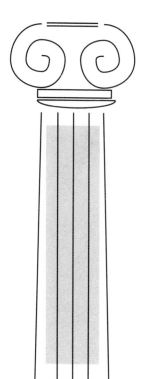

Figures 28a-c.

To create a star:

1. Choose Star from the Create submenu under the Filter menu (**Figure 24**).

2. In the Create Star dialog box, enter a number between 3 and 4000 in the Points field (the number of points on the star) (**Figure 29**). The star will preview in the dialog box.

3. Enter a number in the 1st Radius field (the distance from the center of the object to the outer points).

4. Enter a number in the 2nd Radius field (the distance from the center of the object to the inner points, where the segments bend inward), then press Tab to preview.

5. Click OK or press Return (**Figures 30-31**).

Tips

■ The distance from the center to the outer points of the Star shape will always be the larger of the two Radius values, regardless of which field the larger value is in.

■ The greater the difference between the 1st and 2nd Radius values, the longer the arms of the star.

■ You can use the Rotate tool to rotate the completed star.

■ Values in the Polygon, Spiral, and Star dialog boxes (and all other dialog boxes) are shown in the Ruler units currently selected in the Document Setup dialog box.

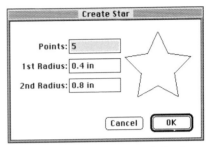

Figure 29. *In the **Create Star** dialog box, enter numbers in the **Points, 1st Radius,** and **2nd Radius** fields.*

Figure 30.

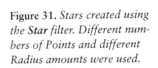

Figure 31. *Stars created using the **Star** filter. Different numbers of Points and different Radius amounts were used.*

Create a Star

SELECT/MOVE

I N CHAPTER 5 you learned how to create various objects. In later chapters you will learn many methods for modifying objects, such as reshaping, recoloring, and transforming. An object must be selected before it can be modified, however, so selecting objects is an essential Illustrator skill to learn. In this chapter you will learn how to use the selection tools to highlight objects and paths, and how to hide, lock, and move objects.

There are three **selection tools** (**Figure 1**):

The **Selection** tool is used to select all the anchor points on an object or path. If you click on the edge or the fill of an object with the Selection tool, you will select all the points on the object.

The **Direct Selection** tool is used to select one or more anchor points or segments of a path. If you click on the edge of an object with the Direct Selection tool, you will select only that segment. If you click on the fill of an object, you will select all the points on the object.

The **Group Selection** tool can be used to select all the anchor points on a path, but its primary use is to select groups within a group in the order in which they were added into the larger group. Click once to select an object; click twice to select that object's group; click three times to select the next group that was added to the larger group, etc.

Selection Tools

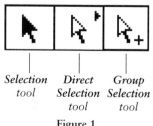

Selection *Direct* *Group*
tool *Selection* *Selection*
tool *tool*

Figure 1.

To select by clicking:

1. To select an anchor point or a segment, choose the **Direct Selection** tool, then click on the point or the segment (**Figures 2-3**).

or

To select a whole path, choose the **Selection** tool or **Group Selection** tool, then click on the edge of the path (**Figure 4**).

or

To select a whole path when your illustration is in Preview view and the Area Select option is on *(see box at right)*, choose any selection tool, then click on the object's Fill.

or

If your illustration is in Artwork view, you can select an object by clicking on its edge with any selection tool.

2. *Optional:* Hold down Shift and click with the Direct Selection tool to select additional anchor points.

or

Hold down Shift and click with the Selection or Group Selection tool to select additional objects.

Tip

■ Hold down Option to use the Group Selection tool while the Direct Selection tool selected.

THE AREA SELECT OPTION

If the **Area Select** box is checked in the **General Preferences** dialog box (opened from the Preferences submenu under the File menu), you can click on an object's Fill when your illustration is in **Preview** view to select the object's entire path. If the Area Select box is unchecked or the object has no Fill, you must click on the edge of the object to select it. If your illustration is in Preview Selection view, you must click on the edge of an object to select it, regardless of the Area Select setting.

(Fill and Stroke are defined in Chapter 9)

Figure 2. *One anchor point selected with the **Direct Selection** tool (Artwork view).*

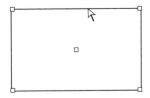

Figure 3. *A segment selected with the **Direct Selection** tool.*

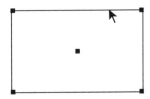

Figure 4. *A path and all its anchor points selected with the Selection tool.*

MORE ABOUT SELECTIONS

A selected anchor point is solid. If an anchor point is hollow, only its adjoining segments are selected.

◆

If a curve segment is selected, the direction lines that control the curve segment are also highlighted and selected. Straight line segments do not have direction lines, they only have anchor points.

◆

If an anchor point on a curve segment is selected, the direction lines that shape the curve segments that join the anchor point are also highlighted and selected.

◆

If you select or move curve segments without their corresponding anchor points, you will reshape the curves and the anchor points will remain stationary *(more about reshaping curves in the next chapter).*

To select by dragging:

1. Choose a selection tool.

2. Position the pointer outside the object or objects you wish to select, drag the pointer diagonally across them (a dotted marquee will define the area as you drag over it), then release the mouse.

If you use the **Direct Selection** tool, only the anchor points or segments you marquee will be selected (**Figure 5**).

If you use the **Selection** tool, the whole object (or objects) will be selected, even if only a portion of the object is marqueed (**Figure 6**).

If you use the **Group Selection** tool, any object you marquee will be selected.

Tip

■ Hold down Command (⌘) to use the last highlighted selection tool when another tool is selected. With Command (⌘) held down, you can click the mouse to select or deselect an object.

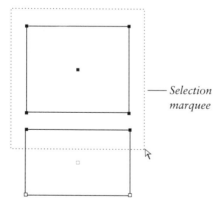

Selection marquee

Figure 5. *A selection being made with the* **Direct Selection** *tool. Only anchor points within the marquee are selected.*

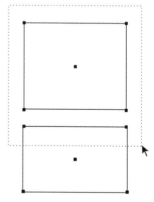

Figure 6. *The* **Selection** *tool selects whole objects.*

To select all the objects in an illustration:

Choose Select All from the Edit menu (**Figure 7**).

or

Hold down Command (⌘) and press "A".

All the objects in your illustration will be selected, whether they are currently showing in the document window or not.

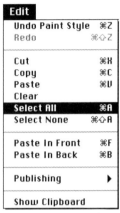

Figure 7. *Choose Select All from the Edit menu.*

Use the **Select filters** to select objects with similar characteristics to a currently selected object. Each filter is named for the attributes it searches for.

To select using a filter:

1. Choose any selection tool.

2. Click on an object with characteristics you wish to search for in other objects (look at the submenu in **Figure 8**).

3. Choose from the Select submenu under the Filter menu:

   Same Fill Color to search for Fill attributes only.

   Same Paint Style to search for all paint attributes.

   Same Stroke Color to search for Stroke attributes only.

   Same Stroke Weight to search for Strokes of the same weight.

   Select Inverse to select objects that were not initially selected and deselect the initially selected objects.

   Select Stray Points to select single points that are not part of any paths so they can be deleted easily.

   Select Masks to select masking objects. This filter is useful because the edges of a masking object display in Preview view only when the object is selected.

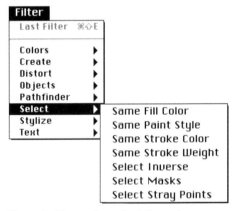

Figure 8. *Choose from the Select submenu under the Filter menu.*

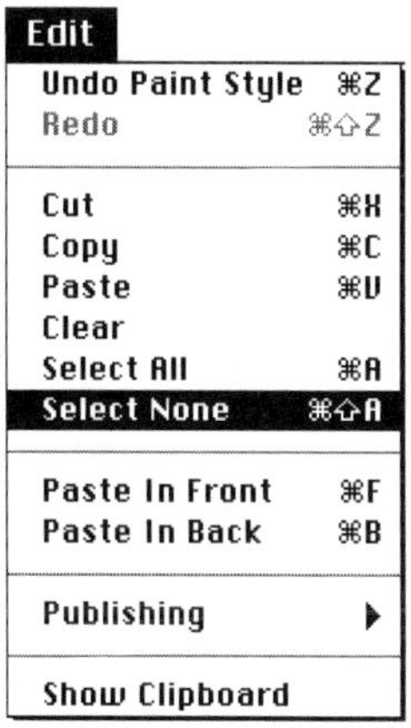

Edit

Undo Paint Style   ⌘Z
Redo   ⌘⇧Z

Cut   ⌘X
Copy   ⌘C
Paste   ⌘U
Clear
Select All   ⌘A
Select None   ⌘⇧A

Paste In Front   ⌘F
Paste In Back   ⌘B

Publishing   ▶

Show Clipboard

Figure 9. Choose Select None from the Edit menu.

To prevent further modifications to a selected object, you must deselect it.

To deselect an object or objects:

1. Choose a selection tool.

2. Click ouside the selected object or objects.
or
Choose Select None from the Edit menu (**Figure 9**).
or
Hold down Command (⌘) and Shift and press "A".

Tip

■ To deselect an individual object within a multiple selection, hold down Shift and click on the object or press and drag over the object.

View

✓Preview   ⌘Y
Artwork   ⌘E
Preview Selection   ⌘⌥Y

Show Template
Show Rulers   ⌘R
Hide Page Tiling
Hide Edges   ⌘⇧H
Hide Guides

Zoom In   ⌘]
Zoom Out   ⌘[
Actual Size   ⌘H
Fit In Window   ⌘M

New View...   ⌘⌃U
Edit Views...

Figure 10. Choose Hide Edges from the View menu.

You can hide an object's anchor points, segments, and direction lines while still keeping the object selected and editable. You can use the **Hide Edges** command when you want to see how different Stroke colors or widths look on an object.

To hide the anchor points and segments of a selected object:

Choose Hide Edges from the View menu (**Figure 10**).
or
Hold down Command (⌘) and Shift and press "H".

Tip

■ To redisplay the anchor points and segments, choose Show Edges from the View menu.

The **Hide** command and the **Lock** command, discussed next, can help you isolate objects to work on. If your illustrations are complex, you'll find these commands particularly useful. A hidden object is invisible in both Artwork and Preview views, and will not print.

To hide an object:

1. Select the object or objects to be hidden.

2. Choose Hide from the Arrange menu (**Figure 11**).

Tip

■ Individual hidden objects cannot be selectively redisplayed. To redisplay all hidden objects, choose Show All from the Arrange menu. You can use the Layers palette to hide or lock objects on an individual layer *(see pages 118-120)*.

A locked object cannot be selected or modified.

To lock an object:

1. Select the object or objects to be locked.

2. Choose Lock from the Arrange menu (**Figure 12**).

Tip

■ Locked items cannot be unlocked individually. If you choose Unlock All from the Arrange menu, all locked items will be unlocked.

LOCK/HIDE TIPS

You can't lock or hide part of an object or path.

◆

To unlock or show only one of several locked or hidden objects, choose Unlock All or Show All from the Arrange menu, choose the Selection tool, hold down Shift and click on the object you wish to unlock or show, then choose Lock or Hide for the remaining selected objects.

◆

If you chose Lock or Hide for an object within a group, you can unlock or show just that object. Select the group, then hold down Option and choose Unlock All or Show All from the Arrange menu.

Figure 11. *Choose **Hide** from the **Arrange** menu.*

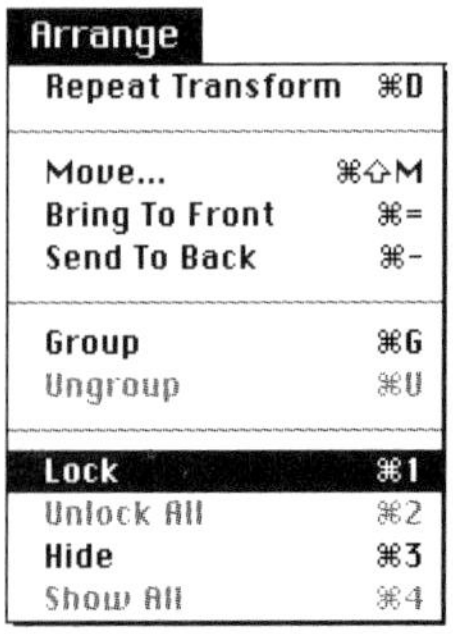

Figure 12. *Choose **Lock** from the **Arrange** menu.*

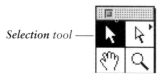

Selection tool —

Figure 13.

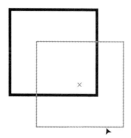

Figure 14. *Press and drag the object's edge.*

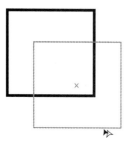

Figure 15. *To copy an object, hold down **Option** and press and drag the object's edge. Note the double arrowhead pointer.*

To move an object by dragging:

1. Choose the Selection tool (**Figure 13**).

2. If your illustration is in Artwork view, press and drag the object's edge (**Figure 14**).

or

If your illustration is in Preview view, press and drag the object's edge or the object's Fill (if there is one, and the Area Select option is on in General Preferences).

Tips

■ The Direct Selection tool can also be used to press and drag an object's Fill.

■ Press any arrow key to move a selected object the Cursor key increment specified in the General Preferences dialog box (File menu).

■ If the Snap to Point box is checked in the General Preferences dialog box, the part of the object directly underneath the pointer will "snap" to the nearest guide or to a point of another object if it comes close to it.

■ Hold down Shift while dragging to constrain the movement to a horizontal or vertical axis or to a 45° angle.

To move a copy of an object by dragging:

1. Choose the Selection tool.

2. Hold down Option and press and drag the Fill or edge of the object you wish to copy (the pointer will turn into a double arrowhead) (**Figure 15**).

3. Release the mouse, then release Option. A copy of the object will appear in the new location.

Tip

■ To create a second copy of the object, choose Repeat Transform from the Arrange menu or hold down Command (⌘) and press "D".

Move an Object; Move a Copy of an Object

What is the Clipboard?

If you select an object or group and then choose the **Cut** or **Copy** command, that object or group is placed onto the **Clipboard**, a temporary storage area in memory. The previous contents of the Clipboard are replaced when you choose Cut or Copy.

The **Paste** command places the current Clipboard contents in the center of the currently active document window. The Clipboard contents can be pasted an unlimited number of times.

To move an object or group from one document to another:

1. Choose the Selection tool.

2. Click on the object or group.

3. Choose Cut from the Edit menu (**Figure 16**).
or
Hold down Command (⌘) and press "X".

The object or group will be removed from the current document.

4. Click in the "destination" document window.

5. Choose Paste from the Edit menu (**Figure 17**).
or
Hold down Command (⌘) and press "V".

Tips

■ To move a copy of an object or group, choose Copy from the Edit menu (or hold down Command (⌘) and press "C") for step 3 above.

■ You can place an object created in Illustrator into a document in another Adobe PostScript application using the Clipboard commands (Cut, Copy, Paste). On a newer Mac operating system with QuickDraw GX, you will be able to Paste into any application.

■ To place a PICT version of an object on the Clipboard, hold down Option when you choose Cut or Copy.

GROUPED OBJECTS

If you copy an object in a group by dragging (use the Direct Selection tool with Option held down), the copy will be **part of** that group. If you use the Clipboard to copy and paste an object in a group, the object will paste **outside** the group *(the Group command is discussed on page 112).*

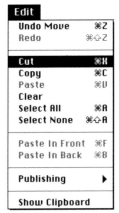

Figure 16. *Choose* **Cut** *from the* **Edit** *menu.*

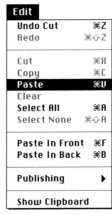

Figure 17. *Choose* **Paste** *from the* **Edit** *menu.*

PATHS

AS YOU LEARNED in Chapter 5, a path is the edge of an object. In this chapter, you will learn how to change the profile of an object by changing the number, position or type of anchor points on its path. Using these techniques, you'll be able to draw just about any shape imaginable.

You will learn how to move anchor points or path segments, how to convert a corner anchor point into a curve anchor point (or vice versa) to reshape the segments that it connects, and how to add or delete anchor points.

You will also learn how to split a path, how to join two open paths into one path, how to close an open path, how to combine paths using the Unite filter, and how to automatically or manually trace a picture. Also included in this chapter are two practice exercises.

What is a Bezier curve?

In Illustrator, a curve segment is also called a Bezier curve. A Bezier curve consists of two anchor points connected by a curve segment, with at least one direction point and direction line attached to each anchor point (**Figure 1**). If an anchor point connects a curve and a straight line segment, it will have one common direction line. If an anchor point connects two curve segments, it will have a pair of direction lines.

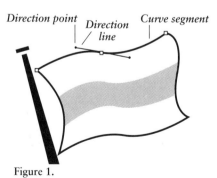

Direction point   *Direction line*   *Curve segment*

Figure 1.

If you move an anchor point, segments connected to it will reshape. If you move a curve segment, connecting anchor points will not move along with it. If you move a straight line segment, connecting anchor points will also move.

To move an anchor point or a segment:

1. Choose the Direct Selection tool (**Figure 2**).

2. Click on an anchor point or a segment.

3. Press and drag the anchor point or segment (**Figures 3a-b**).

Tips

■ Hold down Shift to constrain the movement to a horizontal or vertical axis or to a 45° angle.

■ If all the anchor points on a path are selected, you will not be able to move an individual point or segment. Deselect the object, then select an individual point.

■ Hold down Shift and click to select more than one anchor point at a time.

In the previous instructions, you learned that you can drag a curve segment or an anchor point to reshape a curve. A more precise way to reshape a curve is to lengthen, shorten, or change the angle of the direction lines.

To reshape a curve segment:

1. Choose the Direct Selection tool.

2. Click on an anchor point (**Figure 4**).

3. Press and drag a direction point (the end of the direction line) toward or away from the anchor point (**Figure 5**).

or

Rotate the direction point around the anchor point (**Figure 6**). The anchor point will remain selected when you release the mouse.

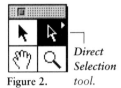
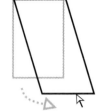

Figure 2.   *Direct Selection tool.*

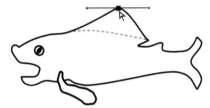

Figure 3a. *A segment is moved.*

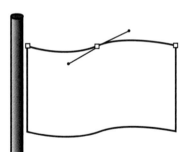

Figure 3b. *An anchor point is moved.*

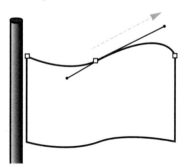

Figure 4. *The original shape with an anchor point selected.*

Figure 5. *A direction point is dragged away from the anchor point.*

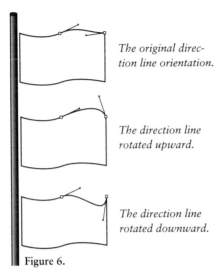

The original direction line orientation.

The direction line rotated upward.

The direction line rotated downward.

Figure 6.

Figure 7. *Convert Direction Point tool.*

To convert a corner anchor point into a curve anchor point:

1. Choose the Direct Selection tool (**Figure 2**), then click on the edge of the object. The anchor points will be hollow.

2. Choose the Convert Direction Point tool (**Figure 7**).

3. Press on an anchor point, then drag away from it. Direction lines will be created as you drag. The further you drag, the rounder the curve will be (**Figure 8**).

4. *Optional:* To further modify the curve, choose the Direct Selection tool, then drag the anchor point or the direction line.

Tips

■ Direction lines on a smooth curve form a straight line in relationship to each other even if one direction line is moved, or the curve segment or anchor point they are connected to is moved.

■ If the new curve segment twists around the anchor point as you drag, keep the mouse button down, rotate the direction line back around the anchor point to undo the twist, then continue to drag in the new direction (**Figure 9**).

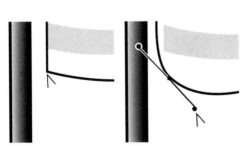

Figure 8. *To convert a corner anchor point into a curve anchor point, click with the **Convert Direction Point** tool on the anchor point, then drag away from it.*

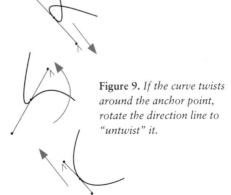

Figure 9. *If the curve twists around the anchor point, rotate the direction line to "untwist" it.*

Convert a Corner Point into a Smooth Point

To convert a curve anchor point into a corner anchor point:

1. Choose the Direct Selection tool (**Figure 2**).

2. Click on the edge of the object to display its anchor points.

3. Choose the Convert Direction Point tool (**Figure 7**).

4. Click on a curve anchor point. Its direction lines will be deleted (**Figure 10**).

Figure 10. *Click with the* **Convert Direction Point** *tool on a curve anchor point to convert it into a corner anchor point.*

To "pinch" a curve, its direction lines must rotate independently of each other rather than remain in a straight line in relationship to each other.

To pinch a curve inward:

1. Choose the Direct Selection tool (**Figure 2**).

2. Click on the edge of an object to display its anchor points.

3. Choose the Convert Direction Point tool (**Figure 7**).

4. Press and drag a direction point at the end of one of the direction lines. The curve segment will reshape as you drag (**Figure 11**).

5. Choose the Direct Selection tool. Click on the anchor point again.

6. Drag the other direction line for that anchor point.

Tip

■ To revert an independent-rotating direction line pair back into its previous straight-line alignment and produce a smooth, "un-pinched" curve segment, choose the Convert Direction Point tool, then click on either direction point.

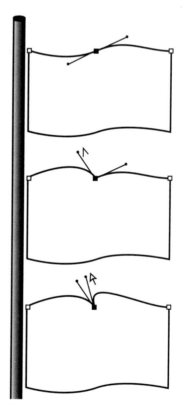

Figure 11. *Direction lines are moved independently to pinch the curve.*

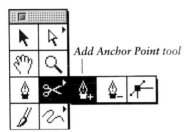

Figure 12.

Add Anchor Point tool

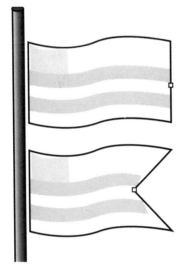

Figure 13. *Click on a segment with the **Add Anchor Point** tool to create a new anchor point, then move the anchor point, if desired.*

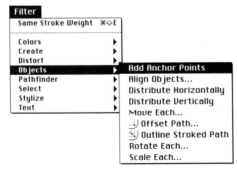

Figure 14. *Choose **Add Anchor Points** from the Objects submenu under the **Filter** menu.*

Another way to reshape an object is to manually add or delete anchor points from its path using the **Add Anchor Point** or **Delete Anchor Point** tool. Adding or deleting points from a path will not split or open it; the path will remain closed. A new anchor point on a curve segment will be a curve anchor point with direction lines. A new anchor point on a straight line segment will be a corner anchor point.

To add points to a path manually:

1. *Optional:* Select an object to display its anchor points *(see page 56).*

2. Choose the Add Anchor Point tool **(Figure 12).**

3. Click on the edge of the object. The new anchor point will be selected **(Figure 13).** Repeat, if desired, to add more points.

4. Use the Direct Selection tool to move or otherwise modify the new anchor point **(Figure 13).**

Tips

■ If you do not click precisely on a segment of an object, a warning prompt will appear. Click OK, then try again.

■ Hold down Option to use the Delete Anchor Point tool when the Add Anchor Point tool is selected and is over an anchor point.

The **Add Anchor Points** filter inserts one anchor point midway between every two existing anchor points.

To add anchor points to a path using a filter:

1. Select an object or objects.

2. Choose Add Anchor Points from the Objects submenu under the Filter menu **(Figure 14).**

3. *Optional:* Reapply the filter to add more points.

Add Points to a Path

To delete points from a path:

1. Select an object *(see page 56)*.

2. Choose the Delete Anchor Point tool (**Figure 15**).

3. Click on an anchor point. The point will be deleted and an adjacent point will become selected (**Figure 16**). Repeat to delete other anchor points, if desired.

Tips

■ If you do not click precisely on an anchor point, a warning prompt will appear. Click OK and try again.

■ Hold down Option to use the Add Anchor Point tool when the Delete Anchor Point tool is selected and over a segment.

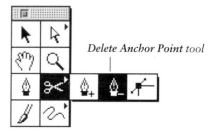

Delete Anchor Point tool

Figure 15.

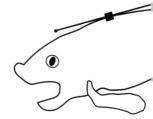

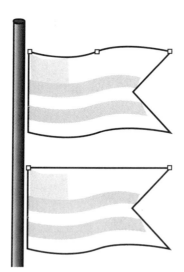

Figure 16. *To delete an anchor point, click on it with the **Delete Anchor Point** tool. The path will reshape.*

Delete Points from a Path

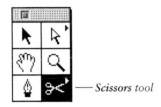

— *Scissors* tool

Figure 17.

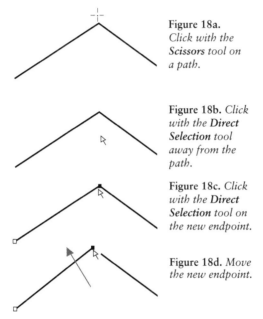

Figure 18a.
Click with the
Scissors *tool on*
a path.

Figure 18b. *Click*
with the ***Direct***
Selection *tool*
away from the
path.

Figure 18c. *Click*
with the ***Direct***
Selection *tool on*
the new endpoint.

Figure 18d. *Move*
the new endpoint.

An open path can be split into two paths and a closed path can be opened using the **Scissors tool**. A path can be split at an anchor point or in the middle of a segment.

To split a path:

1. Choose any selection tool.

2. Click on an object to display its anchor points.

3. Choose the Scissors tool (**Figure 17**).

4. Click on the object's path (**Figure 18a**). If you click on a closed path, it will turn into a single, open path. If you click on an open path, it will be split into two paths. The new endpoints will be selected and will overlap each other.

To move the new endpoints apart:

5. Choose the Direct Selection tool.

6. Click away from the object to deselect it (**Figure 18b**).

7. Click on the object's path.

8. Click on the new endpoint (**Figure 18c**), then drag it away to reveal the endpoint underneath (**Figure 18d**).

Tips

■ You can apply a Fill color to an open path. If you apply a Stroke color, you will be able to see where the missing segment is (**Figure 19**).

■ You cannot split an open path if it has text on it or inside it.

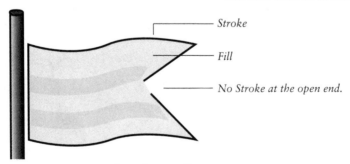

— *Stroke*

— *Fill*

— *No Stroke at the open end.*

Figure 19. *An open path can have a Fill and a Stroke.*

Split a Path

The **Average** command reshapes one or more paths by precisely realigning their endpoints or anchor points to the horizontal and/or vertical axis.

To average anchor points:

1. Choose the Direct Selection tool (**Figure 2**).

2. Hold down Shift and click on two or more anchor points. You might want to zoom in on the objects so you can clearly see the selected points.

3. Choose Average from the Object menu (**Figure 20**).

4. Click **Horizontal** to align the points along the horizontal (x) axis (**Figure 21**).

or

Click **Vertical** to align the points along the vertical (y) axis.

or

Click **Both** to overlap the points along both the horizontal and vertical axes. Choose this option if you want to join them later into one point *(instructions on the following page)*.

5. Click OK or press Return. (**Figure 22**)

Figure 20. *Choose Average from the Object menu.*

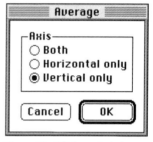

Figure 21. *Click an Axis button in the Average dialog box.*

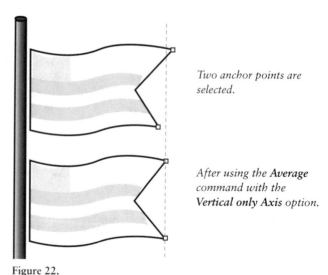

Two anchor points are selected.

After using the Average command with the Vertical only Axis option.

Figure 22.

Average Anchor Points

Figure 23. *Choose Join from the Object menu.*

Figure 24. *Click Corner or Smooth Points in the Join dialog box.*

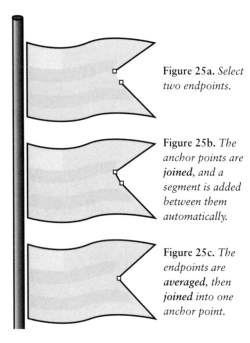

Figure 25a. *Select two endpoints.*

Figure 25b. *The anchor points are joined, and a segment is added between them automatically.*

Figure 25c. *The endpoints are averaged, then joined into one anchor point.*

If you align two endpoints on top of each other and then execute the **Join** command, they will combine into one anchor point. If the endpoints are not on top of each other, a new straight line segment will be created between them. The Join command will not add direction lines to the new anchor point.

To join two endpoints:

1. Choose the Direct Selection tool.

2. *Optional:* If you want to combine two endpoints into one, move one endpoint on top of the other manually or use the Average command (Both Axis) to align them *(instructions are on the previous page)*.

3. Hold down Shift and click on two endpoints (**Figure 25a**).

4. Choose Join from the Object menu (**Figure 23**). If the endpoints are not on top of each other, the Join command will connect them with a straight line segment (**Figure 25b**). If the endpoints are aligned on top of each other, the Join dialog box will open. In the Join dialog box (**Figure 24**):

Click **Corner** to join corner points into one corner point with no direction lines or to connect two curve points (or a corner point and a curve point) into one curve point with independent-moving direction lines. This is the default setting (**Figure 25c**). *or*

Click **Smooth** to connect two curve points into a curve point with direction lines that move in tandem.

5. Click OK or press Return.

Tip

■ To average and join two selected endpoints via one keystroke, hold down Command (⌘) and Option and press "J".

Join Endpoints

Filters under the Pathfinder submenu combine multiple objects into one new object. The **Unite** filter is used in these instructions.

To combine two objects into one using the Unite filter:

1. Position two or more objects so they overlap (**Figure 26**).

2. Choose the Selection tool.

3. Press and drag a marquee around all the objects.

4. Choose Unite from the Pathfinder submenu under the Filter menu (**Figure 27**). The individual objects will combine into one closed object (**Figure 28**).

Tips

- If you apply a Sroke color to the new object, you will see that its previously overlapping segments were removed.

- You can use the new closed object as a masking object. (You could not create a mask with the original objects before they were united.)

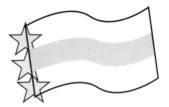

Figure 26. *Overlap two or more objects, then select them all.*

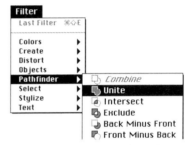

Figure 27. *Choose **Unite** from the Pathfinder submenu under the **Filter** menu.*

Figure 28. *The individual shapes are combined into a single shape.*

Figure 29. *These numbers were converted to outlines before applying the Unite filter.*

Figures 30a-b.

(side margin) **Unite Objects**

Figure 31. *The outer shape of this tag was created by placing a rectangle over a circle and then applying the Unite filter.*

Exercise

Change a square into a star (or clover):

1. If the rulers are not displayed, choose Show Rulers from the View menu.
2. Choose the Rectangle tool.
3. Click on the Artboard.
4. In the Rectangle dialog box, enter 3" in the Width and Height fields.
5. Choose the Selection tool.
6. Click on the rectangle.
7. Press and drag a guide from the horizontal ruler. Release the mouse when the guide is over the rectangle's center point.
8. Press and drag a guide from the vertical ruler. Release the mouse when the guide is over the rectangle's center point (**Figure 33**).
9. Choose the Add Anchor Point tool (**Figure 32**).

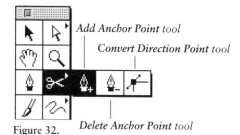

Add Anchor Point tool

Convert Direction Point tool

Delete Anchor Point tool

Figure 32.

(Continued on the following page)

Exercise *(continued)*

10. Position the pointer over the inter-section of a ruler guide and the edge of the rectangle, then click to add a point in the middle of the segment (**Figure 34**).

11. Add points to the other segment midpoints.

12. Choose the Direct Selection tool.

13. Drag each of the midpoints inward toward the center point (**Figure 35**). You should now have a star with four narrow spokes.

14. Choose the Convert Direction Point tool (**Figure 32**).

15. Drag from the outer anchor points to convert the corners into smooth curves (**Figure 37**).

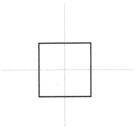

Figure 33.

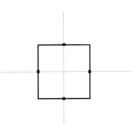

Figure 34.

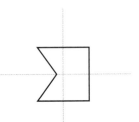

Figure 35.

Change the star back into a square:

1. If the star is not selected, select it with a selection tool.

2. Choose the Convert Direction Point tool (**Figure 32**).

3. Click on the curve points to convert them back into corner points.

4. Choose the Delete Anchor Point tool (**Figure 32**).

5. Click on each of the inner anchor points. The outer points will be reconnected by a single segment, and the object will be square again.

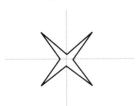

Figure 36.

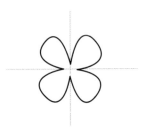

Figure 37.

Exercise

Exercise

Create the flag shown in Figure 1:

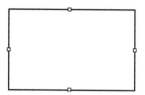

1. Draw a rectangle. Apply a White Fill and a Black stroke. Add points to the middle of the segments using the Add Anchor Point tool.

2. Drag with the Convert Direction Point tool from the top and bottom midpoints.

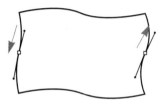

3. Drag with the Convert Direction Point tool from the side midpoints.

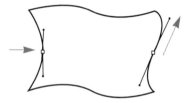

4. Using the Direct Selection tool, move the left midpoint inward, then rotate the direction lines. Drag the right midpoint direction lines away from their anchor point.

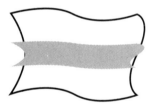

5. Select the whole object, then double-click the Scale tool. Enter Non-uniform: Horizontal 100%, Vertical 30%, then click Copy. Apply a Gray Fill and a Stroke of None.

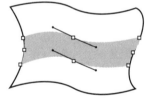

6. Rotate the top and bottom midpoints' direction lines to match the flag's curves. Move the left and right anchor points to fit into larger shape as closely as possible.

7. To cover the edges of the gray shape with a copy of the flag, select the large flag shape, choose Copy from the Edit menu. Select the gray shape, then Choose Paste in Front from the Edit menu. Apply a Fill of None and a Black Stroke in a thick Weight. Marquee all the shapes with the Selection tool, then choose Group from the Arrange menu.

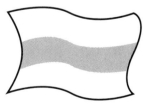

The **Auto Trace tool** automatically traces a path over a PICT template. Unfortunately, the tool is not as magical as it sounds. It usually creates too many anchor points, and places points in inappropriate locations. Also, it does not create perfect rectangles, circles, or straight lines. Autotraced shapes usually need to be cleaned up (use the tools discussed in this chapter).

The exactness with which the Auto Trace tool traces a path is determined by the Freehand tolerance setting in the General Preferences dialog box (File menu). The higher the Freehand tolerance, the less exactly an object will be traced, and the fewer anchor points will be created.

The Adobe Streamline program traces more accurately and offers more options than Illustrator's Auto Trace tool. You can also adjust a bitmapped image in Streamline before using the program to trace it.

To use the Auto Trace tool:

1. Hold down Option and choose New from the File menu.

2. Locate and highlight a PICT file, then Click Open (**Figure 38**).

3. Choose a Fill of None and a Stroke of Black from the Paint Style palette.

4. Choose the Auto Trace tool (**Figure 39**).

5. Click on the edge of the template shape. The shape will be traced automatically (**Figures 40-41**).

6. Click on any other white areas within the template shape (**Figure 42**).

7. Select individual shapes with the Direct Selection tool, and apply Fill and/or Stroke colors (**Figure 43**) *(see page 89)*.

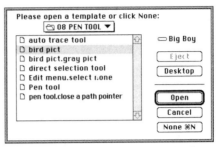

Figure 38. *In the open template dialog box, highlight a PICT file, then click* **Open**.

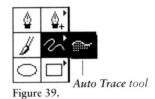

Auto Trace tool

Figure 39.

Figure 40. *The template in the document window.*

Figure 41. *The outer path traced.*

Figure 42. *The outer and inner paths traced.*

Figure 43. *The final objects with Black and White Fills.*

Auto Trace

Figure 44. *The final label.*

Figure 45. *A closeup of the PICT template.*

Figure 46. *A closeup of an Auto Trace of the letters. Note the non-systematic distribution of anchor points and direction lines.*

Figure 47. *The letters drawn manually (the template is hidden). Direction lines are horizontal or on the same diagonal.*

To trace letters manually:

The Auto Trace tool traces quickly and is useful if the "feel" of the relatively coarse rendering it produces is appropriate for your particular project (**Figure 46**). If you need to create smoother shapes, however, you can refine the Auto Trace tool paths or trace the template manually.

The following is a description of how designer Peter Fahrni uses Illustrator to produce his own letterforms. Figure 44 is a label he produced.

1. *Scan the artwork*

To make sure the baseline of your letterwork template squares with the horizontal guidelines in Illustrator, trim the edge of your drawing parallel to the baseline and slide it against the glass frame of the scanner. Scan your artwork (a resolution of 300 dpi is usually sufficient) and save it as a PICT.

2. *Manual trace*

Follow the instructions on the previous page to open the PICT in Illustrator. Most round shapes can be drawn using four anchor points to support the path. In upright letters, place anchor points on the topmost, bottommost, leftmost, and rightmost points of the curve. Hold down Shift if you want to draw out the direction lines horizontally or vertically.

To create the inclined letter shown in **Figure 47**, a line was drawn following the inclination of a stem, (in this case the lower case "t"), and then it was copied and converted into a guide for positioning the direction lines (choose Make from the Guides submenu under the Object menu). The direction lines of the leftmost and rightmost points were drawn out to align with the guides.

(Continued on the following page)

Manual Trace

3. *Fine tune the flow of curves*

Select an anchor point, then move it by pressing the arrow keys (the length and the angle of the direction lines will not change). Select a curve segment, and press the arrow keys to adjust its shape (the length, but not the angle, of the direction lines will change).

The manually traced "B" consisted of two closed crisscrossing paths (**Figure 48**). The Unite filter (Pathfinder submenu under the Filter menu) was applied to combine the two paths into one (**Figure 49**). ■

Figure 48. *The hand drawn "B."*

Figure 49. *The final "B" after applying the Unite filter.*

A comparison of an Auto Traced character and an Adobe font character.

Figure 50a. *The PICT template in Illustrator.*

Figure 50b. *The character Auto Traced.*

Figure 51. *A character in the Goudy 100 Adobe PostScript font, created as type in Illustrator.*

PEN TOOL 8

THE **PEN TOOL** creates precise curve and straight line segments connected by anchor points. If you click with the Pen tool, you will create corner points and straight line segments with no direction lines. If you drag with the Pen tool, you will create smooth curve points and curve segments with direction lines. The distance and the direction in which you drag the mouse determines the shape of the curve segment.

The Pen tool is the most difficult tool in Illustrator to master. Patience and practice are required to become comfortable and adept using it. If you find the Pen tool too difficult to use, remember that you can transform a simple shape into a complex shape using the point and path editing tools, as shown in Chapter 7, *Paths*.

Pen Tool

Miriam Schaer

Click with the Pen tool to create an open or closed straight-sided polygon.

To create a straight-sided object using the Pen tool:

1. Choose the Pen tool (**Figure 1**).

2. Click to create an anchor point.

3. Click to create a second anchor point. A straight line segment will connect the two points.

4. Click to create additional anchor points. They will be also connected by straight line segments.

5. To complete the shape as an **open path:**

Click the Pen tool on the Toolbox.
or
Hold down Command (⌘) and click outside the new shape to deselect it.
or
Choose Select None from the Edit menu (**Figure 2**).

To complete the shape as a **closed path,** position the Pen pointer over the starting point (a small circle will appear next to the pointer), then click (**Figure 3**).

Tips

■ If you use the Pen tool when your illustration is in Preview view and a Fill color is selected on the Paint Style palette, the Pen path will be filled as soon as three points are created. To create segments that appear as lines only, choose a Fill of None and choose a Stroke color before using the Pen tool *(see page 89)*.

■ Hold down Shift while clicking with the Pen tool to constrain the line to the horizontal or vertical axis or to a 45° angle relative to the angle specified in the Constrain Angle field in the General Preferences dialog box (File menu). When the Constrain Angle is 0°, the 45° angle will be measured from the horizontal and vertical x and y axes.

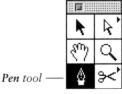

Pen tool —

Figure 1.

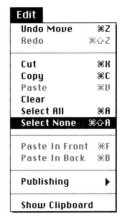

Figure 2. *To complete the polygon as an **open** path, choose **Select None** from the **Edit** menu.*

Figure 3. *The **Pen** tool pointer positioned over the starting point. Note the small circle next to the pointer.*

(sidebar) Create a Straight-Sided Object

Figure 4a. *Press and drag to create the first anchor point.*

Follow these instructions to create continuous curves — smooth anchor points connected by smooth curve segments, each with a pair of direction lines that move in tandem. The longer the direction lines, the larger the curve.

To create continuous curves using the Pen tool:

1. Choose the Pen tool (**Figure 1**).

2. Press and drag to create the first anchor point (**Figure 4a**). The angle of the pair of direction lines that you create will be determined by the direction you drag.

3. **Release the mouse and move it away from the last anchor point,** then press and drag in the direction you want the curve to go to create a second anchor point (**Figure 4b**). A curve segment will connect the first and second anchor points, and a second pair of direction lines will be created. The shape of the curve segment will be defined by the length and direction you drag the mouse.

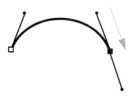

Figure 4b. *Release and reposition the mouse, then drag in the direction you wish the curve to follow.*

4. Drag to create additional anchor points and direction lines (**Figures 4c-d**). The anchor points will be connected by curve segments.

(Continued on the following page)

Figure 4c. *Continue to reposition and press-and-drag.*

Figure 4d. *Continue to reposition and press-and-drag. To complete the object as an open path, click the* **Pen** *tool on the toolbox.*

Create Continuous Curves

5. To complete the object as an **open path**:

Click the Pen tool on the Toolbox.
or
Click a selection tool, then click away from the new object to deselect it.
or
Choose Select None from the Edit menu.

To complete the object as a **closed path**, position the Pen pointer over the starting point (a small circle will appear next to the pointer) (**Figures 5a-e**), drag, then release the mouse.

Tips

■ The fewer the anchor points, the smoother the shape. Too many anchor points will produce bumpy curves.

■ Hold down Command (⌘) to use the Selection tool or Direct Selection tool (whichever was last highlighted) while the Pen tool is selected. Hold down Command (⌘) and Tab to use the Selection tool or Direct Selection tool (whichever was not last highlighted).

■ To turn a curve anchor point into a corner anchor point while drawing with the Pen tool, click on the last anchor point. The direction lines will disappear.

To turn a corner anchor point into a curve anchor point while drawing with the Pen tool, position the pen pointer over the last anchor point, then press and drag. Direction lines will appear.

Figures 5a-e. Another path being created, finishing as a closed path.

Figure 5a.

Figure 5b.

Figure 5c.

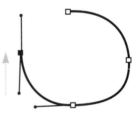

Figure 5d.

Figure 5e. *To close the path, press and drag over the starting point.*

Create Continuous Curves

Figure 6a. *Press and drag to create the first anchor point.*

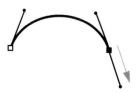

Figure 6b. *Release and reposition the mouse, then press and drag to create a second anchor point.*

Figure 6c. *Hold down **Option** and press and drag from the last anchor point in the direction you wish the new curve to follow. Note that the direction lines are on the same side of the curve segment.*

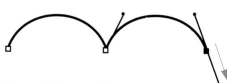

Figure 6d. *Press and drag to create another anchor point, etc.*

You can use the Pen tool to create non-continuous curves — segments that curve on only one side of an anchor point, like a series of archways (**Figure 6d**). (In a continuous curve, segments curve on both sides of an anchor point.) The anchor point that connects non-continuous curves is called a corner point. If you move one direction line from a corner point, only the curve on the same side of the point will reshape. Continuous and non-continuous curves can be combined in the same path.

Two methods for producing non-continuous curves follow. In the first set of instructions, you will press and drag to create an anchor point first, then hold down Option to redraw the direction line for that anchor point.

To create non-continuous curves (Pen tool method):

1. Choose the Pen tool (**Figure 1**).

2. Press and drag to create the first anchor point (**Figure 6a**).

3. **Release the mouse and move it away from the last anchor point,** then press and drag to create a second anchor point (**Figure 6b**). A curve segment will connect the first and second anchor points, and a second pair of direction lines will be created. The shape of the curve segment will be determined by the length and direction you drag.

4. Hold down Option and press and drag from the last anchor point in the direction you wish the new curve to follow (**Figure 6c**). A new direction line will be created.

5. Repeat steps 3 and 4 to create a series of anchor points and curves (**Figure 6d**).

Create Non-Continuous Curves

To create non-continuous curves (Convert Direction Point tool method):

1. Follow the steps on page 81 to create an open path with smooth curves.

2. Choose the Direct Selection tool (**Figure 7**).

3. Click on the path (**Figure 8a**).

4. Click on the anchor point to be modified (**Figure 8b**).

5. Hold down Control to temporarily use the Convert Direction Point tool and rotate the direction line so it forms a "V" shape with the other direction line (**Figure 8c**). The curve segment will be on the same side of the anchor point as the previous curve segment.

6. Release Control.

7. Repeat steps 4-6 to convert other anchor points (**Figure 8d**).

Tips

■ Hold down Option and Control to use the Convert Direction Point tool to move a direction line when the Pen tool is selected.

■ To convert a pair of direction lines back into a smooth curve, choose the Direct Selection tool, click on the anchor point, choose the Convert Direction Point tool (or hold down Control), then click on a direction line point.

Direct Selection tool

Figure 7.

Figure 8a. *Click on the path.*

Figure 8b. *Click with the Direct Selection tool on the anchor point you wish to modify.*

Figure 8c. *Hold down* **Control** *and rotate the direction line, then release Control.*

Figure 8d. *Repeat steps 4-6 for other anchor points you wish to convert.*

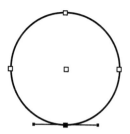

Figure 9. *Click on the bottom edge of the circle.*

Figure 10. *Move the bottom anchor point downward.*

Exercise

Convert a circle into a heart:

1. Draw a perfect circle with the Oval tool (hold down Shift while dragging).

2. Choose the Direct Selection tool (**Figure 7**).

3. Click away from the object to deselect it.

4. Click on the bottom edge of the circle (**Figure 9**).

5. Hold down Shift and drag the bottom anchor point downward (**Figure 10**).

6. Hold down Control to temporarily use the Convert Direction Point tool and press and drag one of the direction lines upward to form a non-continuous curve (**Figure 11**).

7. Release Control.

8. Click on the bottom anchor point to reselect it, then drag the second direction line upward. The bottom of the circle will become a corner point (**Figure 12**).

9. Hold down Shift and drag the anchor point from the top of the circle downward (**Figure 13**).

(Continued on the following page)

Exercise

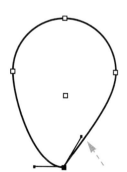

Figure 11. *Hold down* **Control** *and move one of the direction lines upward.*

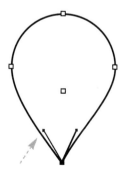

Figure 12. *Reselect the bottom anchor point, then drag the second direction line upward.*

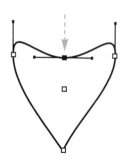

Figure 13. *Move the top anchor point downward.*

10. Hold down Control to temporarily use the Convert Direction Point tool and drag a direction line connected to the top anchor point upward to form a non-continuous curve (**Figure 14**).

11. Release Control.

12. Click on the top anchor point to reselect it, then drag the second direction line upward. The top of the circle will become a corner point (**Figure 15**). ■

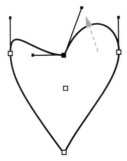

Figure 14. *Hold down Control, drag one of the top direction lines upward, then release Control.*

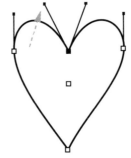

Figure 15. *Click on the top anchor point, then drag the second direction line upward.*

Figure 16. *The completed heart.*

*I*N THIS CHAPTER you will learn to **Fill** the inside of an object with a color, shade, pattern, or gradient, **Stroke** an object's edge with a color or shade, choose stroke styles, mix process colors, append paint styles from another document, use the Eyedropper tool to match colors from the illustration, use the Paint Bucket tool to apply Fill and Stroke colors at the same time, and adjust colors using filters.

Colors are applied using the **Paint Style palette**. You can choose a Fill or Stroke color from premixed swatches, mix your own gray percentage, mix a process color from Cyan, Magenta, Yellow and Black, or choose a Pantone or other named color swatch. You can also Fill a shape with a pattern or gradient and store any custom color, pattern, or gradient Fill on the Paint Style palette. Custom colors are saved with the illustration in which they are created or applied.

The Paint Style palette can also be used to set line style characteristics, such as Stroke color, Stroke thickness, and Stroke style (dashed or solid).

A Fill and/or Stroke can be applied to a closed path or an open path. Any new object you create will automatically be painted with the current Paint Style palette Fill and Stroke settings, which can be changed at any time. When an object is selected, the Paint Style palette displays its paint characteristics.

For the instructions in this chapter, open the **Paint Style** palette *(choose Paint Style from the Object menu, or hold down Command (⌘) and press "I", or choose Show Paint Style from the Window menu)*. Display both the left and right panels of the palette *(instructions are on the following page)*, and check the **Auto** box to apply colors immediately.

Also, work with your illustration in **Preview view** so you can see colors on screen as you apply them *(choose Preview from the View menu)*.

The Paint Style palette

The palette is divided into three panels: Paint swatches on the left panel, color selection method icons and the Stroke Weight field on the right panel, and Stroke attribute options on the bottom panel (**Figure 1**).

You can control which panel or combination of panels are open using the pop-up panel display menu in the upper right corner of the palette. Or, click the section on the miniature palette that corresponds to the panel you wish to display or hide.

Tips

■ To open the left and right panels at the same time, click on the line between the left and right panels on the miniature palette.

■ When the Auto box on the right panel is checked, color attributes apply immediately to the selected object. To apply colors when the Auto box is unchecked, click the Apply button, or double-click a color swatch, or press Enter.

(Overprinting is discussed in Chapter 24)

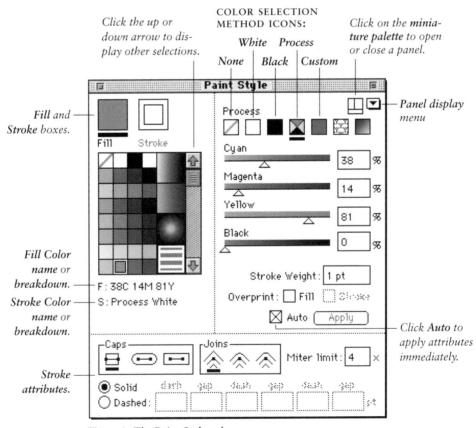

Figure 1. *The Paint Style palette.*

Window

New Window

Hide Toolbox ⌘⌃T
Hide Layers ⌘⌃L
Show Info ⌘⌃I
Show Paint Style
Show Gradient
Show Character
Show Paragraph

✓ junk ai <50%>

Figure 2. *Choose Show Paint Style from the Window menu.*

Note: Instructions for applying a custom (named) color are on page 91, instructions for applying a Gradient Fill are in Chapter 10, *Gradients,* and instructions for applying a Pattern Fill are in Chapter 11, *Patterns.*

To apply a Fill or Stroke color (None, Black, White, or Process):

1. Select an object (not all the anchor points need to be solid).

2. If the Paint Style palette is not displayed, choose Paint Style from the Object menu or choose Show Paint Style from the Window menu (**Figure 2**). Check the Auto box.

The palette will display the paint attributes of the selected object.

3. Click the Fill box at the top of palette.
or
Click the Stroke box at the top of the palette.

4. To Fill or Stroke with **None**, click the color selection method icon with the slash. The Fill or Stroke box will also have a slash through it and any already applied Fill or Stroke color will be removed from the object.

To Fill or Stroke with **White**, click the White color selection method icon. A slider will appear below the Color selection boxes. Leave it all the way to the left to apply white.

To Fill or Stroke with **Black** or **gray**, click the Black color selection method icon. A slider will appear below the color selection boxes. Move the slider to mix a shade of gray. Or, enter a number in the percentage field, then press Tab or Return.

To Fill or Stroke with a **Process** color, click the color selection method icon that is divided into four little wedges. Four sliders will appear below the color selection boxes. Move the

(Continued on the following page)

SWATCH TIPS

If you click on a paint swatch, the color name or the CMYK breakdown of that color will be displayed just below the swatch scroll window.

To store a custom color, pattern, gradient, or new process color in the swatch window, first click the swatch window scroll arrow to display the empty squares. Then drag the color name from the right panel onto an empty square, or drag the Fill or Stroke box color onto an empty square, or hold down Option and click on an empty square.

To replace a swatch, drag a new swatch or color name over it, or hold down Option and drag an existing swatch over it.

You can save up to 255 swatches with a document.

To delete a swatch, hold down Command (⌘) and click on the swatch, then click Delete when the warning prompt appears. You cannot restore a deleted swatch with the Undo command.

Apply a Fill or Stroke Color

sliders. Or, enter numbers in the percentage fields, then press Tab.
or
Click a swatch.
(Figure 3)

Tips

- A Gradient cannot be applied as a Stroke color.
- If the Stroke box is highlighted, you can enter a thickness value in the Stroke Weight field.
- To make the Fill color the same as the Stroke color, or vice versa, drag one box over the other.
- Hold down Shift and drag any slider to change the saturation of a process color while preserving its Cyan, Magenta, Yellow, Black ratios.
- You can paint multiple selected objects. If their Fill and Stroke colors differ, a question mark will appear in the corresponding box. You can apply a new Fill and/or Stroke color to all the objects.
- Don't apply a large Stroke Weight to small type — it will distort the character shapes.

FAIR WARNING

If you've read our other books, you've already heard us beg and plead our readers not to mix process colors or choose spot (Pantone) colors based on how they look on the screen (unless you're working on a very carefully calibrated monitor, which most people aren't). Screen colors — which are seductively bright and luminous — don't accurately simulate printed colors. To avoid an embarassing and costly on-press surprise, **use matching books to choose spot colors or mix process colors**.

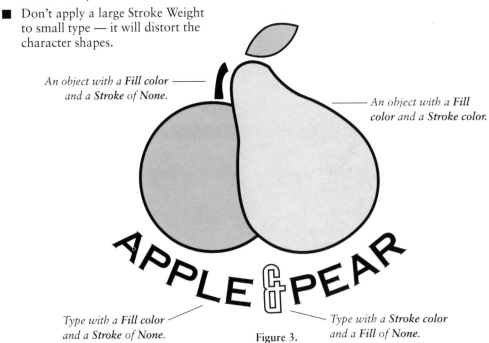

An object with a *Fill color* and a *Stroke* of *None*.

An object with a *Fill color* and a *Stroke color*.

Type with a *Fill color* and a *Stroke* of *None*.

Type with a *Stroke color* and a *Fill* of *None*.

Figure 3.

(instructions are on the next two pages).

What is a Custom Color?

A **custom color** is a process color that you have named or a color from a matching system, such as Pantone or Trumatch. In order to access a custom color in an Illustrator document, you must mix and name it or copy it from one of the color matching system files that are supplied with Illustrator *(instructions are on the next two pages).* Matching system colors are not automatically available in a document.

*Click the **Custom** color selection icon to display the custom color scroll window.*

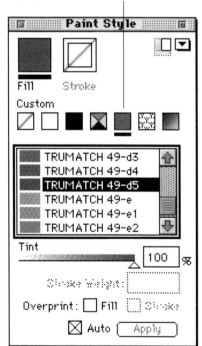

Figure 4. *The right side of the **Paint Style** palette.*

To Fill or Stroke with a custom (named) color:

1. Select an object.

2. Click the Fill or Stroke box at top of the Paint Style palette (the attribute of the object you wish to modify).

3. On the right panel, click the Custom color selection method icon (**Figure 4**). A scroll window will appear.

4. Click a custom color name. The new color will appear in the Fill or Stroke box and in the selected object.

5. *Optional:* For a spot color, move the tint slider or enter a number in the Tint field.

Tips

■ To display the process color breakdown of a color, highlight the color name, then click the Process color selection method icon.

■ To convert a process color into a custom color in a selected object, drag the process color swatch or drag from the Fill or Stroke box onto the Custom color selection method icon or drag a swatch onto the custom color scroll list. Click OK when the Custom Color dialog box opens. (You can also change the color name before you click OK.)

■ If you modify a named color, it will automatically be modified in all the objects to which it has already been applied.

Apply a Custom Color

To name a process color:

1. Choose Custom Color from the Object menu (**Figure 5**).
or
On the Paint Style palette, click the Custom color selection method icon, then double-click a color name on the custom color scroll list.

2. Click New (**Figure 6**).

3. Enter a name for the color in the "Change name to" field.

4. Click the White or Black color selection method icon, then move the slider to mix a shade.
or
Click the Process color selection method icon, then move the sliders or enter numbers in the percentage fields and press Tab.

5. Click OK or press Return. The color name will appear on the Paint Style palette.

Tips

■ To convert a custom color into a process color in a selected object, click on a custom color name on the Paint Style palette, then click on the Process color selection method icon. Or, use Adobe Separator to convert a custom color into a process color (*see page 213*).

■ To delete a custom color, highlight the color name, then click Delete. Objects painted with that color will be painted Black. The color will be deleted from all open documents in which it has been saved. (To retrieve a deleted custom color after closing the Custom color dialog box, choose Undo from the Edit menu.)

■ Beware: if you click Select All Unused and then click Delete, all unused custom and Pantone colors will be deleted from the custom color list of any open document.

Figure 5. *Choose **Custom Color** from the **Object** menu.*

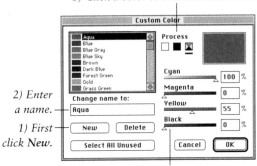

3) Click a color selection method icon.

2) Enter a name.

*1) First click **New**.*

4) Move the sliders (or enter percentages).

Figure 6. *The **Custom Color** dialog box.* **Note:** *In Illustrator 5.0, if you modify the percentages for a CMYK color in the Custom Color dialog box and then click Cancel, the original color is not restored. If necessary, you can choose Undo after closing the dialog box. This bug should be fixed in version 5.0.1.*

Name a Process Color

Figure 7. *Choose* **Open** *from the* **File** *menu.*

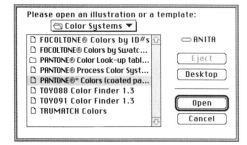

Figure 8. *Click on a matching system name, then click Open.*

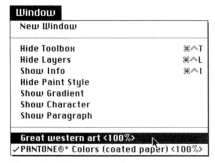

Figure 9. *Choose your document name from the* **Window** *menu.*

To add matching system colors to a document:

1. Choose Open from the File menu (**Figure 7**).

2. Locate and select the desired matching system file in the Color Systems folder inside the Adobe Illustrator folder (**Figure 8**).

3. Click Open.

4. Choose your document name from the Window menu (**Figure 9**).

5. Click the Custom color selection method icon on the Paint Style palette. The matching system color names will appear on the scroll list (click the scroll arrow to display them, if necessary).

6. Press and drag a color name you wish to save onto a blank square in the paint swatch window (scroll, if necessary, to display blank swatches).

7. Choose the matching system document from the Window menu, then click on that document's close box. Don't save over a matching system file if it has been altered. If a warning prompt appears, click Don't Save.

The selected matching system colors will be saved with your document, and can be accessed from the Custom color swatch window and scroll list.

Tip

■ If you use Import Styles to append matching system colors, the document to which they are appended will contain all the colors from that matching system file, and its file storage size will increase.

Use the **Import Styles** command to append custom colors, patterns, and gradients from another Illustrator document or from the Illustrator Gradients and Patterns or Color Systems folder onto the current document palette/s.

To append colors, patterns or gradients:

1. Choose Import Styles from the File menu (**Figure 10**).

2. Locate the document with the color styles you wish to append.

3. Click Import.

Tips

■ Paint swatches on the Paint Style palette in the document from which styles are imported will not be imported.

■ If you append a color (or pattern or gradient) with the same name as a color in the current document, it will replace the color in the current document.

You can change a Stroke's color, weight (thickness), and style (dashed or solid, rounded or sharp corners, and flat or rounded ends).

To change the thickness of a Stroke:

1. Select an object.

2. Click the Stroke box at the top of Paint Style palette.

3. If the bottom panel of the Paint Style palette is not displayed, choose the first icon from the palette panel display menu.

4. Enter a width in the Stroke Weight field (**Figure 11**). Half the Stroke will be applied inside the object, the other half will be applied outside the object.

Tip

■ A line weight of 0 will be a one-pixel wide hairline if it is output on a high resolution printer.

Append Paint Styles; Stroke Thickness

TO APPEND MORE SELECTIVELY

To import colors, patterns, or gradients one at a time, choose Open from the File menu, then locate and open the document you wish to append from. Click on your "destination" document, then drag any individual color, pattern, or gradient name you want to append from the Paint Style palette scroll list to a swatch square.

Figure 10. *Choose* **Import Styles** *from the File menu.*

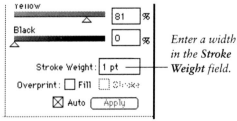

*Enter a width in the **Stroke Weight** field.*

Figure 11. *The right panel of the **Paint Style** palette.*

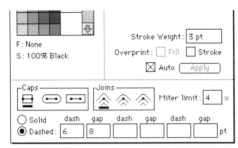

Figure 12. *The bottom panel of the* **Paint Style** *palette.*

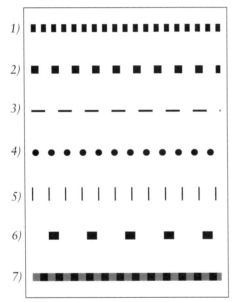

Figure 13. *A variety of dashed lines (the first Caps icon selected for all except #4):*

1) stroke 6, dash 4, gap 4.

2) stroke 6, dash 6, gap 10.

3) stroke 1.5, dash 11, gap 10.

4) stroke 5, dash 0, gap 12 (round caps).

5) stroke 10, dash 1, gap 12.

6) stroke 6, dash 0, gap 10, dash 8, gap 10.

7) stroke 6, dash 6, gap 6 (pasted in front of a 6 point gray Stroked line).

To create a dashed Stroke:

1. Select an object.

2. Click the Stroke box on the Paint Style palette.

3. Make sure the bottom panel is displayed (**Figure 12**).

4. Click the Dashed button.

5. Click a Caps icon (the dash shape).

6. Enter a number in the 1st Dash field (the length of the first dash), then press Tab to apply.

7. *Optional:* To create dashes of varying lengths, enter other amounts in the other Dash fields. If you enter an amount only in the 1st Dash field, that amount will be repeated for all the dashes.

8. Enter an amount in the Gap field (the length of the first gap after the first dash), then press Tab to apply.

9. *Optional:* Enter other amounts in the other Gap fields to create gaps of varying lengths. If you enter an amount only in the 1st Gap field, that amount will be repeat for all the gaps.

(**Figure 13**)

Tip

■ To create a dotted line, click the Round Cap icon, enter a Dash value of 0, and enter a Gap value that is greater than or equal to the Stroke Weight.

Create a Dashed Line

To modify Stroke caps and/or joins:

1. Select an object.
2. Click the Stroke box at the top of Paint Style palette.
3. Make sure the bottom panel of the palette is displayed (**Figure 14**).
4. To modify the endpoints of a solid line or all the dashes in a dashed line:

   Click the left **Caps** icon to create square-cornered ends or square-cornered dashes in which the Stroke stops at the endpoints.

   Click the middle **Caps** icon to create curved ends or round-ended dashes.

   Click the right **Caps** icon to create square-cornered ends or square-cornered dashes in which the Stroke extends beyond the endpoints.

5. To modify the line bends:

   Click the left **Joins** icon to produce pointed bends (miter joins) (**Figure 15**).

   Click the middle **Joins** icon to produce semicircular bends (round joins).

   The right **Joins** icon to produce a square-cornered bend (bevel joins).

   (**Figure 15**)

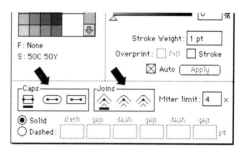

Figure 14. *The Caps and Joins icons on the Paint Style palette.*

Left Caps icon, left Joins icon.

Middle Caps icon, middle Joins icon.

Right Caps icon, right Joins icon.

Figure 15.

Stroke Caps and/or Joins

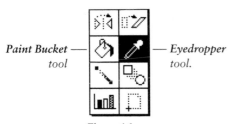

Paint Bucket — tool

— *Eyedropper* tool.

Figure 16.

If you click with the **Paint Bucket** tool on an object, that object will be Filled and Stroked using the current Paint Style palette settings. The Paint Style palette does not have to be displayed for you to use the Paint Bucket tool.

To use the Paint Bucket tool:

1. Choose the Paint Bucket tool (**Figure 16**).

2. Click on an object (the object does not have to be selected). The object will become selected and colored with the current Paint Style palette attributes.

Tip

■ Hold down Option to use the Eyedropper tool while the Paint Bucket tool is selected.

If you click on an object with the **Eyedropper tool**, it picks up the object's paint attributes and displays them on the Paint Style palette. You can then apply those attributes to any other object. The document containing the color you click on does not have to be active.

To use the Eyedropper tool:

1. Choose the Eyedropper tool (**Figure 16**).

2. Click on an object (the object does not have to be selected). The Paint attributes from that object will be displayed on the Paint Style palette.

Tips

■ Hold down Option to use the Paint Bucket tool to paint another object while the Eyedropper is selected. The Paint Style palette does not have to be open.

■ To pick up a color from type, click on the baseline of the type block.

■ To preserve the color, drag the Fill or Stroke box onto a blank swatch square.

Paint Bucket and Eyedropper Tools

To use the Eyedropper tool to Fill multiple objects:

1. Select several objects.

2. Choose the Eyedropper tool.

3. Double-click one of the selected objects or double-click a non-selected object. In either case, the paint attributes of the object you click on will be applied to all the selected objects.

Use the Paintbucket/Eyedropper dialog box to change the default attributes for either or both tools.

To choose paint attributes the Eyedropper picks up or the Paint Bucket applies:

1. Double-click the Paint Bucket or Eyedropper tool.

2. Click check box options on or off (**Figure 17**).

3. Click OK or press Return.

Use the **Adjust Colors filter** to manually adjust colors in one or more selected objects. All the Colors filters automatically convert custom colors into CMYK (process) colors.

To adjust colors:

1. Select the object or objects whose color you wish to modify.

2. Choose Adjust Colors from the Colors submenu under the Filter menu (**Figure 18**).

3. Enter percentages in the Cyan, Magenta, Yellow, or Black fields (the amount of those colors you wish to add or subtract) (**Figure 19**).

4. Click "Increase by %" or "Decrease by %" to add or subtract the color or colors in the percentages entered in step 3.

5. Click Apply to preview.

6. Click OK or press Return.

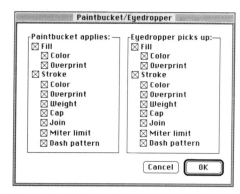

Figure 17. *Click check boxes on or off in the Paintbucket/Eyedropper dialog box.*

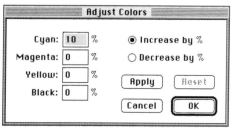

Figure 18. *The Colors submenu under the Filter menu.*

Figure 19. *In the Adjust Colors dialog box, enter percentages in the Cyan, Magenta, Yellow, or Black fields, and click Increase by % or Decrease by %. Click Apply to preview.*

Adjust Colors Filter

GRADIENTS

A GRADIENT FILL is a gradual blend between two or more colors. The simplest Gradient Fill consists of a starting and ending color, with the midpoint (the point where the colors are equally mixed together) midway between the two colors. A gradient can be linear (side to side) or radial (out from center). You can apply a Gradient Fill to one object or across several objects.

You can apply one of the predefined gradients that are supplied with Illustrator, or you can create your own gradient using the **Gradient palette**. The **Paint Style palette** is used to apply a gradient to an object.

Once an object is filled with a gradient, you can use the **Gradient tool** to modify how the Fill is distributed within the object, such as the direction of the gradient, how quickly one color blends into another, and the placement of the center of a radial Gradient Fill.

Note: The Gradient palette and Gradient tool produce color blends. The Blend tool transforms one object into another by producing a series of transitional shapes.

"A cup of coffee a bagel, and you..."

Follow these instructions to apply a predefined Gradient Fill — a gradient supplied with Illustrator or a custom gradient that you have already created. To create your own Gradient Fill, follow the next set of instructions.

To Fill with a gradient:

1. Select an object.

2. If the Paint Style palette is not open, choose Paint Style from the Object menu. Check the Auto box on the palette.

3. Click the Fill box on the palette (**Figure 1**).

4. On the right panel, click the Gradient color selection method icon. A scroll list will appear.

5. Click on a gradient name (**Figure 1**).

6. *Optional:* Enter a new angle for a linear Fill in the Angle field.

Tips

■ To apply a gradient to a Stroke, first apply the Outline Stroked Path filter to convert it into a closed object (Objects submenu under the Filter menu), then follow steps 2-5 above.

■ To Fill type with a gradient, you must first convert it into outlines (choose Create Outlines from the Type menu).

To create a two-color Gradient Fill:

1. Choose Show Gradient from the Window menu (**Figure 3**).
or
Choose Gradient from the Object menu.
or
Double-click a gradient name on the Paint Style palette (**Figure 1**).

2. If the bottom panel of the Gradient palette is not displayed, click the palette display lever.

3. Click the New button (**Figure 4**).

2) Click the Gradient color selection method icon.

3) Click a gradient name.

1) Click the Fill box.

Figure 1. *The Paint Style palette. You can append other gradients supplied with Illustrator or gradients from another document (see page 94).*

Figure 2. *An object filled with a gradient.*

Figure 3. *Choose Show Gradient from the Window menu.*

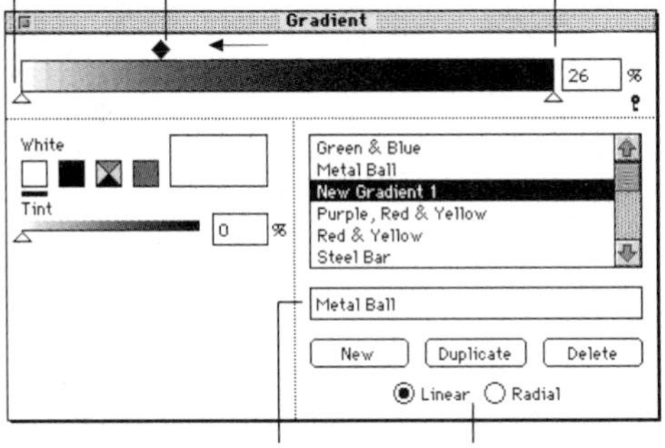

4. Type a name for the gradient in the highlighted field.

5. Press Return.

6. Click the starting color triangle under the left side of the color bar.

7. Click the White or Black color selection icon. Move the slider to choose a shade of gray.
or
Click the Process color selection icon, then move the sliders to mix a color.
or
Click the Custom color selection icon, click a name on the scroll list, and, if desired, move the Tint slider.

8. Click the ending color triangle under the right side of the color bar.

9. Repeat step 7.

10. Click the Linear or Radial button.

11. *Optional:* Move the midpoint diamond (above the color bar) to the right to produce more of the starting color than the ending color, or to the left to produce more of the ending color than the starting color (**Figures 5a-b**).

The new Gradient name will appear on the Gradient and Paint Style palette scroll lists.

Starting color triangle

Midpoint diamond *(where the starting and ending colors are half-and-half).*

Ending color triangle

*Enter a unique **name** for the Gradient.*

*Click the **Linear** or **Radial** button.*

Figure 4. *The Gradient palette. The **midpoint diamond** was moved to the left. The Gradient Fill now contains more of the ending color than the starting color.*

Tips

■ To color separate a gradient containing more than one custom color, assign a different screen angle to each color using Adobe Separator or click the Process color icon on the Gradient palette to translate the custom color into a process color *(see the Illustrator "User Guide" for more information)*. Ask your service bureau for help.

■ To swap the starting and ending colors, drag one triangle over the other.

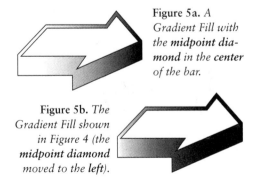

Figure 5a. *A Gradient Fill with the **midpoint diamond** in the **center** of the bar.*

Figure 5b. *The Gradient Fill shown in Figure 4 (the **midpoint diamond** moved to the **left**).*

Two-Color Gradient Fill

A Gradient Fill can contain up to 32 colors.

To create a multi-color Gradient Fill:

1. Follow steps 1-10 on the previous page to produce a two-color Gradient Fill.

or

Click a gradient name on the Gradient palette.

2. Click on the bottom of the color bar where you wish to place the new color. A new triangle will appear (**Figure 6**).

3. Mix a new color.

Steps 4-6 are optional:

4. Move the new triangle left or right to change the location of that color in the gradient (**Figure 6**).

5. Move the midpoint diamond to the left or right of the new color to change the location where the new color is evenly blended with either of the colors adjacent to it.

6. Repeat steps 2-5 to add more colors (**Figure 7**).

Tips

■ To produce a sharp transition between colors, drag the midpoint diamond close to a color triangle or move the color triangles close together.

■ To remove a color triangle, drag it downward off the color bar.

■ To create a variation of a Gradient Fill, click the Duplicate button on the Gradient palette, rename the Fill, then modify it.

■ To delete a Gradient Fill name from the Gradient palette, click on it, then click Delete.

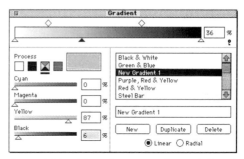

Figure 6. *To add a color to a gradient, click under the color bar to add a new triangle, click a color selection method icon, then mix a process color or click on a custom color name.*

Figure 7. *Six new shades of black have been added to this gradient. Move the **midpoint diamond** between a pair of colors to change the location where those colors are evenly blended, or move a **triangle** to move that individual color.*

Figure 8. *Multi-color gradients.*

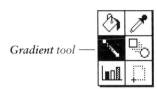

Gradient tool —

Figure 9.

Figure 10a. *A linear Gradient Fill applied using the Paint Style palette only.*

Figure 10b. *The Gradient tool dragged a short distance from **right to left** across the same gradient.*

Once an object is filled with a gradient, you can use the **Gradient tool** to manually change the angle of the Fill, the order of the starting and ending colors, or the location of the center of a radial Gradient Fill.

To use the Gradient tool:

1. Follow the instructions on page 100 to apply a Gradient Fill to an object. Keep the object selected.

2. Choose the Gradient tool (**Figure 9**).

3. To modify a **linear** Gradient Fill, you can press and drag across the object in a new direction (right-to-left or diagonally) (**Figures 10a-b**). To blend the colors quickly, drag a short distance; to blend the colors slowly across a wider span, drag a long distance.

To modify a **radial** Gradient Fill, position the pointer where you wish the center of the fill to be, then press and drag (**Figures 11a-b**).

Tips

■ Repeat step 3 — drag in a different direction to produce a different result. The new gradient will replace the old.

■ Drag in the opposite direction to reverse the order of the Fill colors.

■ If you start to drag or finish dragging outside the edge of an object with the Gradient tool, the colors at the beginning or end of the gradient Fill will not appear in the object.

Gradient tool

Figure 11a. *A radial Gradient Fill before using the Gradient tool.*

Figure 11b. *After dragging the Gradient tool across the same radial Gradient Fill.*

You can Fill multiple objects with the same gradient, including type that has been converted to outlines.

To fill multiple objects with the same gradient:

1. Select the objects.

2. Fill them with a Gradient *(instructions on page 100)* (**Figure 12**).

3. Choose the Gradient tool (**Figure 9**).

4. Drag over the objects in the direction and angle you wish the Gradient Fill to appear (**Figure 13**).

Tip

■ Once multiple objects are filled with the same gradient, do not combine them into a compound path — it may become too complex to print.

Figure 12. *A Gradient Fill applied using the* **Paint Style palette** *only. Each type object is filled with its own gradient.*

Peter Fahrni

Figure 13. *A Gradient Fill produced using the* **Gradient** *tool. One gradient blends across all the type outlines.*

PATTERNS

A PATTERN IS AN ARRANGEMENT of adjacent rectangles, each containing the same shapes. You can fill an object with any of the 50 patterns included with Illustrator, or you can create your own patterns. This chapter contains instructions for applying a pattern to an object, creating a custom pattern, modifying a pattern, and tips for printing and transforming patterns.

To create a custom pattern, objects are placed within a *bounding rectangle* that defines the border of the pattern. The background Fill of the rectangle will be the background color in the pattern. Patterns are applied via the Paint Style palette, and are named, defined and modified using the Pattern dialog box.

Patterns

Follow these instructions to apply a predefined pattern or to apply a custom pattern once it has been created.

To Fill with a pattern:

1. Select an object *(see page 56)*.

2. If the Paint Style palette is not displayed, choose Paint Style from the Object menu. Check the Auto button on the palette.

3. Click the Fill box at top of the palette (**Figure 1**).

4. Click the Pattern color selection method icon on the right panel.

5. Click on a pattern name on the scroll list (**Figures 2a-f**).

Tip

■ To apply a pattern to a Stroke, first apply the Outline Stroked Paths filter from the Objects submenu under the Filter menu. The Stroke will turn into a separate object, to which you can apply a pattern as a Fill.

*1) Click the **Fill** or **Stroke** box.*   *2) Click the **Pattern** color selection method icon.*

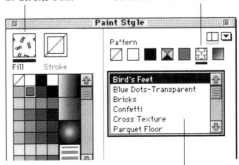

*3) Click a **pattern name**.*

Figure 1. *The **Paint Style** palette. You can append additional Illustrator patterns or patterns from another document (see page 94).*

Figure 2a.
Our pattern.

Figure 2b.
Cross Texture.

Figure 2c.
Tablecloth.

Figure 2d
Mali.

Figure 2e.
Congo Stripes.

Figure 2f.
Haida arrows.

Fill with a Pattern

Figure 3. *Draw objects for the pattern.*

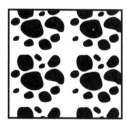

Figure 4. *Draw a bounding rectangle around the objects, then send the rectangle to the back.*

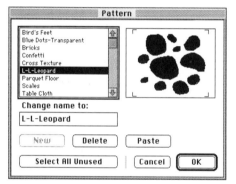

Figure 5. *In the* **Pattern** *dialog box, click* **New**, *then enter a name in the* **Change name to** *field.*

Figure 6. *Our L-L-Leopard Pattern Fill.*

To create a simple pattern:

1. Draw an object or objects to be used as the pattern (**Figure 3**).

2. Choose the Rectangle tool.

3. Draw a rectangle around the objects. Fit the rectangle closely around the objects if you don't want an empty border to be part of the pattern (**Figure 4**).

4. Choose Send to Back from the Edit menu. The bounding rectangle must be behind the pattern objects.

5. Apply a Fill and Stroke of None to the rectangle *(see page 89)*.
   or
   Apply a Fill color to be the background color in the pattern.

6. Choose the Selection tool.

7. Position the cursor outside all the objects, then press and drag diagonally across them.

8. Choose Pattern from the Object menu.

9. Click New. The pattern tile will preview in the dialog box (**Figure 5**).

10. Enter a name in the "Change name to" field.

11. Click OK or press Return (**Figure 6**). The pattern will be saved with your document.

Tips

■ A pattern cannot contain a mask or an object filled with a pattern or gradient.

■ The more complex the pattern, the smaller the bounding rectangle should be. To facilitate printing of a complex pattern, make the rectangle about one-inch square.

■ To reposition the pattern within the object, deselect then reselect the object with the Selection tool, then hold down "P" and press and drag inside the object.

Create a Simple Pattern

Create a Geometric Pattern

You can create a geometric pattern by arranging straight-sided objects around a common center point.

To create a geometric pattern:

1. Create a geometric object (**Figure** 7). Use the Polygon, Spiral, or Star filter to create an object easily, if you wish *(see pages 52-54)*.

2. Choose a selection tool.

3. Hold down Option and press and drag a copy of the object so it abuts the original. Hold down Shift while dragging to constrain the movement horizontally or vertically.

4. Repeat step 3 with other objects to create a symmetrical arrangement (**Figure 8**).

5. *Optional:* Apply different Fill colors to add variety to the pattern.

6. Choose the Rectangle tool.

7. Press and drag a rectangle around the objects. Make sure the symmetry is preserved (**Figure 9**).

8. Follow steps 4-11 on page 107. (**Figure 10**)

Tips

■ You can use the Crop Fill filter to see exactly what the pattern tile will look like *(see page 184)*.

■ To create a pattern that repeats seamlessly, follow the instructions in the Illustrator *User Guide*.

Figure 7. *Draw a geometric object.*

Figure 8. *Copy the object and arrange the copies symmetrically.*

Figure 9. *Draw a bounding rectangle around the objects, then send the rectangle to the back.*

Figure 10. *A geometric Pattern Fill.*

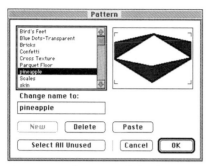

Figure 11. *In the* **Pattern** *dialog box, click the name of the pattern you wish to modify, then click* **Paste.**

Figure 12. *A line is added to the pasted pattern.*

Figure 13. *The modified pattern.*

You can modify any pattern, including those supplied with Illustrator. To change an existing pattern, first it must be pasted back into a document. Objects already filled with the pattern in any open documents will be updated automatically.

To modify a pattern:

1. Display a blank area in your document window, then choose Pattern from the Object menu.

2. Click on the name of the pattern you wish to modify (**Figure 11**).

3. Click Paste.

4. Click OK. The pattern will be pasted into the center of the document window, and will be selected.

5. Modify the pattern objects (**Figure 12**).

6. Choose the Selection tool.

7. Position the pointer outside all the objects, then press and drag a selection marquee over the bounding rectangle and objects.

8. Choose Pattern from the Object menu.

9. Click on the name of the original pattern.

10. Click OK. (**Figure 13**)

Tips

■ To create a variation of a pattern and preserve the original, follow steps 1-8 above, click New, enter a new name in the "Change name to" field, then click OK.

■ To delete a pattern, click on its name, then click Delete. Objects filled with the pattern will be filled with Black, and the pattern will be deleted from all currently open files in which it was used. (To retrieve a deleted pattern after clicking OK in the Pattern dialog box, choose Undo from the Edit menu.)

Modify a Pattern

PRINTING PATTERNS

For a pattern to preview and print, the **Preview and Print Patterns** box must be checked in the **Document Setup** dialog box, opened from the **File** menu. A pattern can cause a document to print slowly. Uncheck the Preview and Print Patterns box to preview and print a document containing a pattern more quickly.

A pattern can also cause a document not to print at all. If a document containing a pattern prints with the Preview and Print Patterns box unchecked, remove or simplify the pattern. Grouping objects of the same color within the pattern may help. A document containing multiple patterns may be particularly problematic.

PATTERNS AND THE TRANSFORMATION TOOLS

If you use a transformation tool (Rotate, Scale, Reflect, Shear, or Blend) and the object you are transforming contains a Pattern Fill, you can transform the pattern when you transform the object. Check the **Pattern tiles** box in the transformation tool dialog box (**Figures 14-15c**).

◆

To transform the pattern and not the object, uncheck the **Objects** box in the transformation tool dialog box. Or, choose the transformation tool, click to establish a point of origin, then hold down "P" and press and drag.

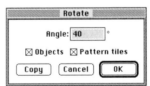

Figure 14. *Check or uncheck the* **Pattern tiles** *box in any transformation tool dialog box.*

Figure 15a. *The original pattern.*

Figure 15b. *The pattern rotated without rotating the object.*

Figure 15c. *The object and pattern sheared.*

●●●

EACH NEW OBJECT you draw in an illustration is automatically positioned on top of the previous object. This positioning is called the **stacking order** (**Figure 1**). By default, all new objects are stacked on a single **layer**. Using the **Layers palette**, you can add new layers to an illustration, each of which can contain a stack of objects. You can change the stacking order of objects within a layer, and you can reorder whole layers. You can also group objects together so they can be moved as a unit. If you place objects on separate layers, you can selectively display, edit, and print them.

In this chapter you will learn to group and ungroup objects and to restack objects. Using the Layers palette, you will learn to create and delete layers, hide/show, lock/unlock, and print individual layers, move an object to a different layer, and reorder layers.

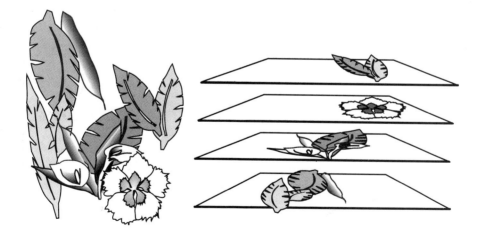

Figure 1. *Imagine your illustration is like modular shelves. You can rearrange (restack) objects on an individual shelf (layer), move an object to a different shelf, or rearrange the order of the shelves (layers).*

Layers and Stacks

If you **group** objects together, you can easily select, cut, copy, paste, or move them as a unit. Also, grouped objects are automatically placed on the same layer, so you can take advantage of the special Layers palette hide/show, lock/unlock, and print options.

To group objects:

1. Choose the Selection tool.

2. Hold down Shift and click on each of the objects to be grouped (**Figures 2a-b**).
   or
   Position the pointer outside all the objects, then press and drag a marquee diagonally across them.

3. Choose Group from the Arrange menu (**Figure 3**).
   or
   Hold down Command (⌘) and press "G".

Figure 2a. *An object is selected.*

Figure 2b. *The other objects are selected with Shift held down.*

Arrange	
Repeat Transform	⌘D
Move...	⌘⇧M
Bring To Front	⌘=
Send To Back	⌘-
Group	**⌘G**
Ungroup	⌘U
Lock	⌘1
Unlock All	⌘2
Hide	⌘3
Show All	⌘4

Figure 3. *Choose* **Group** *from the* **Arrange** *menu.*

To ungroup objects:

1. Choose the Selection tool.

2. Click on a group.

3. Choose Ungroup from the Arrange menu (**Figure 3**).
   or
   Hold down Command (⌘) and press "U".

Group; Ungroup

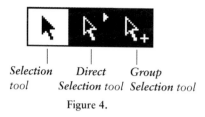

Selection   Direct   Group
tool   Selection tool Selection tool

Figure 4.

To select grouped objects:

To select the entire group, click on any item in the group with the **Selection** tool (**Figure 4**).

or

To select individual anchor points or segments of an object within a group, use the **Direct Selection** tool.

or

Use the **Group Selection** tool to select multiple groups within a larger group in the order in which they were added to the group. Click once to select an object in a group (**Figure 5a**); click again on the same object to select the group that object is part of (**Figure 5b**); click again on the object to select the next larger group the first group is a part of (**Figure 5c**), etc.

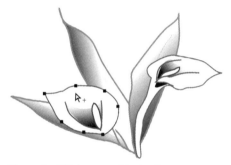

Figure 5a. *Click once with the Group Selection tool to select an individual object.*

Figure 5b. *Click a second time with the Group Selection tool to select that object's group.*

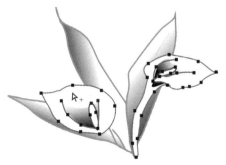

Figure 5c. *Click a third time with the Group Selection tool to select the next larger group the first group is a part of.*

Select Grouped Objects

Use the **Bring To Front** or **Send To Back** command to move an object or a group to the front or the back of its stack.

To place an object on the bottom of its stack:

1. Choose the Selection tool (**Figure 4**).

2. Click on the object or group.

3. Choose Send To Back from the Arrange menu (**Figure 6**).
or
Hold down Command (⌘) and press "–".

The selected object or group will be placed on the bottom of its stack within the same layer (**Figures 7a-b**).

Tip

■ If you select only a portion of a path (a point or a segment), and change its stacking position, the entire object will be moved.

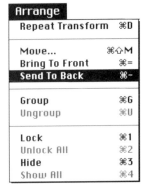

Figure 6. *Choose Send To Back from the **Arrange** menu.*

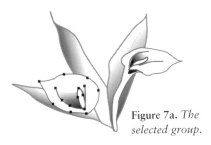

Figure 7a. *The selected group.*

Figure 7b. *After applying the **Send To Back** command.*

To place an object on the top of its stack:

1. Choose the Selection tool.

2. Click on the object or group.

3. Choose Bring To Front from the Arrange menu (**Figure 8**).
or
Hold down Command (⌘) and press "+".

The selected object or group will be placed on the top of its stack within the same layer.

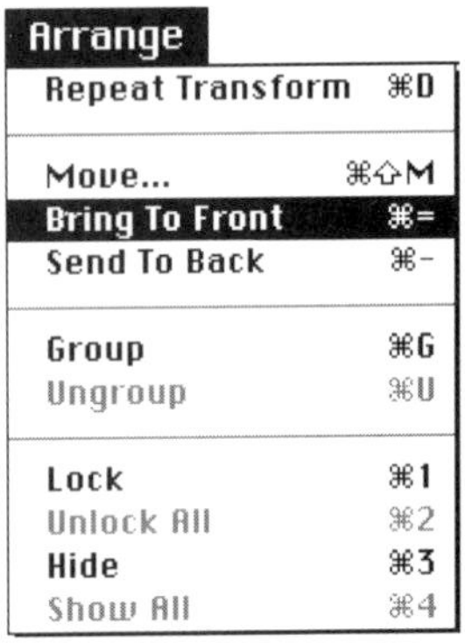

Figure 8. *Choose Bring To Front from the **Arrange** menu.*

Restack an Object

Figure 9. *The gray object is selected and then placed on the Clipboard via the Cut command.*

Edit

Undo Move	⌘Z
Redo	⌘⇧Z
Cut	⌘H
Copy	⌘C
Paste	⌘U
Clear	
Select All	⌘A
Select None	⌘⇧A
Paste In Front	**⌘F**
Paste In Back	⌘B
Publishing	▶
Show Clipboard	

Figure 10. *Choose **Paste In Front** or **Paste In Back** from the **Edit** menu.*

Figure 11. *The inner flower shape is selected. Paste In Back (Edit menu) is chosen to place the gray object behind the inner flower shape.*

The **Paste In Front** and **Paste In Back** commands paste the Clipboard contents just in front of or just behind the currently selected object within the selected object's layer. The object will paste in the same horizontal and vertical position from which it was cut.

To restack an object in front of or behind another object:

1. Choose the Selection tool.

2. Click on an object (**Figure 9**).

3. Choose Cut from the Edit menu to place the object on the Clipboard.

4. Click on an object that you wish to paste just in front of or just behind.

5. Choose Paste In Front from the Edit menu (or hold down Command (⌘) and press "F").
or
Choose Paste In Back from the Edit menu (or hold down Command (⌘) and press "B") (**Figures 10-11**).

Tips

■ To restack part of an object, use the Direct Selection tool to select the part before choosing Cut.

■ If no object is selected when you choose Paste In Front or Paste In Back, the object on the Clipboard will paste on the top or bottom, respectively, of the stack within the currently active layer (the highlighted layer on the Layers palette).

■ You can use the Paste In Front and Paste In Back commands to restack type outlines. For example, you can stack a type outline with a Stroke color and a Fill of None in front of the same character with a wider Stroke of a different color.

■ If you Paste In Front of or Paste In Back of an object in a group, the pasted object will be added to the group.

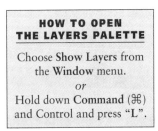

**HOW TO OPEN
THE LAYERS PALETTE**

Choose **Show Layers** from
the **Window** menu.
or
Hold down **Command** (⌘)
and Control and press "**L**".

Figure 12. *Choose* New Layer *from the* Layers
palette pop-up menu.

You can select individual layers to work
on using the **Layers** palette. You can
also reorder layers, display a layer in
Preview or Artwork view, lock a layer,
hide a layer, or print only one layer. Any
new object you create will be placed on
the currently selected layer. *(Other layer
options are discussed on page 118.)*

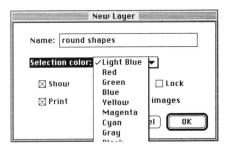

Figure 13. *In the* New Layer *dialog box,
enter a* Name *and choose a* Selection color.

To create a new layer:

1. Choose New Layer from the Layers
palette pop-up menu (**Figure 12**).

2. Enter a name for the new layer
(**Figure 13**).

3. Choose a selection color for items
on that layer from the Selection color
pop-up menu.

4. Click OK or press Return.

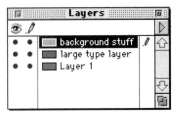

Figure 14a. *Press and drag a layer
name up or down.*

The order of names on the Layers
palette matches the front-to-back order
of layers in the illustration.

To reorder layers:

Press and drag a layer name up or
down (the pointer will turn into a fist
icon). Release the mouse when the
small arrowhead points to the desired
position (**Figures 14a-c**). The illustration
will redraw.

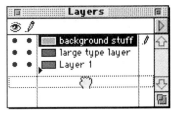

Figure 14b. *Release the mouse when
the arrowhead points to the desired
position.*

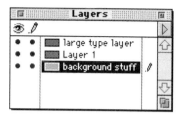

Figure 14c. *The newly moved layer is now on the bottom, and objects on that layer are now in the back of the illustration.*

Figure 15. *The topmost leaf is selected.*

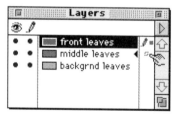

Figure 16. *Move the little square for the selected object. Release the mouse when the arrowhead points to the desired layer name.*

Figure 17. *The object is on a different layer.*

You can move an object to a different layer using just the Layers palette (method 1), or you can use the Clipboard and the Layers palette to move an object to a different layer (method 2). **Open the Layers palette for both methods.**

To move an object to a different layer (method 1):

1. Choose any selection tool, then click on the object or group you wish to move (**Figure 15**). The object's current layer will be highlighted on the Layers palette.

2. Drag the little colored square next to the highlighted layer name up or down (the pointer will turn into a pointing hand icon) (**Figure 16**), then release the mouse when the arrowhead points to the name of the layer you wish to move the object to. The illustration will redraw with the object in the new layer (**Figure 17**).

To move an object to a different layer (method 2):

1. Choose the Selection tool, then click on the object you wish to move.

2. Choose Cut from the Edit menu.

3. Click on the name of the layer on the Layers palette that you wish to move the object to.

4. Choose Paste from the Edit menu. The object will be placed at the top of the stack within the layer you highlighted.

Tip

■ If the object moves only to the top of its stack rather than to a different layer, choose Paste Remembers Layers from the Layers palette pop-up menu to uncheck this option. Paste Remembers Layers can also be turned on or off in the General Preferences dialog box.

Move an Object to a Different Layer

The following options affect all the objects on the currently selected layer.

To choose other layering options:

1. Click on a layer name on the Layers palette, then choose "Layer Options for ....." from the Layers palette pop-up menu.
or
Double-click any layer name on the Layers palette.

2. Check **Show** to display the layer; uncheck to hide it (**Figure 18**).

Check **Preview** to display the layer in Preview View; uncheck to display the layer in Artwork view.

Check **Lock** to prevent all the objects on that layer from being selected; uncheck to allow objects to be selected.

Check to **Print;** uncheck to prevent all the objects on that layer from printing.

Check **Dim placed images** to dim any placed EPS images on that layer; uncheck to display placed images normally.

Tip

■ You can use the Layers palette to Show/Hide or Lock/Unlock all the objects on an individual layer. To quickly Hide or Lock one item at a time, you can choose the Lock or Hide command under the Arrange menu. However, you cannot unlock or show individual items using the Arrange menu; choosing Unlock All or Show All will affect all locked or hidden objects in the illustration.

Choosing the Layers palette option will not affect the status of the menu command, and vice versa. For example, choosing Lock from the Arrange menu will not cause the Lock option box in the Layers Option dialog box to be checked.

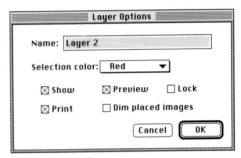

Figure 18. *In the* **Layer Options** *dialog box, check the* **Show, Preview, Lock, Print,** *or* **Dim placed images** *boxes on or off.*

Layer Options

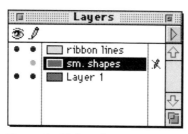

Figure 19. *Click in the Eye column to hide or show a layer. In this illustration, the "sm.shapes" layer is hidden.*

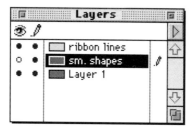

Figure 20. *Option-click in the Eye column to display a layer in Artwork view. In this illustration, the "sm.shapes" layer is in Artwork view.*

Figure 21. *Click on the name of the layer you wish to delete, then choose Delete "...." from the pop-up menu.*

If there is a dot next to a layer name under the Eye icon column, that layer is currently displayed.

To hide a layer:

1. Click on a layer name on the Layers palette.

2. Click on the black dot in the Eye column next to the layer name (**Figure 19**). All objects on that layer will be hidden, whether they are selected or not.

Tips

■ To display the layer again, click in the Eye column where the black dot was.

■ To display a layer in Artwork view, hold down Option and click on the black dot in the Eye column next to the layer name (**Figure 20**). To display the layer in Preview view again, hold down Option and click on the hollow dot.

To delete a layer:

1. Click on the name of the layer you wish to delete on the Layers palette.

2. Choose Delete "...." from the palette pop-up menu (**Figure 21**).

3. If a warning prompt appears, click Delete. **All the objects on the deleted layer will be removed.**

Tip

■ To retrieve the layer and the objects on the layer, choose Undo Delete Layers from the Edit menu.

Hide a Layer; Delete a Layer

119

If there is a dot next to a layer name in the Pencil icon column, objects on that layer are currently editable.

To make a layer editable or non-editable:

1. Click on a layer name on the Layers palette.
2. Click on the black dot in the Pencil column next to the layer name (the dot will disappear) (**Figure 22**). Objects in that layer can no longer be selected or edited.

Tip

■ To make the layer editable again, click where the black dot was in the Pencil column (the dot will reappear).

This icon indicates the layer is locked.

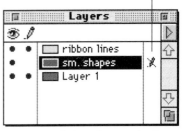

Figure 22. *Click in the **Pencil** column to make a layer editable or non-editable.*

To hide or lock multiple layers:

1. Click on the layer whose options you don't wish to change.
   or
   Hold down Shift and click on multiple layers.
2. Click on the Eye icon to hide all non-highlighted layers (**Figure 23**).
   or
   Click on the Pencil icon to lock all non-highlighted layers so they can't be edited (**Figure 24**).

Tips

■ To show or unlock all the non-highlighted layers again, click the Eye or Pencil icon again.

■ If your illustration is in Preview view, you can hold down Option and click on the Eye icon to display all non-highlighted layers in Artwork view.

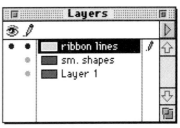

Figure 23. *Click on the **Eye** icon to hide all non-highlighted layers.*

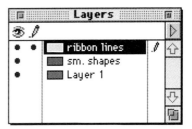

Figure 24. *Click on the **Pencil** icon to lock all non-highlighted layers.*

CREATE TYPE

TYPE CAN BE ENTERED directly in Illustrator, or it can be imported from another application. There are three type tools — the Type tool, the Area Type tool, and the Path Type tool (**Figure 1**) — and they produce different kinds of type objects.

The **Type** tool is used to create blocks of type consisting of one line or several lines. You can create a free-floating block of type with the Type tool that is not associated with an object, called **point** type; you can draw a rectangle with it, then enter text inside the rectangle; and you can use the Type tool to enter type on the outside edge of an open path or inside a closed path.

The **Area Type** tool is used to create type inside an open or closed path. Lines of type created with the Area Type tool automatically wrap inside the object.

The **Path Type** tool is used to enter a line of type on the outside edge of an open or closed path.

You can also convert a type object into **outlines** — objects with anchor points and segments. The "characters" will still look like letters, but will function like graphic objects. You can use this feature to design your own characters.

Typographic attributes are modified using the Character palette and Paragraph palette, which are covered in Chapter 14, along with methods for selecting type.

Type Tools

Type tool   Area Type tool   Path Type tool

Figure 1. *The Type tools.*

Figure 2. *ATM on.*

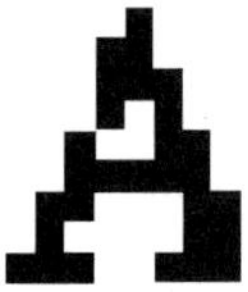

ATM off.

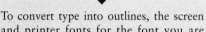

FONTS

Make sure Adobe Type Manager (ATM), the utility that smooths font rendering, is installed and is turned on before you launch Illustrator (Figure 2). See the Illustrator *Getting Started* guide for more information about ATM.

◆

To convert type into outlines, the screen and printer fonts for the font you are using and Adobe Type Manager must be installed in the system.

◆

If you open a document containing type styled in a font whose suitcase is closed or not available, the font will not display on screen. If you open a font suitcase using a utility, such as Suitcase, after launching Illustrator, the font will reappear on Illustrator's font list and the type should display correctly. If it doesn't, choose Artwork view and then Preview view from the View menu to force the screen to redraw.

Point type is type that is not inside an object or along a path.

To create point type:

1. Choose the Type tool (**Figure 3**).

2. Click on the Artboard where you wish the type to start. A flashing insertion marker will appear.

3. Enter type. Press Return if you wish to start a new line (**Figure 4**).

4. Choose a selection tool and click away from the type block to deselect it.
or
Click the Type tool again to complete the block of type and start a new one.

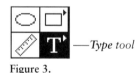

—*Type tool*

Figure 3.

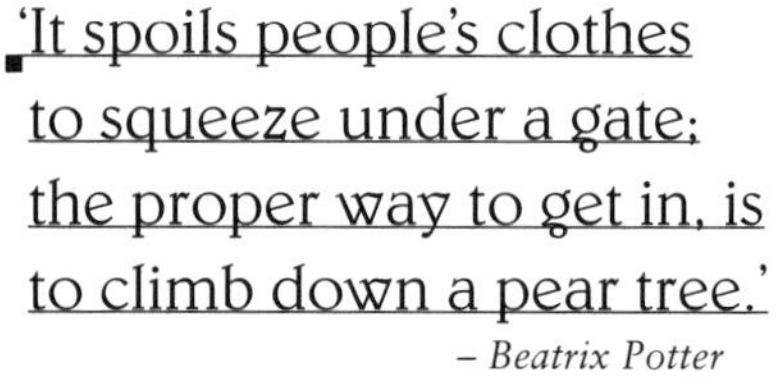

'It spoils people's clothes to squeeze under a gate; the proper way to get in, is to climb down a pear tree.'
— *Beatrix Potter*

Figure 4. *Type created using the **Type** tool.*

TYPE OBJECTS VS. GRAPHIC OBJECTS

When type is placed inside an object or on a path, the object will be Filled and Stroked with None. You can reapply a Fill and/or Stroke if you select the object first with the Direct Selection tool.

◆

Once you place type on or inside a graphic object, it becomes a type object, and it cannot be converted back into a graphic object. To preserve the original graphic object, make a copy of it and convert the copy into a type path.

◆

You cannot enter type into a compound path or a mask object, and you cannot make a mask or compound path out of a text object.

'It spoils people's clothes to squeeze under a gate; the proper way to get in, is to climb down a pear tree.'

Figure 5. *Press and drag with the* **Type** *tool to create a rectangle, then enter type. The edges of the rectangle will be visible in* **Artwork** *view.*

'It spoils people's clothes to squeeze under a gate; the proper way to get in, is to climb down a pear tree.'

Figure 6. *The type rectangle reshaped using the* **Direct Selection** *tool. The edges of the rectangle will be hidden in* **Preview** *view.*

To create a type rectangle:

1. Choose the Type tool (**Figure 3**).

2. Press and drag to create a rectangle. When you release the mouse, a flashing insertion marker will appear in the upper left corner of the rectangle.

3. Enter type. Press Return when you need to create a new paragraph. The type will automatically conform to the rectangle (**Figure 5**).

4. Choose a selection tool and click away from the type block to deselect it.
   or
   Click the Type tool again to complete the type object and start a new one.

Tips

■ If your illustration is in Artwork view, the edges of the rectangle will be displayed as you enter type.

   If your illustration is in Preview view, the type rectangle will only be displayed if you select it.

■ You can reshape a type rectangle using the Direct Selection tool. The type will reflow to fit the new shape (**Figure 6**).

■ To turn an object created with the Rectangle tool into a type rectangle, click on the edge of the path with the Type tool or the Area Type tool, then enter text.

You can import text into a type rectangle or any other type shape from another application, such as Microsoft Word, WordPerfect or MacWrite.

To import type into an object:

1. Choose the Type tool or Area Type tool (**Figure 7**).

2. Press and drag to create a type rectangle with the Type tool (**Figure 8**).
   or
   Click on the edge of a graphic object to create a flashing insertion marker with the Area Type tool.

3. Choose Import Text from the File menu (**Figure 9**).

4. Highlight the name of the text file you wish to import.

5. Click Open. The text file will flow into the object (**Figure 10**).

Tip

◼ If you click with the Type tool to create an insertion point rather than press and drag to create a rectangle, each paragraph of the imported text will appear on a separate, single line, and it may be difficult to work with.

◼ If fewer than ten file formats are listed on the Show pop-up menu in the Import Text dialog box, do a Custom installation from the Illustrator Installer disk. Select the Claris Translators and the Claris XTND System files.

Type tool   Area Type tool

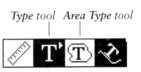

Figure 7.

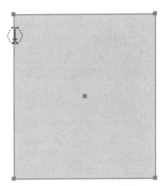

Figure 8. *The object will lose its Fill and Stroke colors as soon as you click on its edge with the Area Type tool.*

Figure 9. *Choose* **Import Text** *from the* **File** *menu.*

Here was peace. She pulled in her horizon like a great fishnet. Pulled it from around the waist of the world and draped it over her shoulder.

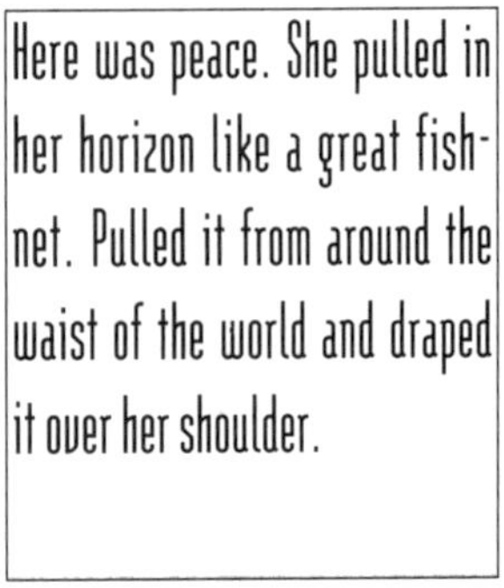

Figure 10. *Text appears in the object.*

Import Type

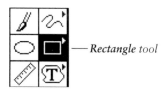

— *Rectangle* tool

Figure 11.

If a type rectangle is not large enough to display all the type inside it, you can flow the hidden, remaining type — called **overflow type** — into a new object.

If your illustration is in Artwork view, the overflow symbol will always be visible (**Figure 12**). If your illustration is in Preview view, the overflow symbol will be displayed only as you move the type rectangle.

Follow the instructions on this page to flow type into a standard rectangle. Follow the instructions on the next page to flow type into a copy of a non-standard type object.

Here was peace. She pulled in her horizon like a great fish-net. Pulled it from around the waist of the world and draped it over

Figure 12. *The overflow symbol.*

Figure 13. *Create a new rectangle.*

To link type to a rectangle:

1. Choose the Rectangle tool (**Figure 11**).

2. Press and drag diagonally to create a new rectangle (**Figure 13**).

3. Choose the Selection tool.

4. Hold down Shift and click on both rectangles.
   or
   Drag a marquee across both rectangles.

5. Choose Link Blocks from the Type menu (**Figure 14**). Extra type from the first rectangle will flow into the new rectangle (**Figure 15**).

Type	
Size	▶
Leading	▶
Alignment	▶
Tracking...	⌘⇧K
Spacing...	⌘⇧O
Character...	⌘T
Paragraph...	⌘⇧T
Link Blocks	⌘⇧G
Unlink Blocks	⌘⇧U
Make Wrap	
Release Wrap	
Fit Headline	
Create Outlines	

Figure 14. *Choose Link Blocks from the Type menu.*

Tips

■ To unlink type objects, choose the Selection tool, click on one of the objects (all the linked objects will be selected), then choose Unlink Blocks from the Type menu. Each block of type will now be separate in its own object.

■ To remove one type object from a series of linked objects, choose the Group Selection tool, click on the edge of the object to be removed (the type shouldn't be underlined), then press Delete. The type will reflow into the remaining objects.

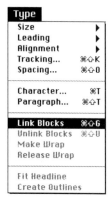

Here was peace. She pulled in her horizon like a great fish-net. Pulled it from around the waist of the world and draped it over

her shoulder. So much of life in its meshes! She called in her soul to come and see.

Figure 15. *Type flows from the first object into the second object.*

Link Type

To link type to a copy of an existing object:

1. Choose the Group Selection tool (**Figure 16**).

2. Click away from the type object to deselect it.

3. Click on the edge of the type object. This may be easiest to do in Artwork view. The type should not be underlined after you click.

4. Hold down Option and drag a copy of the type object away from the original object. Hold down Shift while dragging to constrain the movement to a horizontal or vertical axis.

5. Release the mouse, then release Option (and Shift, if used). The overflow type will be displayed inside the new object (**Figure 17**).

Tip

■ If both the type and the type object are selected when you drag, a copy of the object will be created, but it will not be linked to the first object.

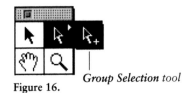

Figure 16. *Group Selection tool*

Link Type

The
kiss of
memory made pic-
tures of love and light
against the wall. Here was peace.

She
pulled in her
horizon like a great
fish-net. Pulled it from around the waist of the world and

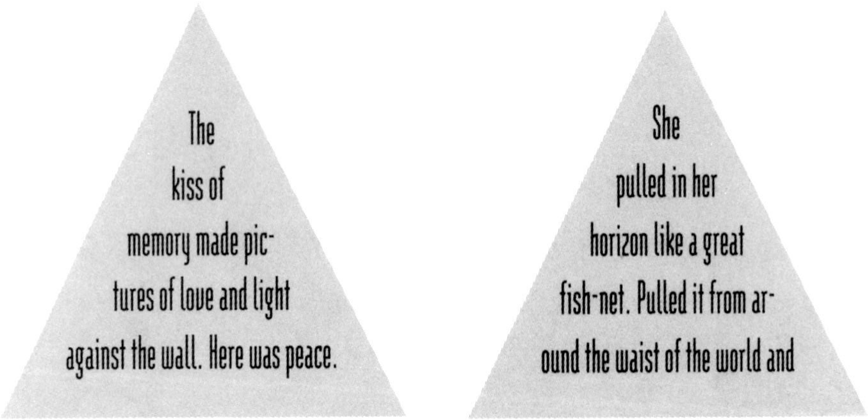

Figure 17. Overflow type from the first object appears in a copy of the object. (A Paragraph indent was applied to the type to move it away from the edge of the objects.)

Use the **Area Type** tool to place type inside a rectangle, an irregularly shaped object, or an open path. The object you use will turn into a type path. You must click precisely on the edge of an object in order to enter type inside it.

To place type inside an object:

1. Choose the Area Type tool (**Figure 7**).

2. Click on the edge of an object. A flashing insertion marker will appear.

3. Enter type. It will wrap inside the object (**Figures 18-19**).

4. Choose a selection tool and click away from the type object to deselect it.

or

Click the Area Type tool again to complete the type object and start a new one.

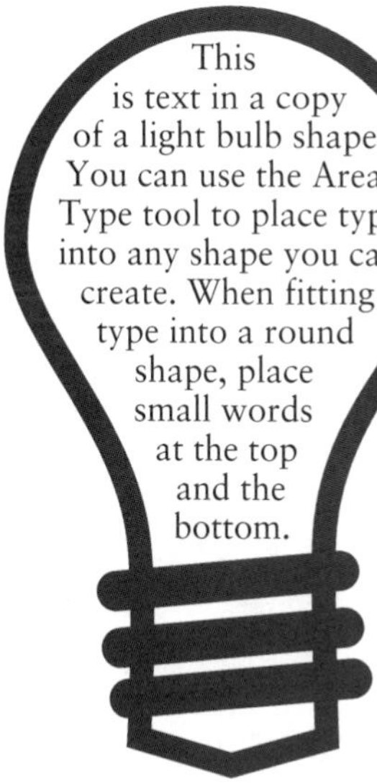

This is text in a copy of a light bulb shape. You can use the Area-Type tool to place type into any shape you can create. When fitting type into a round shape, place small words at the top and the bottom.

Figure 18. *Area type.*

The kiss of memory made pictures of love and light against the wall. Here was peace. She pulled in her horizon like a great fish-net. Pulled it from around the waist of the world and draped it over her shoulder. So much of life in its meshes! She called in her soul to come and see.
ZORA NEALE HURSTON

Figure 19. *Type in a circle.*

Enter Type in an Object

127

Use the **Path Type** tool to place type on the inside or outside edge of an object. Type cannot be positioned on both sides of a path, but it can be moved from one side to the other after it is created *(see the next set of instructions)*. Only one line of type can be created per path.

To place type on an object's path:

1. Choose the Path Type tool (**Figure 20**).

2. Click on the top or bottom edge of an object. A flashing insertion marker will appear.

3. Enter type. Do not press Return. The type will appear along the edge of the object (**Figures 21-22**).

4. Choose a selection tool and click away from the type object to deselect it.

or

Click the Path Type tool again to complete the type object and start a new one.

Tip

■ When you place type on an object, the object's Fill and Stroke revert to None. You can apply a Fill and/or Stroke color to it.

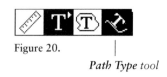

Figure 20.

Path Type *tool*

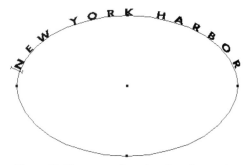

Figure 21. *Type entered on the edge of an oval.*

Figure 22. *Path type.*

To reposition path type:

1. Choose the Selection tool.

2. Click on the path type object.

3. Press and drag the I-beam marker left or right along the edge of the object, move it inside the path, or move it to the other side of the path.

Peter Fahrni

To move or copy type with or without its object, use the **Clipboard**, an invisible temporary storage area in memory. The Clipboard commands are Cut, Copy, and Paste.

To copy a type object from one document to another:

1. Choose the Selection tool.

2. Click on the edge of the object or the baseline of the type.

3. Choose Copy from the Edit menu (**Figure 23**).

4. Click in another document window.

5. Choose Paste from the Edit menu. The type object will reappear.

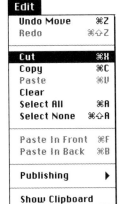

Figure 23. *Choose* **Cut** *or* **Copy** *from the* **Edit** *menu, then later choose* **Paste**.

To move type from one type object to another:

1. Choose the Type tool.

2. Highlight the type.

3. Choose Cut from the Edit menu (**Figure 23**).

4. In the other type object, click to create a flashing insertion marker where you wish the type to reappear (as point type or in another line of type).

5. Choose Paste from the Edit menu.

Copy or Move Type

Type can be converted into graphic objects using the **Create Outlines** command. As outlines, the "characters" can be reshaped, transformed, or used in a compound or a mask. Once type is converted into outlines, it cannot be converted back into type again, and its typeface cannot be changed. If you import type outlines from Illustrator into another application, such as Quark XPress, you do not need the printer fonts for the "characters" to print properly.

To create type outlines:

1. Create type using any type tool.

2. Choose the Selection tool.

3. If the type is not already selected, click on the "x" or on the object's edge (**Figure 24**).

4. Choose Create Outlines from the Type menu (**Figures 25-27**).

Tips

■ To create outlines, the Type 1 font (screen font and printer outlines) or TrueType font for the typeface you are using must be installed in your system.

■ You can Fill type outlines with a gradient *(Chapter 10)* or a pattern *(Chapter 11)*.

■ Group multiple outline "characters" together using the Group command so they're easier to select and move.

■ If the original character had an interior counter — like an "A" or a "P" — you can divide the inside and outside parts of the type outline into separate objects. Choose Release from the Compound Paths submenu under the Object menu. To reassemble the two pieces, select them both, then choose Make from the Compound Paths submenu under the Object menu *(see Figure 8 on page 163)*.

Figure 24. *Click on **point** type with the **Selection** tool.*

Figure 25. *Choose **Create Outlines** from the **Type** menu.*

Figure 26. *The type converted into **outlines**, then reshaped using the Free Distort filter (see page 175).*

Figure 27. *Other outline type examples.*

STYLE TYPE

ONCE YOU HAVE created type, you can change its character-based typographical attributes (font, size, leading, baseline shift, horizontal scale, and tracking) using the **Character palette,** and paragraph-based attributes (alignment and indentation) using the **Paragraph palette.** You can modify the paint attributes of type using the Paint Style palette *(see Chapter 9).*

Before you can modify type, you must select it. If you use the **Selection tool,** both the type and its object will be selected (**Figure 1**). If you use the **Direct Selection tool,** you can select just the type object or the type object and the type (**Figure 2**). If you use **a type tool,** only the type itself will be selected, not the type object (**Figure 3**).

If you select point type (not on or inside a type object) with the Selection or Direct Selection tool, the block will have a solid anchor point before the first character and every line of type will be underlined.

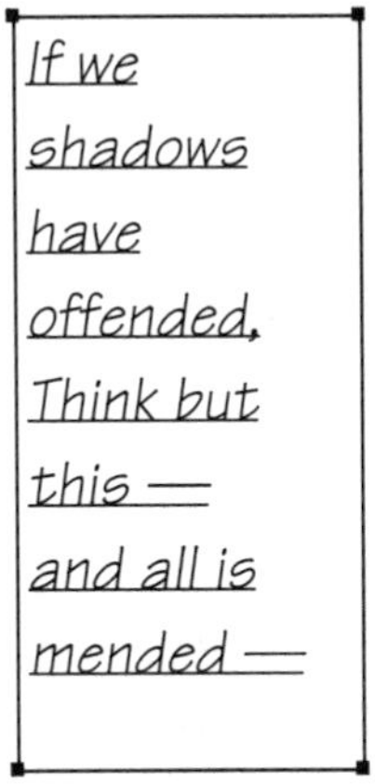

If we

shadows

have

offended,

Think but

this —

and all is

mended —

Figure 1. *Type and type object selected with the **Selection** tool.*

If we

shadows

have

offended,

Think but

this —

and all is

mended —

Figure 2. *Type object selected with the **Direction Selection** tool.*

If we

shadows

have

offended,

Think but

this —

and all is

mended —

Shakespeare

Figure 3. *Type selected with the **Type** tool.*

To select type and a type object:

1. Choose the Selection tool (**Figure 4**).

2. Click on the **edge** of the type object. This may be easiest to do in Artwork view.

or

For point type, with your illustration in Artwork view, you can click on the little "**x**" before the first character (**Figures 5-6**)

or

Click on the **baseline** of any character in the type object in any view.

Selection tool ——

Figure 4.

ₓThink but this — and all
is mended —

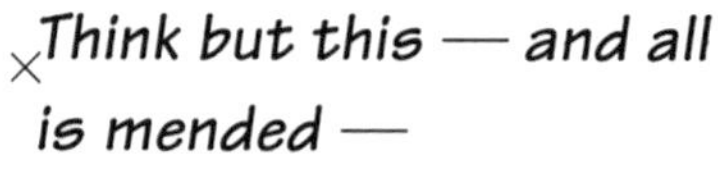

Figure 5. *For* point type *in Artwork view, click on the "***x***."*

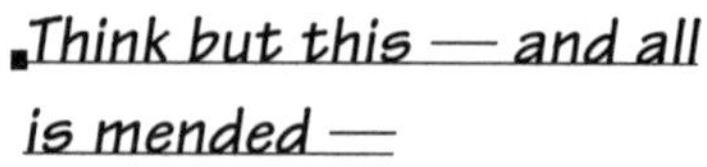

■Think but this — and all
is mended —

Figure 6. *The* type *and* type object *are selected.*

To select a type object (not type):

1. Choose the Direct Selection tool (**Figure 7**).

2. Click on the **edge** of the type object. This may be easiest to do in Artwork view (**Figure 8**).

Modifications you make will affect only the type object, and not the type.

—— *Direct Selection* tool

Figure 7.

Think but this — and
all is mended —

Figure 8. *The* type object *is selected.*

Select Type

To select type:

1. Choose any type tool.

2. Drag horizontally to select a word or a line of type (the pointer will turn into an I-beam) (**Figures 9-10**).
or
Drag vertically to select lines of type.
or
Double-click a word to select only that word.
or
Choose Select All from the Edit menu to select all the type in the block, including any type it is linked to.

3. After modifiying the type, click on the selected type to deselect it but keep the flashing insertion marker in the type block for further editing.
or
Choose a selection tool and click away from the type object to de-select it.

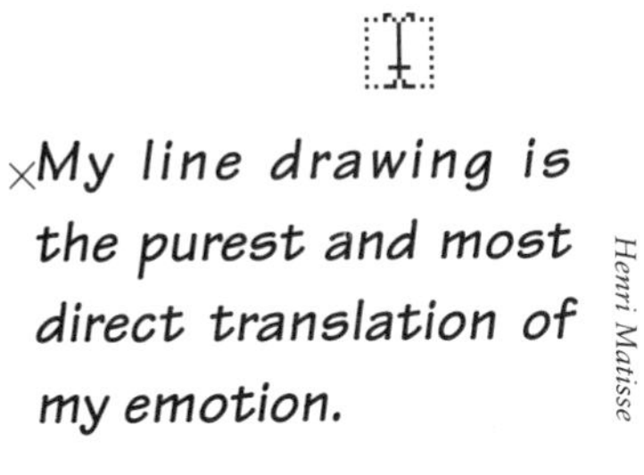

_x*My line drawing is the purest and most direct translation of my emotion.*

Henri Matisse

Figure 9. *The Type tool pointer will have a dotted outline until it is moved over type.*

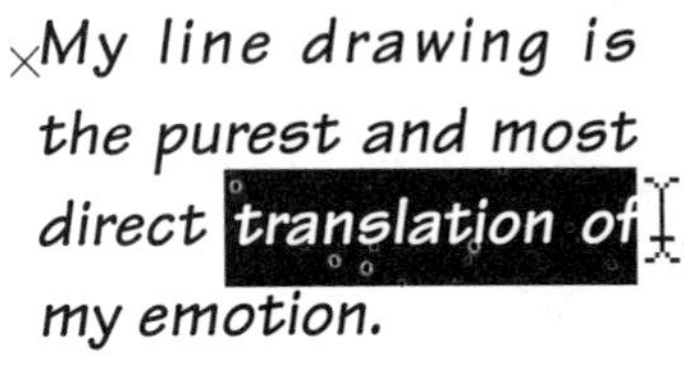

_x*My line drawing is the purest and most direct* **translation of** *my emotion.*

Figure 10. *Two words are selected. Note the I-beam pointer.*

Select Type

The Character and Paragraph palettes

Use the **Character** palette (**Figure 11**) to modify type size, font, leading, tracking/kerning, baseline shift and horizontal scale.

Use the **Paragraph** palette (**Figure 12**) to modify paragraph alignment, indentation, or leading. (A paragraph is created when the Return key is pressed within a type block. There is no on-screen character symbol for a Return.)

The **Info** palette displays the font name, size, and tracking values of type if it is selected with a type tool. Choose Show Info from the Window menu to open the Info palette. Attributes cannot be changed using this palette; it is for information only (**Figure 15**).

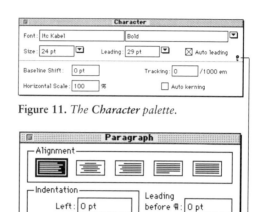

Figure 11. *The Character palette.*

Figure 12. *The Paragraph palette.*

To open or close the bottom panel of the Character or Paragraph palette, click the **palette display** lever.

TO OPEN THE PARAGRAPH PALETTE

Choose **Paragraph** from the **Type** menu.
or
Choose **Show Paragraph** from the **Window** menu.
or
Hold down **Command** (⌘) and **Shift** and press "T".

TO OPEN THE CHARACTER PALETTE

Choose **Character** from the **Type** menu.
or
Choose **Show Character** from the **Window** menu.
or
Hold down **Command** (⌘) and press "T".

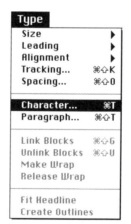

Figure 13. *Choose Character or Paragraph from the Type menu.*

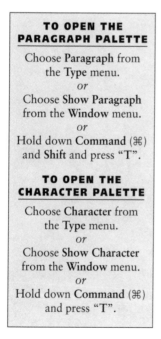

Figure 14. *Or choose Show Character or Show Paragraph from the Window menu.*

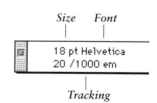

Figure 15. *The Info palette when type is selected.*

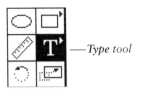

—*Type tool*

Figure 16.

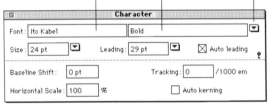

Figure 17. *Select the type you wish to modify.*

To choose a font:

1. Choose the Type tool (**Figure 16**).

2. Select the type you wish to modify (**Figure 17**).

3. On the Character palette, choose a font from the Font pop-up menu (**Figure 18a**). Choose from a submenu if the font name has an arrowhead next to it (**Figure 18b**).
   or
   Type the name of a font and type the name of a style in the Font fields. You need only enter the first few letters of the font name or style; the name or style with the closest spelling match will appear in the field (press Return or Tab) (**Figure 19**).

Tip

■ You can also choose a font from the Font menu.

*Enter a **font name** and **style**.*   *Or choose from the Font pop-up menu.*

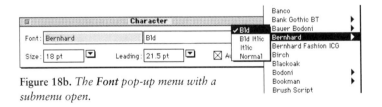

Figure 18a. *The **Character** palette.*

Figure 18b. *The **Font** pop-up menu with a submenu open.*

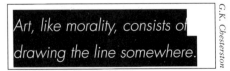

G.K. Chesterston

Figure 19. *The font is changed from Tekton Oblique to Futura Light Oblique.*

Choose a Font

To resize type:

1. Select the type you wish to modify.

2. Enter a number between .1 and 1296 in the Size field on the Character palette (press Return or Tab) (**Figures 20-21**). You do not need to reenter the unit of measure.
or
Choose a preset size from the Size pop-up menu.

Tips

■ You can also choose a preset size from the Size submenu under the Type menu. To choose a custom size, choose Other from the same submenu. The Character palette will open (if it is not open already) and the Size field on the palette will automatically highlight. Enter a size, then press Return.

■ To resize type via the keyboard, select it, then hold down Command (⌘) and Shift and press ">" to enlarge it or "<" to reduce it. The increment the type size changes each time you use this shortcut is specified in the Size/leading field in the General Preferences dialog box (File menu).

Note: If a field on the Character palette is highlighted or contains a flashing cursor, the Keyboard shortcuts will not work. Deselect and then reselect the type.

■ If you select type in more than one point size, the Size field will be blank. You can enter a number in the blank field, and it will apply to all the selected type.

■ You can scale a selected type object using the Scale tool *(see pages 154-155)*. Both the object and the type will resize. To scale type uniformly without condensing or extending it, click, then drag using the Scale tool with Shift held down.

Figure 20. *On the **Character** palette, enter a number in the **Size** field, or choose a preset size from the pop-up menu.*

Figure 21. *Type in three sizes.*

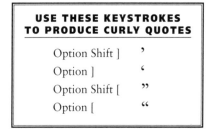

USE THESE KEYSTROKES TO PRODUCE CURLY QUOTES

Option Shift]	'
Option]	'
Option Shift [	"
Option [	"

Resize Type

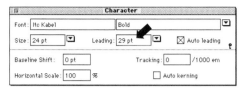

Figure 22. *On the **Character** palette, enter a number in the **Leading** field, or choose a preset leading amount from the pop-up menu, or check the **Auto leading** box.*

ACT III.

Scene I.

The Wood. The Queen of Fairies *lying*

asleep.

Enter QUINCE, SNUG, BOTTOM, FLUTE,
SNOUT, *and* STARVELING.

Bot. Are we all met?

Quin. Pat, pat; and here is a marvel-lous convenient place for our rehearsal. This green plot shall be our stage, this hawthorn brake our tiring-house; and we will do it in action, as we will do it before the duke.

— *"Loose" Leading*

Figure 23.

ACT III.

Scene I.

The Wood. The Queen of Fairies *lying*

asleep.

Enter QUINCE, SNUG, BOTTOM, FLUTE,
SNOUT, *and* STARVELING.

Bot. Are we all met?
Quin. Pat, pat; and here is a marvel-lous convenient place for our rehearsal. This green plot shall be our stage, this hawthorn brake our tiring-house; and we will do it in action, as we will do it before the duke.

— *"Tight" Leading*

Figure 24.

Leading is the distance from baseline to baseline between lines of type. Each line of type in a block can have a different leading amount.

(To add space between paragraphs, follow the instructions on page 142)

To change leading:

1. Select the type you wish to modify.

2. Enter a number in the Leading field on the Character palette (press Return or Tab) (**Figures 22-24**).
or
Choose a preset leading amount from the Leading pop-up menu.
or
Check the Auto leading box to set the leading to 120% of the type size.

Tips

■ You can choose a preset Leading amount from the Leading submenu under the Type menu. To choose a custom leading amount, choose Other from the same submenu. The Character palette will open (if it is not open already) and the Leading field on the Character palette will automatically highlight. Enter a leading amount, then press Return.

■ If a line of type contains more than one type size and the Auto leading box is checked on the Character palette, the leading for that line will be calculated relative to the largest character on the line.

■ Hold down Option and press the up arrow on the keyboard to decrease leading in selected text or the down arrow to increase leading. The increment the leading changes each time you use this shortcut is specified in the Size/leading field in the General Preferences dialog box (File menu).

Leading

Kerning is the adjustment of space between a pair of characters. The cursor must be inserted between a pair of characters in order to kern them.

Tracking is the adjustment of space to the right of one or more highlighted characters. To track type, first select one or more characters with the Type tool or select an entire type block with the Selection tool.

To kern or track type:

1. Select the type you wish to modify.

2. If the bottom of the Character palette is not open, click the palette display lever.

3. Enter a new number in the Tracking/ Kerning field on the Character palette (press Return or Tab) (**Figures 25-28**).
or
Check the Auto kerning box to use the font's built-in kerning values.

Tips

■ You can also apply tracking values by choosing Tracking from the Type menu or kerning values by choosing Kern from the same menu. The Character palette will open automatically (if it is not already open), and the Tracking/Kerning field will highlight automatically.

■ Hold down Option and press the right arrow on the keyboard to add space between letters or the left arrow to decrease space between letters. The amount of space that is added or removed each time you press an arrow is specified in the Tracking field in the General Preferences dialog box (File menu).

Figure 25. *Enter a number in the Tracking/ Kerning field on the Character palette.*

Figure 26. *Normal type.*

Figure 27. *Space added between the first two characters.*

Figure 28. *Space removed between the last five characters.*

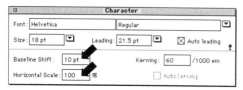

Figure 29. *Enter a number in the* **Baseline Shift** *field or in the* **Horizontal Scale** *field on the* **Character** *palette. (If the bottom of the Character palette is not open, click the palette display lever.)*

Figure 30. *Baseline shifted characters.*

Figure 31. *The "A" baseline shifted downward.*

DANIELLE

Figure 32. *Normal type.*

DANIELLE

Figure 33. *Condensed type.*

DANIELLE

Figure 34. *Extended type.*

The **Baseline Shift** command repositions characters above or below the baseline. You can use this command to offset curved path type from its path, to create superscript or subscript characters (there is no superscript or subscript type style in Illustrator), or to create logos.

To baseline shift type:

1. Select the type you wish to modify.
2. In the Baseline Shift field on the Character palette, enter a negative number to baseline shift characters downward or a positive number to baseline shift characters upward (press Return or Tab) (**Figures 29-31**).

Tip

■ Hold down Option and Shift and press the up arrow to shift selected characters upward, or the down arrow to shift characters downward. The amount type shifts each time you press an arrow is specified in the Baseline shift field in the General Preferences dialog box (File menu).

The **Horizontal Scale** command extends characters (makes them wider) or condenses characters (makes them narrower). The default horizontal scale is 100%. Some designers like to stylize type this way; other designers think it's a sacrilege. You decide.

To horizontally scale type:

1. Select the type you wish to modify.
2. In the Horizontal Scale field on the Character palette, enter a number above 100 to extend the type or a number below 100 to condense it (press Return or Tab) (**Figures 32-34**).

Tip

■ You can also horizontally scale a selected type block using the Scale dialog box. Double-click the Scale tool, click Non-uniform, then enter a number other than 100 in the Horizontal field and enter 100 in the Vertical field.

Baseline Shift

139

Alignment, indent, and leading values affect whole paragraphs. To create a new paragraph in a text block, press Return. Type preceding a Return is part of one paragraph; type following a Return is part of the next paragraph. Type that wraps automatically is part of the same paragraph. To create a line break within a paragraph, press Tab.

To change paragraph alignment:

1. Select the type you wish to modify.

2. Click the Left, Center, Right, Justify, or Justify Last Line Alignment icon on the Paragraph palette (**Figures 35-37**).

Tips

■ The Justify and Justify Last Line alignment options cannot be applied to path type or to point type (type not in a box or in a block), because there is no container to justify the edges to.

■ You can also choose an alignment option from the Alignment submenu under the Type menu.

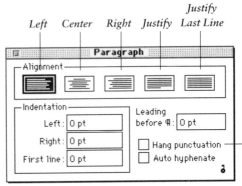

Figure 35. *Click one of the five* **Alignment** *icons on the* **Paragraph** *palette.*

Hanging punctuation looks classy. (We wish QuarkXPress had an automatic hanging punctuation feature.)

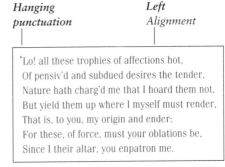

Figure 36.

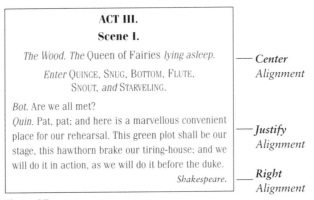

Figure 37.

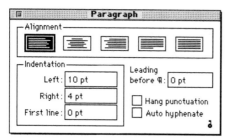

Figure 38. *The **Indentation** fields on the Paragraph palette.*

Left and Right **Indentation** values can be applied to a paragraph within a type rectangle. Only a Left Indentation value can be applied to point type.

To change paragraph indentation:

1. Select the type you wish to modify.

2. Enter new numbers in the Left and/or Right Indentation fields on the Paragraph palette (**Figure 38**).
or
To indent only the first line of each paragraph, enter a number in the "First line" field.

3. Press Return or Tab (**Figure 39**).

Tip

■ You can enter negative values in the Left or First line Indentation field to move the type to the left. If it is pushed outside the type rectangle or object, it will still display and print.

Paragraph Indentation

ACT II.

Scene I.

A Wood near Athens.

Enter a FAIRY *at one door, and* PUCK *at another.*

Puck. How now, spirit! whither wander you?

Fai. Over hill, over dale,
Thorough bush, thorough brier,
Over park, over pale,
Thorough flood, thorouh fire,
I do wander everywhere,
Swifter than the moon's sphere;

Shakespeare

Figure 39. *Left Indentation.*

ACT III.

Scene I.

The Wood. The Queen of Fairies *lying asleep.*

Enter QUINCE, SNUG, BOTTOM, FLUTE,
SNOUT, *and* STARVELING.

Bot. Are we all met?

Quin. Pat, pat; and here is a marvellous convenient place for our rehearsal. This green plot shall be our stage, this hawthorn brake our tiring-house; and we will do it in action, as we will do it before the duke.

Shakespeare

Figure 40. *To create **hanging indentation**, as in this illustration, enter a number in the **Left Indentation** field and the same number with a minus sign in front of it in the **First line Indentation** field.*

Use the **Leading before ¶** field on the Paragraph palette to add or reduce space between paragraphs. Point type cannot be modified using this feature. *(To adjust the space between lines of type within a paragraph, follow the instructions on page 137)*

To adjust the space between paragraphs:

1. Select the type you wish to modify *(instructions on page 133)*. To modify the leading before only one paragraph in a type block, select the paragraph with the Type tool.

2. Enter a number in the "Leading before ¶" field on the Paragraph palette (**Figure 41**).

3. Press Return or Tab (**Figure 42**).

Tips

■ To create a new paragraph, press Return. To create a line break within a paragraph, press Tab.

■ To move paragraphs close together, enter a negative number in the "Leading before ¶" field.

■ To change the horizontal word or letter spacing for justified paragraphs, add higher or lower numbers in the Minimum, Desired, or Maximum fields on the Paragraph palette (click the palette display lever to display the bottom panel). For non-justified type, you can enter values only in the Desired fields.

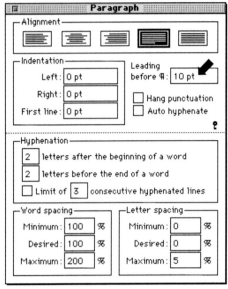

Figure 41. *The **Leading before ¶** field on the Paragraph palette.*

*Different **Leading before ¶** values were applied to these paragraphs to add space between them.*

ACT III.

Scene I.

The Wood. The Queen of Fairies *lying asleep.*

Enter QUINCE, SNUG, BOTTOM, FLUTE, SNOUT, *and* STARVELING.

Bot.   Are we all met?

Quin. Pat, pat; and here is a marvellous convenient place for our rehearsal. This green plot shall be our stage, this hawthorn brake our tiring-house; and we will do it in action, as we will do it before the duke.

Shakespeare

Figure 42.

Paragraph Spacing

PLAY WITH TYPE

H AVING LEARNED how to create type *(Chapter 13)* and style type *(Chapter 14)*, you might like to try some of the simple type exercises in this chapter. There are instructions for creating slanted type, shadow type, and type on a circle, and for wrapping type around an object.

Peter Fahrni

To slant a block of type:

1. Choose the Rectangle tool, then draw a rectangle.

2. Choose the Area Type tool.

3. Click on the edge of the rectangle, then enter type (**Figure 2**).

4. With the rectangle still selected, double-click the Rotation tool.

5. Enter 30 in the Angle field.

6. Click OK or press Return (**Figure 3**).

7. Choose Artwork from the View menu to display the rectangle's segments (or hold down Option and click on the dot in the Eye column for the highlighted layer on the Layers palette).

8. Choose the Direct Selection tool.

9. Drag the top segment diagonally to the right until the side segments are vertical (**Figure 4**).

10. *Optional:* Drag the right segment of the rectangle a little to the right to enlarge the object and reflow the type.

11. Choose Preview from the View menu (**Figure 5**).

Tip

■ You can also use the Shear tool to slant a block of type (**Figures 1a-b**).

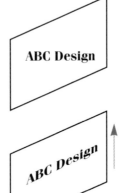

Figure 1a. *The original type block.*

Figure 1b. *Select the type, click with the **Shear** tool on the center of the type, then drag upward or downward from the edge of the type block.*

Figure 2. *The original type object.*

Figure 3. *Rotate the type 30°.*

Figure 4. *Drag the top segment diagonally to the right.*

Figure 5. *The reshaped type object (Preview view).*

the bakery

Figure 6. *Select a type block.*

the bakery

Figure 7. *Position the shadow close to the original type. Leave the lighter type in front...*

the bakery

Figure 8. *...or send it to the back.*

To create type with a shadow:

1. Create point type *(see page 122)* (**Figure 6**).

2. *Optional:* Select the type with the Type tool, then track the characters out *(see page 138)*.

3. Choose the Selection tool.

4. Click on the type block.

5. Choose Preview from the View menu.

6. Apply a dark Fill color and a Stroke of None.

7. Hold down Option and drag the type block by its baseline or its anchor point slightly to the right and downward. Release the mouse, then release Option.

8. With the copy of the type block still selected, apply a lighter shade of the original type (**Figure 7**).

9. *Optional:* Choose Send To Back from the Arrange menu (**Figure 8**).

10. Reposition either type block — press any arrow key to move it in small increments.

Tip

■ To create an even more three-dimensional effect, as in Figure 9, duplicate the type block again, then apply the background Fill color to the middle type block.

Shadow Type

Figure 9. *Three layers of type. The type on the top layer has a White Fill and a Black Stroke, the type on the middle layer has a 50% Black Fill to match the background, and the type on the bottom has a 100% Black Fill.*

To create type with a slanting shadow:

1. Follow the steps on the previous page.
2. Choose the Selection tool.
3. Click on the baseline or anchor point of the shadow type.
4. Double-click the Scale tool (**Figure 10**).
5. Click Non-uniform (**Figure 11**).
6. Enter 100 in the Horizontal field.
7. Enter 60 in the Vertical field.
8. Click Copy.
9. With the shadow type still selected, double-click the Shear tool (**Figure 10**).
10. Enter 45 in the Angle field (**Figure 12**).
11. Click Horizontal Axis.
12. Click OK or press Return.
13. Use the arrow keys to move the baseline of the shadow text so it aligns with the baseline of the original text (**Figure 14**).

Shadow slant variation:

1. Follow all the steps above.
2. Choose the Selection tool.
3. Click on the shadow type.
4. Double-click the Reflect tool (**Figure 10**).
5. Click Horizontal axis.
6. Click OK or press Return.
7. Move the shadow block down so it aligns with the baselines of the two blocks of letters (**Figure 15**).

Tip

■ If you cannot select the shadow type layer in back, select the original type first, press the up arrow key to move it upward, then click on the baseline or anchor point of the shadow type.

Reflect tool — · —*Scale* tool —*Shear* tool

Figure 10.

Figure 11. *Scale dialog box.*

Figure 12. *Shear dialog box.*

MARTINE

Figure 13. *The original type.*

MARTINE

Figure 14. *Reduce the shadow type, then Shear it.*

MARTINE

Figure 15. *After reflecting the shadow.*

Shadow Type

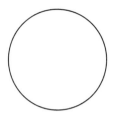

Figure 16. *Create a 3-inch circle.*

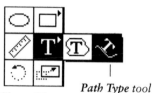

Path Type tool

Figure 17.

Figure 18. *Create path type on the top of the first circle.*

Figure 19. *Create path type on the bottom of the second circle.*

Figure 20. *Drag the path type inside the circle.*

Exercise

Create a logo — type on a circle.

1. Open the Layers, Character, and Paint Style palettes from the Window menu.

2. Choose General Preferences from the Preferences submenu under the File menu, then choose Inches from the Ruler units pop-up menu.

3. Double-click Layer 1 on the Layers palette, then rename it "Circle type."

4. Choose the Oval tool, then click on the Artboard (don't drag).

5. Enter "3" in the horizontal field, and "3" in the vertical field.

6. Click OK (**Figure 16**).

7. On the Character palette, enter 24 in the Size field, then press Return.

8. Choose the Path-Type tool (**Figure 17**).

7. Click on the top of the circle.

8. Type "Type & Design" (**Figure 18**).

9. Choose the Selection tool.

10. Drag the I-beam to the left.

11. Choose the Oval tool, then click on the Artboard.

12. Click OK. (Don't change the dimensions in the Oval dialog box.)

13. Choose Path-Type tool.

14. Click on the bottom of new circle.

15. Enter the text "Form & Function" (**Figure 19**).

16. Choose the Selection tool.

17. Drag the I-beam icon inside the circle (**Figure 20**).

18. On the Character palette, enter -24 in the Baseline Shift field, then press Return.

19. Move the path type to the left (move the I-beam icon) (**Figure 21**). Do not cross over the edge of the circle.

20. Apply a Fill color.

21. Apply a Stroke of None.

22. Apply the same Fill color to the other type block.

23. Choose the Selection tool.

24. Choose Artwork from the View menu.

25. Drag one circle over the other until the centers perfectly align. Press the arrow keys for precision (**Figure 22**).

26. Choose Preview from the View menu.

27. Choose the Selection tool.

28. Drag a marquee around both circles.

29. Choose Group from Arrange menu.

30. Double-click the Scale tool.

31. Click Uniform.

32. Enter 125 in the Uniform field.

33. Click OK.

34. Choose Repeat Transform from the Arrange menu.

35. Save the document.

To create point type for the "Art & Industry" logo:

1. Create a new layer called "Type Block" using the Layers palette.

2. Select the Type tool.

3. Type "Art," press Return, type "&," press Return, then type "Industry" (**Figure 23**).

4. Use the Type tool to select the type.

5. Choose Center from the Alignment submenu under the Type menu.

6. Choose a font, point size, leading, and horizontal scale. Enter a Baseline shift value of 0.

7. Select the "A," choose a different font and size, and change the Fill color.

8. Select the "I," then change the font and size, and the Fill color (**Figure 24**).

Figure 21. Baseline shift the path type on the second circle downward, and center it on the circle.

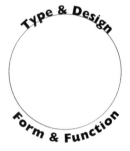

Figure 22. Drag one circle over the other, then group both circles together.

Figure 23. The original plain type.

Figure 24. The type centered, repainted, and restyled.

Figure 25. The small characters baseline shifted upward.

9. Select "rt" and Baseline shift it upward.

10. Select "ndustry" and Baseline shift it upward (**Figure 25**).

Figure 26. The ampersand Cut and Pasted into a separate type block, then resized and restyled. Place with the other type block.

To make the "&" into a separate type block so you can resize, restack or reposition it easily:

1. Choose the Type tool, then Select the "&".

2. Choose Cut from Edit menu.

3. Click the Type tool.

4. Click on the page to create an insertion point.

5. Choose Paste from Edit menu.

6. Choose the Selection tool, then select the "&".

7. Choose a font, Horizontal scale, Fill color, and large point size (**Figure 26**).

8. Drag the "&" into position with the other type block.

9. With the "&" still selected, choose Send to Back from the Arrange menu (**Figure 27**).

10. Select the "&" and the type block.

11. Choose Group from Arrange menu.

12. Save the document.

Figure 27. The final type block.

To combine the type blocks for the logo:

1. Choose the Selection tool.

2. Move the "ART" type block inside the circles.

To resize the type block:

1. Select the "ART" type.

2. Double-click the Scale tool.

3. Enter numbers in the Uniform or Non-uniform fields to enlarge or reduce the type block to fit nicely inside the circle.

4. Choose the Selection tool and adjust the position of the type block.

5. Save the document (**Figure 28**).

Figure 28. The type blocks moved inside the circle. Scale the type block, if necessary.

To add a backdrop to the logo:

1. Choose New Layer from the Layers palette pop-up menu, enter the name "Gradient," choose a Selection color, then click OK.

2. On the Layers palette, drag the "Gradient" layer name below the other two layers.

3. Choose the Oval tool.

4. Hold down Option and click on the center of the circles.

5. Enter 4.3 (inches) in the Width and Height fields.

6. Click the Gradient color selection method icon on the Paint Style palette.

7. Choose a gradient.

8. Choose the Gradient tool.

9. Drag diagonally across the circle.

Figure 29. *Further developed logo, with a radial Gradient Fill and a linear Gradient Fill.*

To wrap type around an object:

1. Create area type inside an object.

2. Choose the Selection tool.

3. Select the object the type is to wrap around (**Figure 30**).

4. Choose Bring To Front from the Arrange menu.

5. Drag a marquee around both objects.

6. Choose Make Wrap from the Type menu (**Figure 31**).

Tips

▪ Use the Direct Selection tool to move the object the type is wrapping around. To move multiple objects, first click on each one with Shift held down.

▪ To move the type away from the edge of the wrap object, enter values in the Left or Right Indentation fields on the Paragraph palette.

▪ To undo the type wrap, choose Release Wrap from the Type menu.

For fine dining, try the food at the Eaterie. Sample the extraordinary entrees and extravagant desserts. And don't forget to taste one of our many fine wines. A true dining pleasure. For fine dining, try the food at the Eaterie, the extraordinary entrees, extravagant desserts. And don't forget to taste one of our fine wines. A true dining pleasure.

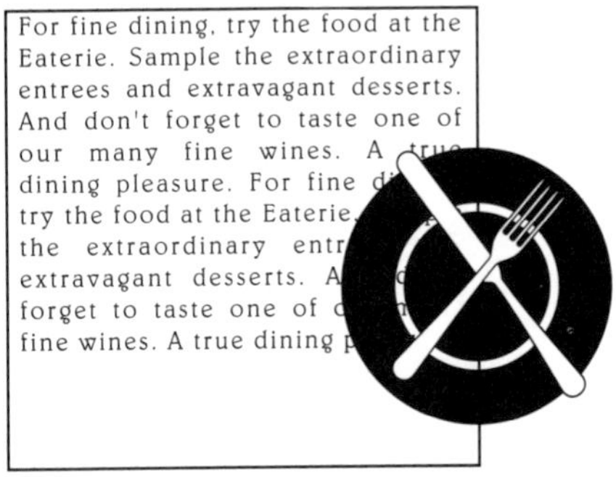

Figure 30. *Select a type object and the object the type is to wrap around.*

For fine dining, try the food at the Eaterie. Sample the extraordinary entrees and extravagant desserts. And don't forget to taste one of our many fine wines. A true dining pleasure. For fine dining, try the food at the Eaterie. Sample the extraordinary en-trees and extravagant desserts. And don't forget to taste one of our many fine wines. A true dining pleasure.

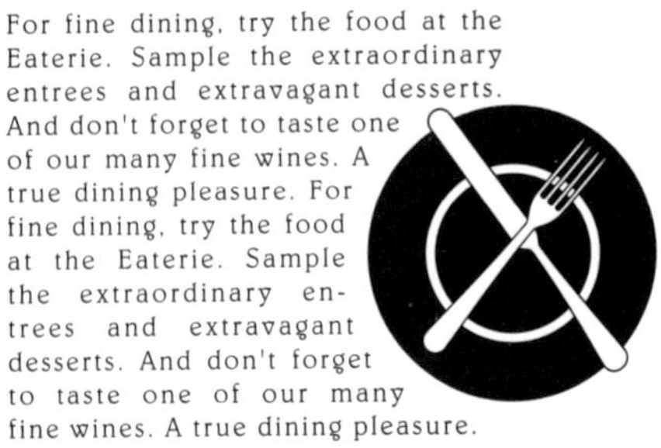

Figure 31. *The type wrap in Preview view.*

T HERE ARE FIVE **transformation tools:** Scale, Rotate, Reflect, Shear, and Blend (**Figure 1**).

The **Rotate** tool rotates an object around its center or around a specified point.

The **Scale** tool enlarges or reduces the size of an object proportionately or non-proportionately.

The **Reflect** tool creates a mirror image of an object across a specified axis.

The **Shear** tool slants an object in a specified direction.

The **Blend** tool transforms one object into another by creating a multi-step progression between them.

The Transformation Tools

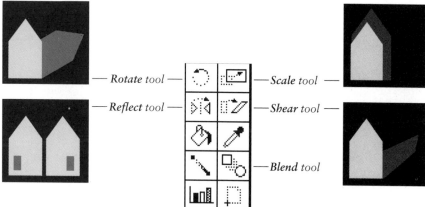

— *Rotate tool* —

— *Reflect tool* —

Scale tool —

Shear tool —

— *Blend tool*

Figure 1.
The Transformation tools.

Transformation Tool Methods

HOW TO USE THE TRANSFORMATION TOOLS

A point of origin must be established before you can transform an object (**Figures 2a-c**).

Dialog box method

Select the object, then double-click the tool to open the tool dialog box. The object's center point will be the point of origin.

or

To select a point of origin other than the object's center point, select the object, choose the transformation tool, hold down Option and click to establish a point of origin, then enter numbers in the tool dialog box.

Press-and-drag method

Select the object, choose the tool, click to establish a point of origin, release and reposition the mouse, then press and drag away from, around, or toward the point of origin.

or

To use the object's center point as the point of origin, select the object, choose the tool, position the pointer outside the object, then press and drag immediately. The further you drag, the greater the transformation.

Press-and-drag method tips

If you use either drag method, after the point of origin is established, the mouse pointer turns into an arrowhead. For optimal control, position the arrowhead a few inches away from the point of origin before dragging.

◆

To choose a different point of origin, click again to redisplay the crosshair pointer, then follow the remaining instruction steps.

◆

Hold down Option while dragging to transform a copy of the original. Release the mouse, then release Option.

To repeat a transformation

Once you have transformed an object, you can transform it again or transform another selected object by choosing **Repeat Transform** from the **Arrange** menu (or hold down **Command** (⌘) and press "**D**"). If you transform *and* copy an object and then choose Repeat Transform, another copy of the original object will be produced. A Blend cannot be repeated.

Figure 2a. *Click to establish a point of origin.*

Figure 2b. *Reposition the mouse.*

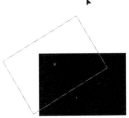

Figure 2c. *Press and drag to transform.*

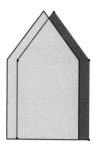

Figure 3. *The shadow object is selected.*

Rotate tool —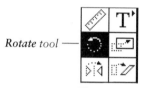

Figure 4.

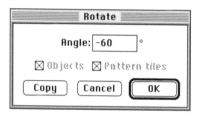

Figure 5. *Enter a number in the Angle field in the Rotate dialog box. Click Copy to rotate a copy of the object.*

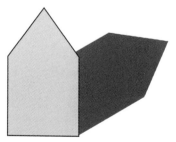

Figure 6. *The shadow was rotated -60°, then moved.*

To rotate an object (dialog box method):

1. Select an object (**Figure 3**).

2. Double-click the Rotate tool (**Figure 4**).

3. Enter a number between 360 and -360 in the Angle field. Enter a positive number to rotate the object counterclockwise or a negative number to rotate the object clockwise (**Figure 5**).

4. *Optional:* If the object contains a Fill pattern and you check the "Pattern tiles" box, the pattern will rotate with the object. (This option can also be turned on or off in the General Preferences dialog box.)

5. *Optional:* Click Copy to rotate a copy of the original (not the original object) and close the dialog box.

6. Click OK or press Return. The object will rotate from its center point and will remain selected (**Figure 6**).

To rotate an object by dragging:

1. Select an object.

2. Click the Rotate tool (**Figure 4**).

3. Click to establish a point of origin (the pointer will turn into an arrowhead), release and reposition the mouse, then drag to rotate the object (**Figures 2a-c**).
or
Without clicking first, press and drag immediately around the object to use the object's center as the point of origin. The object will remain selected when you release the mouse.

Tip

■ Hold down Shift while dragging to rotate in 45° increments. Release the mouse before you release Shift.

Rotate

To scale an object (dialog box method):

1. Select an object.

2. Double-click the Scale tool (**Figure 7**).
or
Choose the Scale tool, then hold down Option and click on the object.

3. To scale the object **proportionately**:
Click **Uniform** (**Figure 8**).
and
In the Uniform field, enter a number above 100 to enlarge the object or a number below 100 to shrink the object.

   Optional: Check the "Scale line weight" box to scale the Stroke thickness proportionately.

   To scale the object **non-proportionately**:
Click **Non-uniform** (**Figure 9**).
and
In the Horizontal and/or Vertical fields, enter a number above 100 or below 100 to enlarge or reduce that dimension. Enter 100 to leave the dimension unchanged.

4. *Optional:* Click Copy to scale a copy of the original (not the original object) and close the dialog box.

5. *Optional:* If the object contains a Fill pattern and you check the "Pattern tiles" box, the pattern will rescale with the object.

6. Click OK or press Return. The object will be scaled from its center point (**Figures 10a-c**).

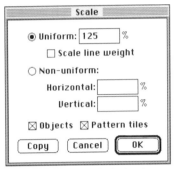

Figure 7.

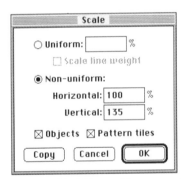

Figure 8. *In the Scale dialog box, click* **Uniform** *to scale proportionately, and enter a percentage.*

Figure 9. *Click* **Non-uniform** *to scale non-proportionately, and enter* **Horizontal** *and* **Vertical** *percentages.*

Figure 10a. *The original object.*

Figure 10b. *The object and the pattern scaled* **Uniformly** *(125%).*

Figure 10c. *The object and pattern scaled* **Non-uniformly** *(100% Horizontal, 135% Vertical).*

To scale an object by dragging:

1. Select an object.

2. Click the Scale tool (**Figure 7**).

3. Click to establish a point of origin (**Figure 11**) (the pointer will turn into an arrowhead), release and reposition the mouse (**Figure 12**), then drag away from the object to enlarge it or drag toward the object to shrink it (**Figure 13**). The object will remain selected when you release the mouse (**Figure 14**).

or

To scale from the object's center, without clicking first, press and drag away from or toward the object.

Tip

■ Hold down Shift while dragging diagonally to scale the object proportionately. Release the mouse before you release Shift.

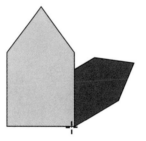

Figure 11. *Click to establish a point of origin.*

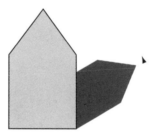

Figure 12. *Release and reposition the mouse.*

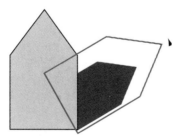

Figure 13. *Press and drag away from the object.*

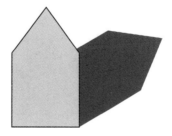

Figure 14. *The shadow object is enlarged.*

To reflect (flip) an object (dialog box method):

1. Select an object.

2. Double-click the Reflect tool (**Figure 15**).

3. Click the Horizontal or Vertical button (the axis the mirror image will flip across) (**Figure 16**).
or
Enter a number between 180 and -180 in the Angle field. Enter a positive number to rotate the object counterclockwise or a negative number to rotate the object clockwise. The angle is measured from the horizontal (X) axis.

4. *Optional:* If the object contains a Fill pattern and you check the "Pattern tiles" box, the pattern will reflect with the object.

5. *Optional:* Click Copy to reflect a copy of the original (not the original object) and close the dialog box.

6. Click OK or press Return. The object will reflect from its center point (**Figures 17-18**).

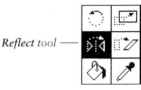

Reflect tool —

Figure 15.

Figure 16. *In the **Reflect** dialog box, click **Horizontal** or **Vertical**, or click **Angle** and enter a number in the **Angle** field.*

To reflect an object by dragging:

1. Select an object.

2. Click the Reflect tool (**Figure 15**).

3. Click to establish a point of origin (the pointer will turn into an arrow-head).

4. Release and reposition the mouse, then press and drag. The object will flip across the axis you create by dragging.

Tip

■ Hold down Shift while dragging to mirror the object in 45° increments. Release the mouse before you release Shift.

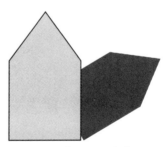

Figure 17. *The original objects.*

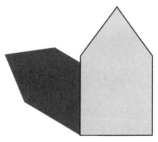

Figure 18. *The shadow **reflected** along the **Vertical Axis**.*

Reflect

Figure 19. *The shadow object is selected.*

— *Shear* tool

Figure 20.

Figure 21. *In the Shear dialog box, enter an Angle, then click an Axis button.*

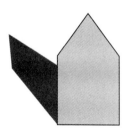

Figure 22. *The shadow object sheared at a -35° Angle on the Horizontal Axis.*

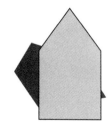

Figure 23. *The shadow object sheared at a -35° Angle on a 35° Axis Angle.*

To shear (slant) an object (dialog box method):

1. Select an object (**Figure 19**).

2. Double-click the Shear tool (**Figure 20**).

3. Enter a number between 360 and -360 in the Angle field. Enter a positive number to slant to the right or a negative number to slant to the left (**Figure 21**).

4. Click the Horizontal or Vertical button (the Axis along which the object will be sheared) (**Figure 22**).
   or
   Click the Axis Angle button, then enter a number in the Axis Angle field (the angle will be calculated relative to the horizontal (x) axis) (**Figure 23**).

5. *Optional:* Check the "Pattern tiles" box to shear a Pattern Fill with the object.

6. *Optional:* Click Copy to shear a copy of the original (not the original object) and close the dialog box.

7. Click OK or press Return. The object will shear from its center.

To shear an object by dragging:

1. Select an object.

2. Click the Shear tool (**Figure 19**).

3. Click to establish a point of origin, release and reposition the mouse, then drag.
   or
   Without clicking, position the pointer outside the object, then press and drag away from the object. The object will slant from its center along the line that you drag.

Tips

■ Start dragging, then hold down Shift to shear the object in 45° increments. Release the mouse, then release Shift.

■ Use the Shear tool to create a shadow for type (*instructions are on page 146*).

Shear

The **Blend** tool creates a multi-step progression between two objects. The objects can have different shapes and can have different Fills and Strokes. You can blend two open paths — like lines — or two closed paths, but you cannot blend an open and a closed path.

To blend (transform) one object into another:

1. Move two open or two closed objects apart to allow room for the transition objects that will appear between them.

2. Choose the Selection tool.

3. Hold down Shift, then click on both objects.

4. Choose the Blend tool (**Figure 24**).

5. Click on a point on the first object.

6. Click on a corresponding point on the second object (**Figure 25**). For example, if you clicked on the top left corner of the first object, click on the top left corner of the second object. If the objects are open paths, click on an endpoint on each.

7. Enter a number in the Steps field (**Figure 26**). The fewer the steps and the farther apart the original objects are, the less the transition objects will overlap. Try a low number first. *(See the box at right)*

8. Click OK or press Return. A series of transition objects will appear between the first and last objects. Only the transition objects will be selected (**Figure 27**).

BLEND STEPS

Illustrator automatically inserts a suggested number of steps in the Blend dialog box based on the difference in CMYK percentages between the two objects and the assumption that the output device will be high-resolution (1200 dpi or higher). To produce a smooth transition between objects, use the suggested step number. To output on a lower resolution printer or to produce a noticeable, banded transition, enter a lower number.

Illustrator's Gradient feature may produce smoother color blends than the Blend tool. Gradients are designed for high-resolution printing.

If you create a color blend across a wide distance (more than seven inches), banding may result. Use Adobe Photoshop to produce a wide color blend.

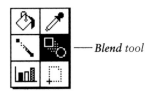

— *Blend tool*

Figure 24.

Figure 25. *Click on corresponding points on two objects.*

Figure 26. *In the **Blend** dialog box, enter a number of transition **Steps** for the blend.*

Tips

- After producing a blend, group the original objects and the transition objects together so you can select and move them easily *(see instructions on page 112)*.

- If you do not like the blend, press Delete while the transition objects are still selected. The original objects will not be deleted. Select the original objects again and redo the blend, if desired.

- If the two original objects contain different colors, the transition objects will be painted with process colors. If you blend two tints of the same spot color, the transition objects will be painted with graduated tints of that color.

- If you click with the Blend tool on non-corresponding points of similar objects (such as the top of one shape and the bottom of the other), the transition objects will be "twisted."

- If one object has more points than the other, rather than selecting the whole objects, as in step 3 on the previous page, you can use the Direct Selection tool to select the same number of similarly located points on each object.

- If the original objects have a Stroke color, the transition objects will be clearly delineated.

Blend

Figure 27. *A military plane transformed into a bird.*

To make the edge of an object look three-dimensional:

1. Select an object (**Figure 28**).

2. Apply a Fill color and a Stroke of None *(see page 89)*.

3. Double-click the Scale tool.

4. Click Uniform.

5. Enter a number between 60 and 80 in the Percentage field.

6. Click Copy.

7. With the copy still selected, choose a lighter or darker variation of the original Fill color (**Figure 29**). For a process color, you can hold down Shift and drag a process color slider on the Paint Style palette.

8. Choose the Selection tool.

9. Marquee both objects, or hold down Shift and click on both objects.

10. Click the Blend tool.

11. Click on a point on one object.

12. Click on a similarly located point on the other object.

13. Enter a number between 30 and 60 in the Steps field (**Figure 30**).
   or
   Leave the suggested number as is.

14. Click OK or press Return (**Figure 31**).

Tip

■ Make sure the smaller object is in front of the larger object before blending them.

■ If the objects have many points, click on non-similar points on the first and last objects to produce a different-looking blend.

Figure 28. *The original object.*

Figure 29. *A reduced-size copy of the object is created, and a darker Fill color is applied.*

Figure 30. *In the* **Blend** *dialog box, enter a number of transition* **Steps**.

Figure 31. *The two objects are blended together.*

3-D Blend

● ●

T HE COMPOUND PATH command joins two or more objects into one object. Where the original objects overlapped, a transparent "hole" is created, through which shapes or patterns behind the object are revealed.

In this chapter, you will learn to create a compound path using the **Make Compound Paths** command or the **Back Minus Front** filter, to release a compound path, and to recolor parts of a compound path. The **Divide Fill** filter is also discussed because it can be used to create "cutouts" or translucent effects.

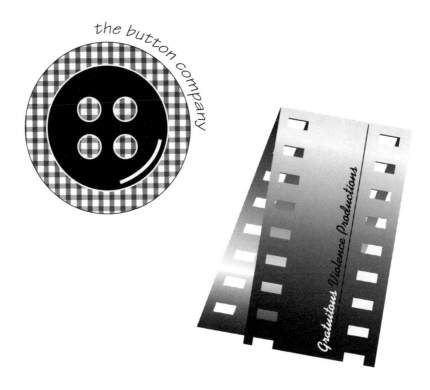

Regardless of their original paint attributes, all the objects in a compound path are painted with the attributes of the backmost object.

To create a compound path:

1. Arrange several objects: place objects you want to see through in front of a larger shape (**Figure 1**).

2. Choose the Selection tool.

3. Marquee all the objects, or hold down Shift and click on all the objects.

4. Choose Make from the Compound Paths submenu under the Object menu (**Figure 2**). The frontmost objects will "cut" through the backmost object (**Figures 3-4**).

Tips

■ Areas where the original frontmost objects overlap each other, and parts of the original frontmost objects that extend beyond the edge of the backmost object, will be painted with the color of the backmost object.

■ Use the Selection tool to select and move a whole compound path; use the Direct Selection tool to select and move a part of a compound path.

■ Regardless of the layers the original objects are on, the final compound path will be placed on the frontmost object's layer.

■ Only one Fill color can be applied to a compound path.

■ To add an object to a compound path, select the compound path and the object you wish to add to it, then choose Make from the Compound Path submenu under the Object menu.

■ In order to use type outline "characters" in a mask, you must first combine them into a compound path. Don't use more than seven or eight characters in a compound path.

Figure 1. *Several objects are placed on top of a larger object, and all the objects are selected.*

Figure 2. *Choose Make from the Compound Paths submenu under the Object menu.*

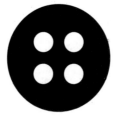

Figure 3. *The objects converted into a compound path.*

Figure 4. *A background object is placed behind the compound path. (A White Stroke was applied.)*

Create a Compound Path

Figure 5. *Click on the compound path.*

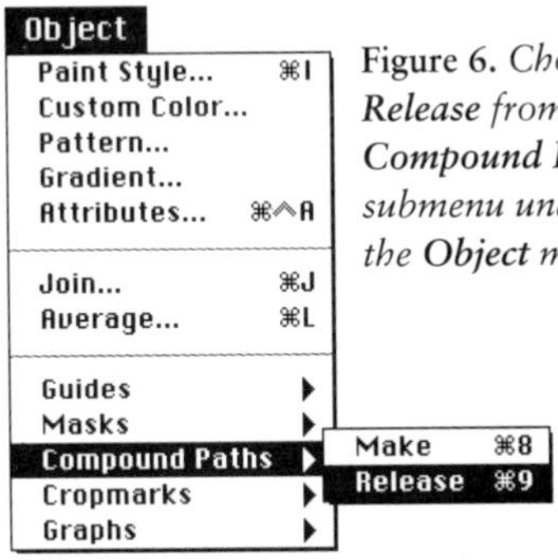

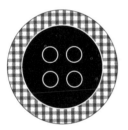

Figure 6. *Choose Release from the Compound Paths submenu under the Object menu.*

You can convert a compound path back into individual objects.

To release a compound path:

1. Choose the Selection tool.

2. Click on the compound path (**Figure 5**).

3. Choose Release from the Compound Path submenu under the Object menu (**Figure 6**).

All the objects will be selected and painted with the attributes from the compound path (**Figure 7**).

Tips

■ If you release a type outline/compound path that has a counter (interior shape), the counter will become a separate shape with the same paint attributes as the outer part of the letterform (**Figures 8a-b**).

■ To delete an object within a compound path without releasing the compound, select the object with the Direct Selection tool, then press Delete. Or, Cut and Paste the object if you want to save it.

■ All objects released from a compound path will have the same Stroke and Fill. It may be difficult to distinguish overlapping objects if your illustration is in Preview view; they will be easier to distinguish in Artwork view. The objects will also stay on the same layer, regardless of which layer they were on before being assembled into a compound.

Figure 7. *The released compound path. The buttonholes are no longer transparent.*

Figure 8a. *Type outlines (a compound path).*

Figure 8b. *The compound path released into separate objects. (The counter of the "P" was moved for illustration purposes.)*

Release a Compound Path

The paint colors in areas that are "cut out" in a compound path can be reversed.

To reverse the Fill of an object in a compound path:

1. Choose Direct Selection tool.

2. Click on the object in the compound path you wish to modify (**Figure 9**).

3. Choose Attributes from the Object menu (**Figure 10**).

4. If the "Reverse path direction" box is checked, uncheck it, or vice versa (**Figure 11**).

5. Click OK or press Return.

The selected path will now have the opposite Fill (the compound path Fill Color or a Fill of None) (**Figure 12**).

Tip

■ If the Reversed path direction box is gray, you have selected the whole compound path. Be sure to select one path within the compound instead.

Figure 9. *Click on an object in the compound path.*

Figure 10. *Choose* **Attributes** *from the* **Object** *menu.*

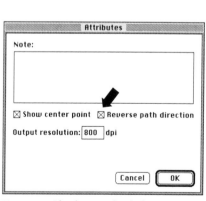

Figure 11. *Check or uncheck the* **Reverse path direction** *box in the* **Attributes** *dialog box.*

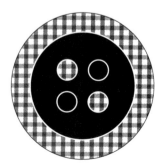

Figure 12. *The color of two of the buttonholes has been reversed.*

Reverse the Fill of an Object in a Compound

Figure 13. *The front-most object does not extend beyond the edge of the black square.*

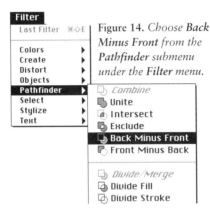

Figure 14. *Choose Back Minus Front from the Pathfinder submenu under the Filter menu.*

Figure 15. *The box is a compound path.*

Figure 16a. *The lines extend beyond the box.*

Figure 16b. *After applying the Back Minus Front filter, the box is divided into three separate objects, and is **not** a compound path.*

To create a compound path using the Back Minus Front filter:

1. Arrange the objects you wish to use in the compound path. Make sure the frontmost objects do not extend beyond the edge of the backmost object, otherwise you will not create a compound path (**Figure 13**).

2. Choose the Selection tool.

3. Select all the objects.

4. Choose Back Minus Front from the Pathfinder submenu under the Filter menu (**Figure 14**). The frontmost objects will "cut through" the back-most object (**Figure 15**).

Tips

■ If objects extend beyond the edge of the backmost object before you apply the Back Minus Front filter, the backmost object will be divided into separate objects, and the over-hanging objects will be deleted (**Figures 16a-b**). The result will not be a compound path, but you can create interesting effects by applying different Fill colors to the separate objects.

■ You can arrange smaller objects behind a larger object and then apply the Front Minus Back filter. The smaller objects will "cut" through the frontmost object.

■ If the frontmost object is a line, apply the Outline Stroked Path filter (from Objects submenu under Filter menu) to convert it into a closed path before applying the Back Minus Front filter. Using a line in a compound path may produce irregular cutout shapes.

Back Minus Front Filter

165

The **Divide Fill** filter does not create a compound path, but it can be used to create compound-like effects, illusions of translucency, or cutouts.

To apply the Divide Fill filter:

1. Arrange objects so they at least partially overlap (**Figure 17**).

2. Choose the Selection tool.

3. Press and drag a marquee across all the objects.

4. Choose Divide Fill from the Pathfinder submenu under the Filter menu (**Figure 18**). Each area where the original objects overlapped will become a separate object.

5. Click away from all objects to deselect them.

6. Choose the Direct-Selection tool.

7. Click on any of the objects and apply new Fill colors or apply a Fill of None to make an object transparent (**Figure 19**).

Tips

■ The Divide Fill filter will remove any Stroke color from the original objects. You can reapply a Stroke color to any object after applying the filter.

■ Move or remove individual objects to create cutouts.

Figure 17. *The original objects. The type was converted into outlines.*

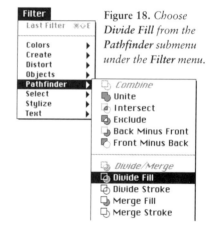

Figure 18. *Choose* **Divide Fill** *from the* **Pathfinder** *submenu under the* **Filter** *menu.*

Figure 19. *After applying the Divide Fill filter. Unlike in a compound path, the areas where the original objects overlapped are now separate objects. Different Fill colors were applied to parts of the letters.*

A MASK IS also called a clipping path, because it "clips" away the parts of other shapes that extend beyond its border. Only parts of objects that are within the confines of the mask will show. Masked objects can be moved, restacked, reshaped, or repainted.

In this chapter you will learn how to create a mask, how to restack, add, delete, or repaint masked objects, and how to release a mask.

Masks

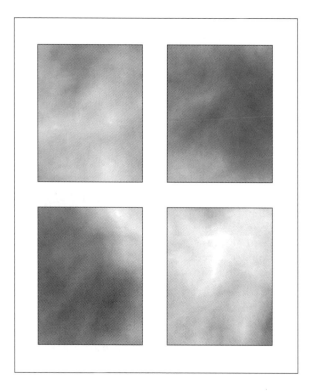

Note: To use a group of objects or use type outlines as a mask, you must first convert them into a compound path (choose Make from the Compound Paths submenu under the Object menu).

To create a mask:

1. *Optional:* Follow the instructions on the next page to place the masking object and the objects to be masked on one layer before you create the mask so you can easily reposition them using the Layers palette.

2. Arrange the objects to be masked (**Figure 1**).

3. Select the masking object, then choose Bring to Front from the Arrange menu or move the object to the top layer using Layers palette (**Figure 2**).

4. Choose the Selection tool.

5. Select all the objects, including the masking object.

6. Choose Make from the Masks submenu under the Object menu (**Figures 3-4**). The mask will have a Stroke and Fill of None and all the objects will be selected. You can move masked objects individually using the Selection or Direct Selection tool.

Tips

■ If the mask is too complex, it may not print. Don't make a mask out of a complex shape with dozens of points or out of an intricate compound path. Don't use more than seven or eight type outline "characters" per mask.

■ The mask can be an open or closed path.

■ If you want to copy a masked object, use the Copy and Paste commands rather than the Option-drag shortcut.

Figure 1. *Arrange the objects to be masked.*

Figure 2. *Place the masking object in front of the other objects.*

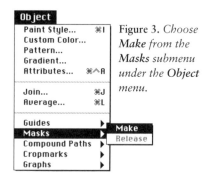

Figure 3. *Choose* **Make** *from the* **Masks** *submenu under the* **Object** *menu.*

Figure 4. *A Stroke color was applied to the mask in this illustration.*

Create a Mask

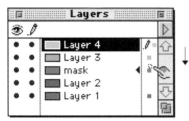

Figure 5a. *The little square from Layer 4 being moved down to the layer called "mask."*

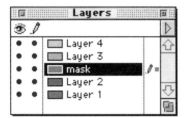

Figure 5b.

Arrange

Repeat Transform	⌘D
Move...	⌘⇧M
Bring To Front	**⌘=**
Send To Back	⌘-
Group	⌘G
Ungroup	⌘U
Lock	⌘1
Unlock All	⌘2
Hide	⌘3
Show All	⌘4

Figure 6. *Choose Bring To Front or Send To Back from the Arrange menu.*

Any objects on the same layer as, or on a layer in between, the layers of objects to be masked may also be masked. You can avoid this problem by following these steps.

To position the objects to be masked on one layer:

1. If the Layers palette is not displayed, choose Show Layers from the Window menu.

2. Choose New Layer from the Layers palette pop-up menu, enter a name, then click OK.

3. Choose the Selection tool.

4. Hold down Shift and click on the masking object and the objects to be masked.

5. On the Layers palette, drag the little square in the rightmost column up or down to the new layer (**Figures 5a-b**).

6. Follow the instructions on the previous page to create a mask.

Stacking is explained in Chapter 10.

To restack a masked object:

1. Choose the Selection tool.

2. Select the object to be restacked.

3. Choose Bring To Front or Send To Back from the Arrange menu (**Figure 6**).

   or

   Choose Cut from the Edit menu, select another masked object, then choose Paste In Front or Paste In Back from the Edit menu.

Re-Layer or Re-Stack Masked Objects

To select mask objects:

To select **the mask and the masked objects**, choose the **Group Selection** tool, then double-click on any of the objects.

To select one or more **individual masked objects**, use the **Selection** tool.

If you haven't applied a Fill or Stroke color to the mask, it will be invisible in Preview view. To select **only the mask** when your illustration is in **Preview** view, choose the **Selection** tool, then drag across where you think the edge of the mask is. If your illustration is in Artwork view, choose the Selection tool, then click on the edge of the mask.
or
Choose Select Mask from the Select submenu under the Filter menu.

To add an object to a mask:

1. Choose the Selection tool.

2. Select the object to be added.

3. Move the object over the mask (**Figures 7a**).

4. Choose Cut from the Edit menu.

5. Click on a masked object.

6. Choose Paste In Front or Paste In Back from the Edit menu. The new object will be masked and will be stacked in front of or behind the object you selected (**Figure 7b**).

Tip

■ Follow the instructions on the previous page to change the stacking position of the newly pasted object.

Figure 7a. *Move the object you wish to add over the mask.*

Figure 7b.

Figure 8. *Select the object you wish to unmask.*

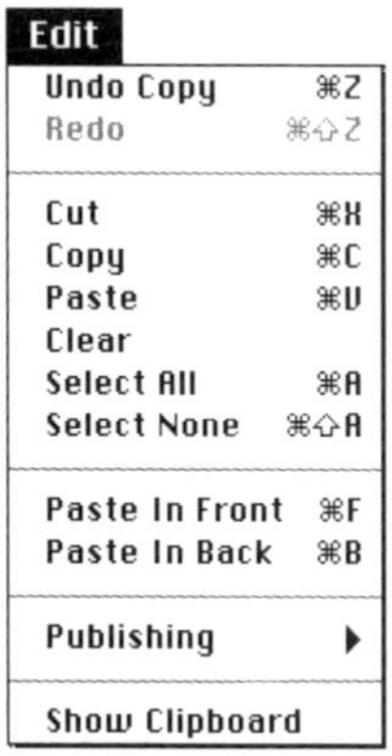

Figure 9. *Choose **Cut** from the **Edit** menu, deselect the mask, then choose **Paste**.*

Figure 10. *The object is now unmasked.*

Figure 11. *Choose **Release** from the **Masks** submenu under the **Object** menu.*

To unmask an object:

1. Choose the Selection tool.

2. Click on the object you want to unmask (**Figure 8**).

3. Choose Cut from the Edit menu (**Figure 9**).

4. *Optional:* If the mask and masked objects are on more than one layer, highlight a layer on the Layers palette that is above or below those layers.

5. Choose Paste from the Edit menu.

The pasted object will now be independent of the mask. Reposition it, if desired (**Figure 10**).

Tip

■ To unmask an object another way, select the object, then, on the Layers palette, drag the little square for the selected object to a different layer.

■ To unmask an object and delete it from the illustration, select it, then press Delete.

■ To determine whether an object is being masked, select the object, then choose Attributes from the Object menu. If the object is being masked, you'll see the words *"The current selection is affected by a mask."*

When you release a mask, the complete objects are displayed again.

To release a mask:

1. Choose the Group Selection tool.

2. Double-click on the mask or a masked object.

3. Choose Release from the Masks submenu under the Object menu (**Figure 11**).

To apply a Fill and/or Stroke color to a mask for the first time, you must use the Paint Style palette and the Fill and Stroke for Mask filter. To repaint a masked object, just use the Paint Style palette.

To Fill and/or Stroke a mask:

1. Choose the Selection tool.

2. Drag over or click on the edge of the mask (**Figure 12**).

3. Choose a Fill and/or Stroke on the Paint Style palette.

4. Choose Fill & Stroke for Mask from the Create submenu under the Filter menu (**Figure 13**).

5. Click OK when the prompt appears. The new Stroke and Fill will be separate objects. You can now select either object with the Selection tool and repaint it without having to reapply the Fill & Stroke for Mask filter (**Figures 14-15b**).

The Stroke object will be in front of, but not part of, the mask.

If the masked objects are on the same layer, the Fill object will be masked. If the masked objects are on more than one layer, the Fill object will be separate from the mask.

6. *Optional:* To group the Stroke object with the mask, choose the Selection tool, press and drag a marquee across the mask and the Stroke object, then choose Group from the Arrange menu.

Tip

■ Use the Direct Selection tool to select a masked object if it is part of a group.

Figure 12. *The original mask.*

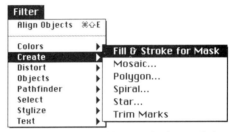

Figure 13. *Choose Fill & Stroke for Mask from the Create submenu under the Filter menu.*

Figure 14. *A Black Fill was applied to the mask. The masked objects were also repainted.*

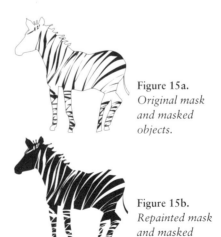

Figure 15a. *Original mask and masked objects.*

Figure 15b. *Repainted mask and masked objects.*

FILTERS  19

FILTERS ARE AMONG Illustrator's most powerful and easy-to-use features, and they perform a variety of operations. Some of the filters are covered in other chapters *(see the box below)*. Seven filter submenu categories are covered in this book:

Color: adjust color in one or more objects.

Create: draw geometric shapes, create trim marks, or paint a mask.

Distort: reshape or stylize objects.

Objects: align or distribute objects, or convert Strokes into closed objects.

Pathfinder: unite, divide, merge, crop, or recolor overlapping objects.

Select: select objects with the same characteristics as the currently selected object.

Stylize: reshape objects for special effects.

Some filters are applied just by selecting the filter name from a submenu (**Figure 1**). Other filters are applied via a dialog box in which special options are selected. Filters can be applied only to a selected object or objects.

Note: For a filter to be accessible in Illustrator, it must be in the Plug-Ins folder when the application is launched. To access certain Objects filters (Offset Path, Outline Stroked Path) and all the Pathfinder filters, a math coprocessor must be installed on your Macintosh.

Filters

The last used filter. Select to reapply the filter with the same settings.

Filter
Invert Colors ⌘⇧E
Colors ▶
Create ▶
Distort ▶
Objects ▶
Pathfinder ▶
Select ▶
Stylize ▶
Text ▶

Figure 1. *The Filter menu.*

The **Mosaic** filter breaks a PICT into little "pixel" squares. The squares are separate objects that can be moved individually.

To "pixelate" a PICT:

1. Choose Mosaic from the Create submenu under the Filter menu (**Figure 2**).

2. Locate and highlight a PICT file to become the mosaic.

3. Click Open.

4. The Current Size field displays the width and height of the image in points (**Figure 3**).

Enter new numbers in the New Size Width and Height fields.

or

Click the Use Ratio button to have Illustrator automatically calculate a width and height proportionate to the original dimensions.

5. Enter the number of tiles to fill the width and height dimensions. If you clicked Use Ratio, the Number of Tiles will be calculated automatically.

6. *Optional:* To add space between each tile, enter numbers in the Tile Spacing Width and Height fields.

7. Click Color or Grayscale.

8. Click OK or press Return (**Figures 4a-c**).

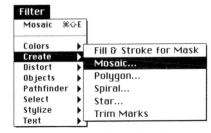

Figure 2. *Choose* **Mosaic** *from the* **Create** *submenu under the* **Filter** *menu.*

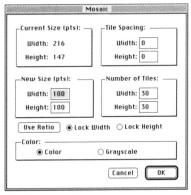

Figure 3. *In the Mosaic dialog box, enter numbers in the* **New Size** *and* **Number of Tiles** **Width** *and* **Height** *fields.*

Figure 4a. *The original PICT.*

Figure 4b. *The* **Mosaic** *filter applied,* **Use Ratio** *option clicked.*

Figure 4c. *The* **Mosaic** *filter applied,* **Use Ratio** *option not clicked.*

Mosaic filter

Figure 5. *Select an object. The type in this logo was converted into outlines.*

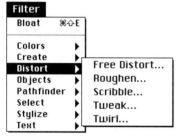

Figure 6. *Choose **Free Distort** from the **Distort** submenu under the **Filter** menu.*

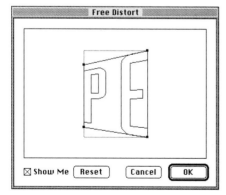

Figure 7. *Drag any corner points of the rectangle in the **Free Distort** dialog box.*

To use the Free Distort filter:

1. Select an object or objects (**Figure 5**).

2. Choose Free Distort from the Distort submenu under the Filter menu (**Figure 6**).

3. Drag any corner point or points of the rectangle that surrounds the object(s) (**Figure 7**). You can drag it beyond the edges of the dialog box.

4. Check the Show Me box to preview the shape in the dialog box.

5. *Optional:* Click Reset if you want to restore the original object and the surrounding rectangle.

6. Click OK or press Return (**Figure 8**).

Tips

- If the object is complex, it may not be drawn accurately in the preview box, but the object will be drawn accurately in the illustration.

- To apply the Free Distort filter to type, you must first convert the type to outlines (choose Create Outlines from the Type menu).

- The last rectangle shape used in the Free Distort dialog box will be displayed next time the dialog box is opened. Click OK to apply the same distortion to another object or click Reset to restore the rectangle to its normal shape.

Figure 8. *After using the Free Distort filter on the "PE" and "ER."*

Free Distort Filter

To randomly distort an object:

1. Select an object or objects (**Figure 9**).

2. Choose Scribble from the Distort submenu under the Filter menu.

3. Enter numbers in the Horizontal and Vertical fields (calculated as a percentage of the longest segment of the object) to specify how much an anchor point or a segment can be moved (**Figure 10**).

4. Check the Anchor Points, "In" Control Points or "Out" Control Points boxes to choose which points on the path will be moved.

5. Click OK or press Return (**Figure 11**). Direction lines will be added automatically to the corner points of paths with straight sides, and whether these new direction lines are moved depends on the "In" and "Out" options you chose.

Tips

■ The more anchor points there are on the path, the greater the Scribble filter effect. To increase the number of points, apply the Add Anchor Points filter from the Objects submenu.

■ To produce different Scribble filter results, check only one or two of the three boxes in the dialog box.

■ The **Tweak** filter works like the Scribble filter, except the numbers entered in the Horizontal and Vertical fields are the actual distances points can move.

Figure 9. *Select an object.*

Figure 10. *The **Scribble** dialog box.*

Figure 11. *After applying the Scribble filter. Low settings (2%) were used to make the cactus a little "prickly."*

Figure 12.
*Select an object
or objects.*

Figure 13.
*The **Roughen**
dialog box.*

Figure 14. *After
applying the
Roughen filter
(Size 2, Detail 6,
Rounded).*

Figure 15. *The original type, converted into outlines.*

Figure 16. *After applying the Twirl
filter to some of the "characters."*

The **Roughen** filter makes an object look
"hand drawn" by adding and moving
anchor points.

To rough up a shape:

1. Select an object or objects (**Figure 12**).

2. Choose Roughen from the Distort
   submenu under the Filter menu.

3. Enter a number in the Size field (a
   percentage of the longest segment
   on the object) to specify how far
   points can be moved (**Figure 13**).

4. Enter a number in the Detail field
   (how many points will be added to
   each inch of the path segments).

5. Click Rounded or Jagged (whether
   the new anchor points will be curved
   or corner).

6. Click OK or press Return (**Figure 14**).

To spin path points around an object's center:

1. Select an object or objects (**Figure 15**).

2. Choose Twirl from the Distort submenu under the Filter menu.

3. Enter a number between 4000 and
   -4000 in the Angle field. Enter a
   positive number to twirl the paths
   clockwise; enter a negative number
   to twirl them counterclockwise.

4. Click OK or press Return (**Figure 16**).

Tips

- To add points to a path and increase
  the Twirl filter effect, apply the Add
  Anchor Points filter from the Objects
  submenu before applying the Twirl
  filter.

- Points close to the center of the object
  will move more than the outer points.

- If several objects are selected, the
  center of the twirl will be their common center.

Roughen and Twirl Filters

The **Calligraphy** filter produces a "thick-thin" line that is similar to that produced by the Brush tool when used with its calligraphic option. Unlike the Brush tool, however, the Calligraphy filter can be applied to an existing object.

To create a calligraphic edge:

1. Select an object (**Figure 17**).

2. Choose Calligraphy from the Stylize submenu under the Filter menu (**Figure 18**).

3. Enter a number in the Pen Width field (the width of the thickest part of the stroke) (**Figure 19**).

4. Enter a number in the Pen Angle field.

5. Click OK or press Return (**Figure 20**).

Tip

■ The Calligraphy filter will convert an open path — like a line — into a closed path. If the object is a filled, closed path, the filter will remove its center area and create a thick-and-thin Fill along its edge, like a ribbon.

Figure 17. *Select an object. This flower was drawn with the Freehand tool.*

Figure 18. *Choose **Calligraphy** from the **Stylize** submenu under the **Filter** menu.*

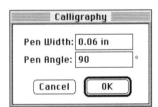

Figure 19. *Enter numbers in the **Pen Width** and **Pen Angle** fields in the **Calligraphy** dialog box.*

Figure 20. *After applying the **Calligraphy** filter.*

Figure 21. *Type outlines are selected.*

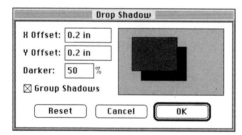

Figure 22. *Choose Drop Shadow from the Stylize submenu under the Filter menu.*

Figure 23. *In the Drop Shaadow dialog box, enter X and Y Offset values and the percentage the shadow color will be Darker than the object's Fill color.*

A drop shadow object produced by the **Drop Shadow** filter will be colored in a darker shade of the object's Fill and Stroke colors.

(To produce a shadow by copying an object, see page 145)

To create a drop shadow:

1. Select an object or objects (**Figure 21**).

2. Choose Drop Shadow from the Stylize submenu under the Filter menu (**Figure 22**).

3. Enter a number in the X Offset field (the horizontal distance between the object and the shadow) and a number in the Y Offset field (the vertical distance) (**Figure 23**).

4. Enter the Percentage of Black to be added to the object's Fill color to produce the shadow color. 100% will produce solid black.

5. Click OK or press Return (**Figure 24**).

Tips

■ Check the "Group shadows" box to group the object with its shadow.

   If the objects are type outlines and you check the Group Shadows box, each character will be grouped individually with its shadow. Instead, you can group the original type shapes first (select them with the Selection tool), apply the Drop Shadow filter, then group the shadow objects as another group. (If you drag a type outline with the Direct Selection tool, the outlines will be separated from the inside areas.)

■ You can enter a negative percentage to remove Black and make the shadow lighter than the object. Too large a negative percentage, though, could create a White Drop Shadow or it might match the object color.

Figure 24. *After applying the Drop Shadow filter.*

Drop Shadow Filter

To make the edges of an object jagged:

1. Select an object or objects (**Figure 25**).

2. Choose Punk from the Stylize sub-menu under the Filter menu.

3. Enter a number between -200 and 200 in the Amount field. The higher the number, the greater the distortion. Enter a low number (between 5 and 15) to distort the object only slightly.

4. Click OK or press Return (**Figure 26**).

Tip

■ To add points to the path and increase the Punk effect, apply the Add Anchor Points filter from the Objects submenu before applying the Punk filter.

Figure 25. *The original*

Figure 26. *After applying the Punk filter.*

Third-party filters:

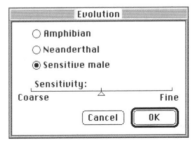

Figure 27a. *A fish is selected.*   Figure 27b. *The **Gefilte** dialog box.*   Figure 27c.

Figure 27d. *An amphibian is selected.*   Figure 27e. *The **Evolution** dialog box.*   Figure 27f. *Sensitive male.*

Punk Filter

Figure 28. *Select an object with a Stroked path. To produce the button shown below, a Gradient Fill was applied to the object before applying the* **Outline Stroked Path** *filter.*

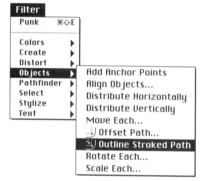

Figure 29. *Choose* **Outline Stroked Path** *from the* **Objects** *submenu under the* **Filter** *menu.*

The **Outline Stroked Path** filter should be applied to an open path before applying a Pathfinder filter, or if you want to apply a Gradient or Pattern Fill to an object's Stroke. This filter produces the most predictable results when applied to objects with wide curves. It may produce odd corner shapes if applied to objects with sharp corners.

To turn a Stroke or an open path into a closed, filled object:

1. Select an object with a Stroke color (**Figure 28**).

2. Choose Outline Stroked Path from the Objects submenu under the Filter menu (**Figure 29**). The width of the new filled object will be the same thickness the Stroke was (**Figure 30**).

Tips

■ The original Stroke path will be deleted by the Outline Stroked Path filter. You can copy it to save it before applying the filter.

■ If you apply the Outline Stroked Path filter to a closed path to which Fill and Stroke colors have been applied, the object will turn into a compound path. To divide the shape into separate objects, choose Release from the Compound Paths submenu under the Object menu.

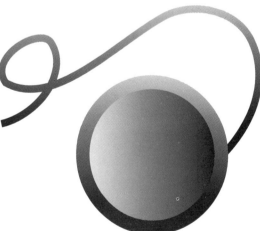

Figure 30. *The* **Outline Stroked Path** *filter converted the Stroke into a closed path. To produce this button, the Stroked path was selected with the Direct Selection tool and a Gradient Fill was applied to it. Then the Gradient tool was dragged across it to contrast with the Gradient Fill in the inner circle.*

The thread was created using the Freehand tool. The **Outline Stroked Path** *filter was applied to it, and then it was also Filled with a Gradient.*

THE PATHFINDER FILTERS

The Pathfinder filters are among the most powerful and useful Illustrator features. There are four Pathfinder filter categories: **Combine, Divide/Merge, Crop,** and **Mix. They create a new, closed object or a compound path (a group of two or more closed shapes) from two or more selected objects that overlap.**

Notes: 1) The Pathfinder filters (except Divide Fill and Divide Stroke) produce unpredictable results or no result when applied to open paths. You can apply the Outline Stroked Path filter (Object menu) to convert an open path into a closed path before applying a Pathfinder filter.

2) All filters other than the Combine filters remove Gradient Fills.

Figure 31a. *The original objects.*

Figure 31b. *Unite filter.*

Combine filters

Unite: joins selected objects into one compound path object. Overlapping segments will disappear. The paint attributes of the frontmost object are applied to the new object (**Figures 31a-b**) *(see also pages 72-73).*

Figure 32a. *The original objects.*

Figure 32b. *Intersect filter.*

Intersect: deletes any non-overlapping areas from overlapping, selected objects. The paint attributes of the frontmost object are applied to the new object (**Figures 32a-b**).

Figure 33a. *The original objects.*

Figure 33b. *Exclude filter.*

Exclude: deletes areas where selected objects overlap. The paint attributes of the frontmost object are applied to the new object (**Figures 33a-35b**).

Figure 34a. *The original objects. The white circle is placed over the black circle.*

Figure 34b. *Exclude filter. One new object is formed. The "white" area is transparent.*

Figure 35a. *The original objects.*

Figure 35b. *The Exclude filter.*

Combine Filters

Figure 36a. *The original objects.*

Figure 36b. *Back Minus Front filter.*

Figure 37a. *The original objects.*

Figure 37b. *Back Minus Front filter.*

Figure 38a. *The original objects.*

Figure 38b. *Front Minus Back filter.*

Back Minus Front: the backmost selected object is "cut away" where selected objects overlap it. Objects overlapping the backmost object are deleted. The paint attributes of the backmost object are preserved. This filter works like the Make Compound Paths command if the original frontmost objects do not extend beyond the edge of the backmost object (**Figures 36a-37b**). *(see also page 165)*

Front Minus Back: the frontmost selected object is "cut away" where selected objects overlap it. Objects overlapping the frontmost object are deleted; the paint attributes of the frontmost object are preserved (**Figures 38a-b**).

Divide and Merge filters

These filters divide overlapping areas of selected objects into individual, non-overlapping closed objects (Fills) or lines (Strokes).

Divide Fill: the new objects retain their previous Fill colors. Stroke colors are removed (**Figures 39a-40b**). *(see also page 166)*

(Continued on the following page)

Figure 39a. *The original objects.*

Figure 39b. *Divide Fill filter (pulled apart for emphasis).*

Figure 40a. *The original objects.*

Figure 40b. *Divide Fill filter (pulled apart for emphasis).*

Divide and Merge Filters

Divide Stroke: objects turn into Stroked lines. The Fill colors of the original objects become the Stroke colors, and Fill colors are removed (**Figures 41a-b**).

Merge Fill: objects retain their previous Fill colors, and Stroke colors are removed (**Figures 42a-b**). The frontmost object shape is preserved.

Merge Stroke: objects turn into stroked lines. Segments that were previously behind the frontmost object are removed. The Fill colors of the original objects become the Stroke colors, and Fill colors are removed (**Figures 43a-b**).

Figure 41a. *The original objects.*

Figure 41b. *Divide* **Stroke** *filter (pulled apart for emphasis).*

Figure 42a. *The original objects.*

Figure 42b. **Merge Fill** *filter (pulled apart for emphasis).*

Figure 43a. *The original objects.*

Figure 43b. **Merge Stroke** *filter (pulled apart for emphasis).*

Crop filters

Crop Fill: the frontmost object "trims" areas of selected objects that extend beyond its borders. Non-overlapping objects retain only their Fill colors; Stroke colors are removed. The frontmost object is also removed (**Figures 44a-45b**). Unlike a mask, the original objects cannot be restored.

Crop Stroke: works like the Crop Fill filter, except objects are Stroked with their previous Fill colors and their Fills are removed. Areas that extend beyond the frontmost object are removed (**Figures 46a-47b**).

 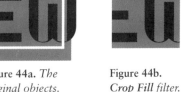

Figure 44a. *The original objects.*

Figure 44b. *Crop Fill filter.*

Figure 45a. *The original objects.*

Figure 45b. *Crop Fill filter.*

Crop Filters

Figure 46a. *The original objects.*

Figure 46b. **Crop Stroke** *filter (paths moved for emphasis).*

Figure 47a. *The original objects.*

Figure 47b. **Crop Stroke** *filter.*

Figure 48a. *The original objects.*

Figure 48b. **Mix Hard** *filter.*

Figure 49a. *The original objects.*

Figure 49b. **Mix Soft** *filter (90%).*

Figure 50a. *The original objects.*

Figure 50b. **Mix Soft** *filter (40%).*

Mix filters

The Mix filters turn areas where objects overlap into separate objects. The new Fill colors are a mixture of the overlapping colors. Stroke colors are removed.

Mix Hard: simulates overprinting. The highest CMYK values from each object are mixed in areas where they overlap. The effect is most noticeable where colors differ most (**Figures 48a-b**).

Mix Soft: creates an illusion of transparency. The higher the Rate you enter in the Mix Soft dialog box, the greater the transparency of the frontmost object (**Figures 49a-50b**).

To create a painterly effect, layer three color objects, then apply the Mix Soft filter at about 75%. Or, to lighten the underlying colors, place an object with a white Fill across other filled objects and enter a Rate between 75% and 100%.

Mix Filters

Exercise

Create a light bulb using filters.

1. *Draw a* **circle** *and a* **rectangle**. *Apply a Fill of None and a 2 point gray Stroke to both objects.*

2. *Select the bottom point of the circle with the* **Direct Selection** *tool. Drag the point downward. Select both objects.*

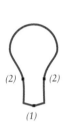

3. *Apply the* **Unite** *filter (Pathfinder submenu). Use the* **Add Anchor Point** *tool to add a point on the bottom segment (1), then use the* **Direct Selection** *tool to drag it downward. Rotate the direction lines upward for the points where the curve meets the straight line segment (2).*

(2)   (2)

(1)

4. *Apply the* **Outline Stroked Path** *filter (Objects submenu).*

5. *Create an oval slightly wider than the base of the bulb. Rotate it using the* **Rotation** *tool. Option-Shift-drag two copies downward.*

6. *Position the ovals on the bottom of the bulb. Select all four shapes. Apply the* **Unite** *filter.*

7. *Use the* **Star** *filter (Create submenu) to create a 20 point star (1st radius: .4", 2nd radius: .69"). Apply a gray Fill that is lighter than the Fill on the bulb, and a Stroke of None.*

8. *Position the star over the bulb. Select the Star, then choose* **Send to Back** *(Edit menu).*

9. *Apply the* **Merge Fill** *filter to the star and bulb shapes to divide the star. Select and Delete the part of the star inside the bulb (use the Direct Selection tool).*

10. *Use the* **Freehand** *tool to draw a filament line inside the bulb. Apply a Fill of None and a Black Stroke to the filament.*

11. *Bulb variation: Before applying the Merge Fill filter (step 9), apply the* **Roughen** *filter (Distort submenu) to the star (Size: 2, Detail: 10, Jagged).*

S IX DIFFERENT **GRAPH** STYLES can be created in Illustrator: **Grouped column, Stacked column, Line, Pie, Area,** and **Scatter.** Explaining Illustrator's somewhat difficult-to-use graphing features in depth is beyond the scope of this book. However, this chapter contains learn-by-example instructions for creating a simple Grouped column graph and then customizing the graph design. Also included are general guidelines for creating other types of graphs. Alternate design and graph style variations are discussed in the "Tips." See the Illustrator *User Guide* for more information about creating graphs.

A graph created in Illustrator is a group of objects. As long as a graph remains grouped, its data and/or style can be changed. As with any group, individual elements in a graph can be selected using the Direct Selection or Group Selection tool and then modified without having to ungroup the whole graph.

THE BASIC GRAPH-MAKING STEPS

- ■ Define the graph **area**
- ■ Enter graph **data** and **labels**
- ■ Choose **graph style** options
- ■ Add custom **design** elements

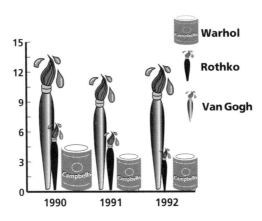

To define the graph area:

Choose the Graph tool (**Figure 1**), then press and drag diagonally.

or

Choose the Graph tool, click on your page, enter numbers in the Width and Height fields, then click OK (**Figure2**). The Graph data dialog box will open automatically.

Tip

■ You can use the Scale tool to resize the whole graph later on.

The **Graph Data** dialog box is like a worksheet, with rows and columns for entering numbers and labels. Most graphs are created in an X/Y **axis** formation. The Y-axis (vertical) is numerical and shows the data in quantities. The X-axis (horizontal) represents information categories.

To enter graph data:

1. For this exercise, enter the data shown in **Figure 4** directly into the cells in the Graph data dialog box. Be sure to enter quotation marks with the dates in the first column. (For other graphs, you can click Import to import a tab-delineated text file or a file from a spreadsheet application.)

Press **Tab** to move across a row.

or

Press **Return** to move down a column.

or

Click on any row or column cell.

or

Press an arrow key.

2. On the top row of the worksheet, enter the **labels**. These will appear next to the legend boxes in the graph.

3. Click OK (**Figure 5**).

Tips

■ If you make a mistake when entering data, click on the incorrect data cell, correct the error in the highlighted

Graph tool. ——

Figure 1.

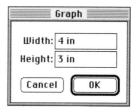

Figure 2. *Enter Width and Height dimensions for the graph in the* Graph *dialog box.*

Figure 3. *The* Graphs *submenu.*

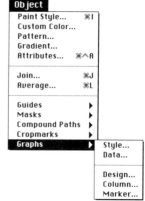

Do not enter any data in this first cell for a Column graph.

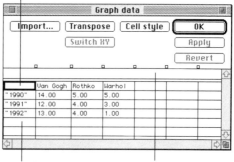

Type these numbers, including the quotaton marks.

Type onto this entry line to fill the currently highlighted cell.

Figure 4. *The* Graph data *dialog box.*

Graphs

Drag this square to the right to make the second column wider.

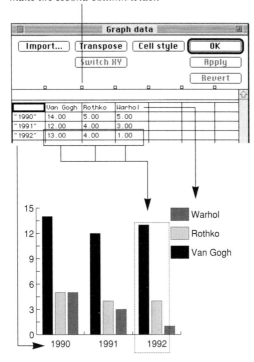

Figure 5. *The relationship between data on the worksheet and the parts of the graph.*

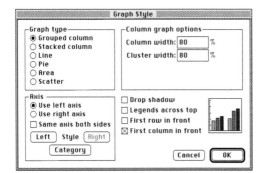

Figure 6. *The Graph Style dialog box.*

entry line, then press Tab or Return to accept the correction.

■ To make a column wider to accommodate a long label name, drag the small square at the top right of that column to the right.

■ To have a legend name appear on two lines, enter "|" (hold down Shift and press the key just above the Return key) in the entry line where you want the name to break.

■ To preview the new graph while the Graph data dialog box is open, click Apply. Move the dialog box to the side if you need to.

When you click on different graph types in the **Graph Style** dialog box, a thumbnail preview of the graph displays in the dialog box.

To style the graph:

1. Select the whole graph (use the Selection tool), then choose Style from the Graphs submenu under the Object menu (**Figure 3**).

2. For this exercise, click the Grouped column button (**Figure 6**). This graph style is a good choice if you want to compare two or three entities over several time periods.

3. Enter 80 in the Column width field to make the individual columns narrower. With a Cluster width of 80%, the three column shapes will spread across only 80% of the horizontal area allotted for each X-axis category.

4. For this exercise, click the Use left axis button. The Axis options affect how and where the X/Y axis appears.

5. To style the axis, click the Left button. For this exercise, leave the default "Calculate axis values from data" button selected (**Figure 7**). Illustrator will scale the Y-axis automatically based on the largest and

Graphs

smallest numbers entered on the worksheet. (Select "Use manual axis values" to enter your own maximum and minimum values for the Y-axis.)

6. The lower part of the dialog box is used for styling the axis **tick lines** (the small lines perpendicular to the axis lines). For this exercise, click the Short button (the default) and enter 2 in the "Draw... tick marks per tick line" field to add an extra tick mark between each Y-axis number.

7. Click OK in both dialog boxes (**Figure 8**).

To Customize the Graph

You can move, transform or modify the Fill and/or Stroke of an individual object in a graph if you select it first with the Group Selection tool.

Tip

■ To restack part of a graph, select a whole group (i.e., the bars and their legend or an axis and its tick marks) with the Group Selection tool, then choose Bring To Front or Send To Back from the Arrange menu.

To recolor the columns/legends:

(In this "Artists Graph": Warhol, Rothko, Van Gogh)

1. Choose the Group Selection tool.

2. Double-click on a legend rectangle to select the legend and its three related columns.

3. Change the Fill and/or Stroke for the legend and the related column objects (**Figure 9**).

Tip

■ You can also click on a column with the Group Selection tool to select it, click a second time to add its related columns to the selection, and click a third time to add its legend to the

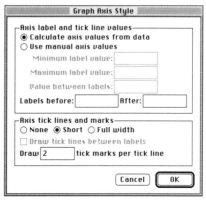

Figure 7. *In the Graph Axis Style dialog box, choose labels for and size of the vertical axis, and choose Axis tick lines and marks options.*

Tick lines.

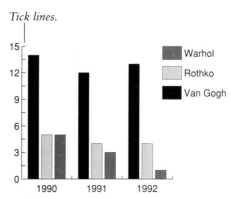

Figure 8.

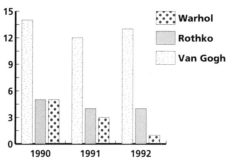

Figure 9. *To restyle this column graph, new Fill patterns were applied to each legend and related column, a heavier Stroke weight was applied to the axes, and the type in the graph was changed.*

Graphs

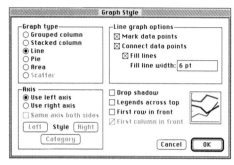

Figure 10. *The Graph Style dialog box.*

selection. Or, use the Direct Selection tool with Option held down instead of using the Group Selection tool.

To change the type in a graph:

1. Choose the Group Selection tool.

2. Click once on the baseline of a type block to select just that block.
or
Click twice to select all the type in the legends or all the labels.
or
Click three times to select all the type in the graph.

3. Modify the type as usual (**Figure 9**).

To combine different styles in one graph:

1. Choose the Group Selection tool.

2. Click twice on the legend box for the category you wish to have in a new style.

3. Choose Style from the Graphs submenu under the Object menu.

4. Click a new Graph type and modify the options for that type. For this exercise, click the **Line** button (**Figure 10**).

5. In the options area, check the "Fill lines" box and enter 6 in the "Fill line width" field.

6. Click the "Use left axis" button.

7. Click OK (**Figure 11**).

Tips

■ To select the line bar in the graph, click twice with the Group Selection tool on the small line bar in the legend (not on the small square marker), or click on the line bar segments in the graph.

■ To modify the marker squares (the points on the line), double-click on the marker in the legend with the Group Selection tool.

Click on the line (not the square marker) to select the legend and its line bar.

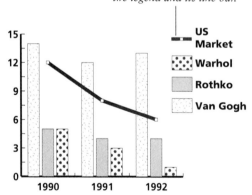

Figure 11. *The Grouped column style and Line style are combined this "Artist's Graph." A new legend name and a column of new data was entered into the Graph data dialog box. The new legend box and its bars were selected, then Line was selected as the Graph type in the Graph Style dialog box. The new line and the legend were selected with the Goup Selection tool (two clicks) and Bring to Front was chosen from the Arrange menu.*

You can replace the rectangles in a graph with graphic objects.

To create a custom graph design:

1. Create a graphic object. Draw a rectangle around the object. Apply a Fill and Stroke of None (unless you want the rectangle to display in the graph). With the rectangle selected, choose Send To Back from the Arrange menu.

2. Choose the Selection tool, and press and drag a marquee over the rectangle and the graphic object.

3. Choose Design from the Graphs submenu under the Object menu.

4. Click New (**Figure 13**).

5. Enter a name for the graphic object. For this exercise, enter "Brush," then click OK.

6. Click on a legend box twice with the Group Selection tool (the legend and its bars should be selected).

7. Choose Column from the Graphs submenu under the Object menu.

8. Choose a "Column design type" (**Figure 14**). The selected type will preview in a thumbnail. For the "Artists Graph," we chose Uniformly scaled to keep the brush wide and we unchecked the "Rotate legend design" box.

9. Click OK (**Figure 15**).

Tips

■ Choose the "Vertically scaled" option to stretch the entire design object.

■ Choose the "Repeating design" option to create a stacked column of design objects. The top of the stack can be scaled or cropped to fit the numeric value of that column. To keep the design object from becoming too small, enter a larger number in the "Each design represents" field.

■ Choose the "Sliding" option to stretch the design object across a section you designate.

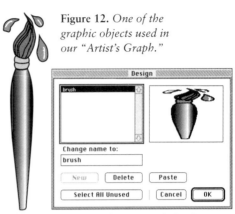

Figure 12. *One of the graphic objects used in our "Artist's Graph."*

Figure 13. *The Design dialog box.*

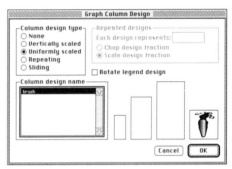

Figure 14. *The Graph Column Design dialog box.*

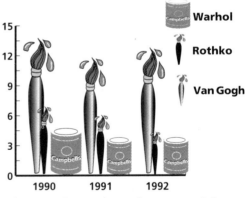

Figure 15. *Custom design elements in a Column graph. Column design type: Uniformly scaled. In the Graph Style dialog box, we increased the Column width value to further widen the brush (we chose 100%). You can also use the Scale tool to resize a selected graph object.*

Graphs

PRECISION TOOLS

THERE ARE many tools that you can use to make your work easier or more precise. In this chapter you will learn how to use **rulers** and **guides** to measure, align, and position objects. How to move an object a specified distance via the **Move dialog box**. How to use the **Info palette** and the **Measure tool** to calculate the dimensions of an object or the distance between objects. And how to **align** or **distribute** objects.

The ruler origin

The rulers are located on the bottom and right edges of the document window. The ruler origin is the point from which all measurements are read — the point where the 0 is on each ruler. By default, the ruler origin is positioned at the lower left corner of the page, but it can be moved in an individual document.

To move the ruler origin, make sure the rulers are displayed (choose Show Rulers from the View menu or hold down Command (⌘) and press "R"), then drag the square where the two rulers intersect to a new position (**Figures 1a-b**). To restore the ruler origin to its default position, drag the square where the two rulers intersect back to the lower left corner of the page.

*(**Note:** If you move the ruler origin, the position of a Pattern Fill in a selected object may change)*

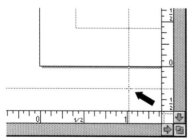

Figure 1a. *Press and drag diagonally away from the intersection of the rulers.*

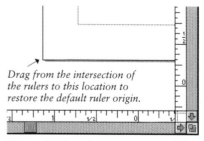

Drag from the intersection of the rulers to this location to restore the default ruler origin.

Figure 1b. *Note the new position of the 0's on the rulers.*

To change the ruler units for the current document only:

1. Choose Document Setup from the File menu (**Figure 2**).

2. Choose Picas/Points, Inches, or Centimeters from the Ruler units pop-up menu (**Figure 3**).

3. Click OK or press Return.

Tips

■ To choose a unit of measure for the current *and* future documents, use the General Preferences dialog box, opened from the File menu.

■ The Ruler units you select will also be the increment used in dialog boxes.

■ The larger the view size, the finer the ruler increments. Dashed lines on the rulers indicate the current location of the pointer.

Figure 2. *Choose Document Setup from the File menu.*

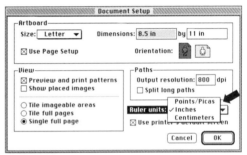

Figure 3. *Choose Points/Picas, Inches, or Centimeters from the Ruler units pop-up menu in the Document Setup dialog box.*

Guides are non-printing dashed lines that you can use to mechanically align or arrange objects. The area of an object under the pointer will snap to a guide if it is moved within two pixels of the guide, and if the Snap to Point box is checked in the General Preferences dialog box (opened from the File menu). You can create a guide by dragging from the horizontal or vertical ruler, and you can turn any object into a guide.

To create a ruler guide:

1. If the rulers are not displayed, choose Show Rulers from the View menu.

2. Drag a guide from the horizontal or vertical ruler onto your page (**Figure 4**). A newly created guide will be locked.

Tip

■ Choose Hide Guides or Show Guides from the View menu to hide or display guides.

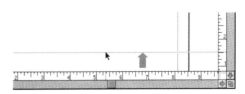

Figure 4. *Press and drag a **guide** from the horizontal or vertical ruler.*

Change Ruler Units; Create a Ruler Guide

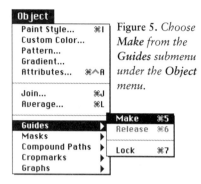

Figure 5. *Choose Make from the Guides submenu under the Object menu.*

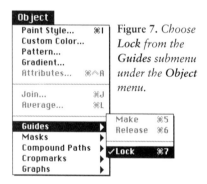

Figure 6. *A circle turned into a guide.*

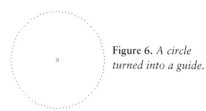

Figure 7. *Choose Lock from the Guides submenu under the Object menu.*

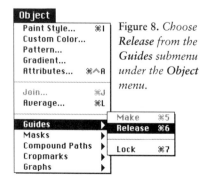

Figure 8. *Choose Release from the Guides submenu under the Object menu.*

To turn an object into a guide:

1. Select an object or a group.

2. Choose Make from the Guides submenu under the Object menu (**Figure 5**). The object will have a dashed border and a Fill and Stroke of None (**Figure 6**).

To unlock guides:

1. Choose Lock (to deselect the command) from the Guides submenu under the Object menu (**Figure 7**). All the guides will unlock.

2. *Optional:* Select any unlocked guide with the Selection tool, then move it or press Delete to remove it.

Tip

■ To move a locked guide, choose the Selection tool, then hold down Control and Shift and drag the guide.

To turn a guide back into an object:

1. If the guides are locked, choose Lock (to deselect the command) from the Guides submenu under the Object menu (**Figure 7**). All the guides will unlock.

2. Choose the Selection tool.

3. Click on the guide you wish to convert.

4. Choose Release from the Guides submenu under the Object menu (**Figure 8**). The guide will turn into a selected object with its former Fill and Stroke.

Tip

■ Choose the Selection tool, then hold down Control and Shift and double-click a guide to quickly release it.

Turn an Object into a Guide; Unlock Guides

You can precisely reposition an object by entering values in the **Move** dialog box. Move dialog box settings remain the same until you change them, move an object using the mouse, or use the Measure tool, so you can repeat the same move as many times as you like.

To move an object a specified distance:

1. Choose the Selection tool.

2. Click on the fill or the edge of the object you wish to move to select it entirely. All its anchor points should be solid.

3. Choose Move from the Arrange menu (**Figure 9**).

or

Hold down Option and click the Selection tool.

4. Enter a positive number in the **Horizontal** and/or **Vertical** field to reposition the object to the right or above its present position. Enter a negative number to move the object to the left or below its present position (**Figure 10**). *(You can use any of these units of measure: "p", "pt", "in", or "cm")*

or

Enter a positive **Distance** amount and a positive **Angle** between 0 and 180 to move the object above the x axis. Enter a positive Distance amount and a negative Angle between 0 and -180 to move the object below the x axis. The other fields will change automatically.

5. *Optional:* Click Copy to close the dialog box and move a copy of the object (not the object itself).

6. Click OK or press Return.

Tip

■ When you open the Move dialog box, the current Distance values indicate the distance the last object was moved, even if it was moved manually.

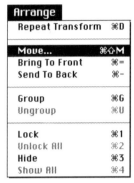

Figure 9. *Choose* **Move** *from the* **Arrange** *menu.*

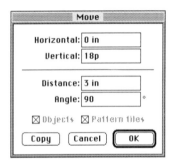

Figure 10. *In the* **Move** *dialog box, enter numbers in the* **Horizontal** *and* **Vertical** *fields, or enter a* **Distance** *and* **Angle** *you wish to move the object.*

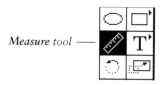

Measure tool —

Figure 11.

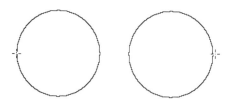

Figure 12a. *Click a starting point. The Info palette will open.*

Figure 12b. *Click an ending point. The distance between clicks will be displayed on the **Info** palette.*

You can use the **Measure** tool to calculate the distance and/or angle between two points in an illustration. When you use the Measure tool, the amounts it calculates are displayed on the **Info** palette, which opens automatically.

To measure a distance using the Measure tool:

1. Choose the Measure tool (**Figure 11**).

2. Click the starting and ending points spanning the distance or angle you wish to measure (**Figures 12a-b**).
or
Press and drag from the first point to the second point.

Measurements will be displayed on the Info palette (**Figure 13**).

Tips

■ Hold down Shift while clicking or dragging with the Measure tool to constrain the measurement to a horizontal or vertical axis.

■ The distances calculated using the Measure tool, as displayed on the Info palette, become the current values in the Move dialog box, so you can use the Measure tool as a guide to judge how far to move an object first, then open the Move dialog box and click OK.

Use the Measure Tool

Horizontal distance from the ruler origin

Horizontal distance from the starting point

Diagonal distance from the starting point

X: 5.056 in	W: 3.403 in	D: 3.403 in
Y: -16.236 in	H: -0.042 in	∠ -0.701°

Vertical distance from the ruler origin

Vertical distance from the starting point

Angle from the starting point

Figure 13. *The **Info** palette after clicking a starting and ending point with the **Measure** tool. (The x and y positions are measured from the ruler origin.)*

To align or distribute objects:

1. Select two or more objects.

2. Choose Align Objects from the Objects submenu under the Filter menu (**Figure 14**).

3. Click the Horizontal or Vertical **None, Left, Center,** or **Right** button (**Figure 15**) (the edge the objects will align to). A thumbnail of generic objects will preview in the dialog box.

or

Click the Horizontal or Vertical **Distribute** button to evenly spread the selected objects between the two objects that are farthest apart.

4. Click OK or press Return (**Figures 16a-b**).

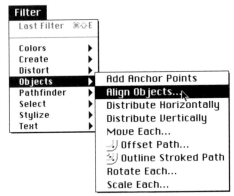

Figure 14. *Choose* **Align Objects** *from the* **Objects** *submenu under the* **Filter** *menu.*

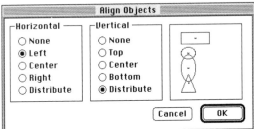

Figure 15. *In the* **Align Objects** *dialog box, click the* **None, Left, Center,** *or* **Right** *Horizontal or* **Vertical** *button, or click* **Distribute***.*

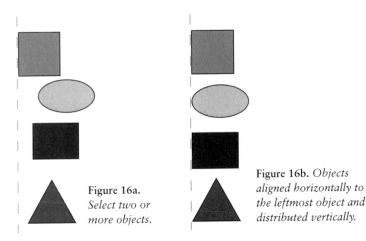

Figure 16a. *Select two or more objects.*

Figure 16b. *Objects aligned horizontally to the leftmost object and distributed vertically.*

Align or Distribute Objects

PREFERENCES

*I*N THIS CHAPTER you will learn to choose default settings for many features, tools, and palettes. You can create a **startup file** with colors, patterns, gradients, and document settings that you work with regularly so they will automatically be part of any new document you create. Using the **General Preferences** dialog box, you can set **Tool Behavior, Keyboard increments, Ruler units,** and **Edit behavior** defaults for the current *and future* documents. And using the **Color Matching** dialog box, you can enhance, albeit slightly, the accuracy of your color monitor.

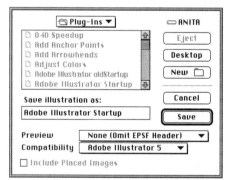

Figure 1. *Enter "Adobe Illustrator Startup" in the Save illustration as field, open the Plug-Ins folder, then click Save.*

To create a custom startup file:

1. Create a new file without a template.
   or
   Open an existing file.

2. Create or import colors, patterns, or gradients; choose Document Setup or Page Setup options; choose a view size; choose a document window size.

3. Choose Save As from the File menu.

4. Enter "*Adobe Illustrator Startup*" in the "Save illustration as" field (**Figure 1**).

5. Locate and open the Plug-Ins folder in the Adobe Illustrator application folder.

6. Click Save.

General Preferences

*(Choose **General** from the **Preferences** submenu under the **File** menu)*

Tool behavior ❶

Constrain angle

The angle for the x and y axes. The default setting is 0° (parallel to the edges of the document window). Tool and dialog box measurements are calculated relative to the current Constrain angle.

Corner radius

The amount of curvature in the corners of objects drawn with the Rounded Rectangle tool. 0 produces a right angle.

Freehand tolerance

The value (between 0 and 10) that determines whether many or few anchor points will be created when you draw an object using the Freehand tool. 1 will produce many points on a line; 10 will produce fewer points. The Freehand tolerance also affects how many points will be created on a path rendered by the Auto Trace tool.

Auto Trace gap

(0-2) how closely the Auto Trace tool traces the contour of a PICT template. The lower the gap, the more closely an image will be traced, and the more anchor points will be created.

Snap to point

When checked, if the area under the pointer is moved within two pixels of a stationary point or a guide, that area will snap to the point or guide.

Transform pattern tiles

When checked, the transformation tools will modify an object *and* any pattern fill it may contain. (You can also turn this option on or off for an individual transformation tool in its own dialog box.)

Scale line weight

Check this box to scale an object's Stroke Weight when you use the Scale tool. (You can also turn this option on or off for the Scale tool in its own dialog box.)

Area select

When checked, if you click with a selection tool on an object's Fill when your illustration is in Preview view, the whole object will be selected.

Use precise cursors

The drawing and editing tool pointers display as a crosshair icon.

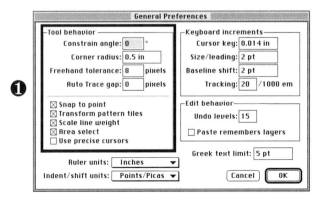

Figure 2. *The **Tool behavior** section of the **General Preferences** dialog box.*

General Preferences

Ruler units ❷

Ruler units

The unit of measure for the rulers and all dialog boxes for the current document *and* all new documents *(see the instructions on page 194 to change Ruler units for an individual document)*.

Indent/shift units

The unit of measure in the type Size, Leading, and Baseline shift fields on the Character palette, and in the Indentation fields on the Paragraph palette.

Keyboard increments ❸

Cursor key

The distance a selected object moves when a keyboard arrow is pressed.

Size/leading, Baseline shift, Tracking

The amount selected text is altered each time a keyboard shortcut is executed for the respective command.

Edit behavior ❹

Undo levels

The number of undo and redo steps (0-200) available at a time. (The Undo and Redo commands are accessed via the Edit menu.)

Paste remembers layers

Whether an object cut or copied to the Clipboard can be pasted onto a different layer from where it originated, (unchecked), or can only be pasted back onto its current layer (checked). Paste remembers layers can also be turned on or off from the Layers palette pop-up menu.

Greek text limit

The point size at which type displays on the screen as gray bars rather than as readable characters. Greeking speeds screen redraw. It has no effect on how a document prints.

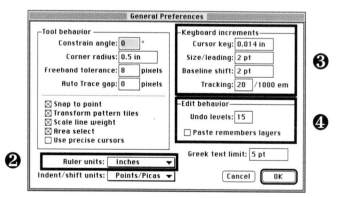

Figure 3. *The Ruler units, Keyboard increments, and Edit behavior sections of the General Preferences dialog box.*

General Preferences

You can enhance the simulation (calibration) of on-screen color using the **Color Matching** dialog box.

To calibrate your color monitor:

1. Choose Color Matching from the Preferences submenu under the File menu (**Figure 4**).

2. If you move files between Adobe Photoshop and Adobe Illustrator, check the "CIE calibration" box so Illustrator can be set up to match Photoshop's RGB-to-CMYK conversion settings (**Figure 5**).

Follow steps 3-5 if you checked the CIE box.

3. Choose the ink your final printer will use from the Ink pop-up menu.

4. Choose your monitor from the Monitor pop-up menu for better translation between on-screen color and printed color.

5. Enter an amount in the Gamma field — the same amount as in Photoshop's Gamma Control Panel (usually 1.8).

Follow steps 6-8 if you unchecked the CIE box.

6. Compare the nine swatches with a printed progressive color bar from your print shop. (There is a sample progressive color bar on page 172 of the Adobe Illustrator *User Guide.* It may not match your printer's inks exactly, however.) If a swatch does not closely match the color on the printed bar, click on it.

7. In the Apple Color Picker, click the up or down arrow to make the color match the color bar, then click OK.

8. Repeat step 6-7 for any other non-matching swatches.

9. Click OK or press Return.

Tip

■ To restore the original Color Matching dialog box settings and swatches, click Use Defaults.

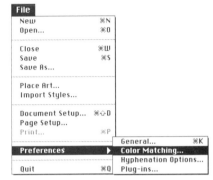

Figure 4. Choose **Color Matching** *from the* **Preferences** *submenu under the* **File** *menu.*

Figure 5. The **Color Matching** *dialog box.*

PRINT

・・・・・・・・・・・・・・・・・・・・・・・・・・・・・・・・

*I*N ADOBE ILLUSTRATOR, objects are described and stored as mathematical commands, but they are rendered as dots when they are printed. The higher the resolution of the output device, the finer and sharper the rendering of lines, curves and gradients.

In this chapter you will learn to print an illustration on a PostScript black-and-white or composite color printer, to create crop marks, to print an oversized illustration, and to troubleshoot printing problems.

(To print color separations, you must use Adobe Separator, which is covered in Chapter 24)

Miriam Schaer

To print on a black-and-white or a color PostScript printer:

1. Select the Chooser from the Apple menu, click on the desired printer name, then close the Chooser.

2. In Adobe Illustrator, choose Page Setup from the File menu (**Figure 1**).

3. Click a Paper size button (**Figure 2**).
or
If you are printing on a color printer, choose the printer driver from the Tabloid pop-up menu.

4. Make sure the correct Orientation icon is selected (to print vertically or horizontally on the paper). *(See page 28)*

5. Click OK or press Return.

6. Choose Print from the File menu.

7. Enter the desired number of Copies (**Figure 3**).

8. To print a single full page document or a Tile imageable areas document, leave the Pages: All button selected.
or
Enter a range of tiled pages in the From and To fields.

9. Check the Color/Grayscale button so colors will print in color on a color printer or in shades of gray on a black-and-white printer.

10. Click the Destination: Printer button.

11. Click Print or press Return.

Tip

■ On a Tile imageable areas document, only tile pages with objects on them will print. If a direction line from a curved anchor point extends onto a blank tile, that page will also print.

PRINTER HALFTONES

If your printer has halftone enhancing software like Photograde, check the "Use printer's default screen" box in the Document Setup dialog box, opened from the File menu, before printing. This will enable the printer's halftone method and disable Illustrator's built-in halftone method.

The "Use printer's default screen" option will automatically be turned off if the file is output on a high-resolution printer or is color separated.

Figure 1. *Choose* **Page Setup** *from the* **File** *menu.*

Figure 2. *In the* **Page Setup** *dialog box for a black-and-white printer, click a* **Paper** *size button. For a* **color** *printer, choose the printer name from the* **Tabloid** *pop-up menu.*

Figure 3. *In the* **Print** *dialog box, enter a number of* **Copies,** *the* **Pages** *you wish to print, and click the* **Black & White** *or* **Color/Grayscale** *button.*

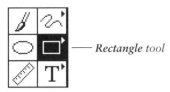

Figure 4.

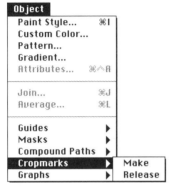

Figure 5. *Choose Make (or Release) from the Cropmarks submenu under the Object menu.*

— *Rectangle* tool

Crop marks are short perpendicular lines around the edge of a page that a printer uses as a guide to trim the paper. Illustrator's Cropmarks command creates crop marks around a rectangle that you draw.

To create cropmarks:

1. Choose the Rectangle tool (**Figure 4**).

2. Draw a rectangle to encompass some or all of the objects in the illustration.

3. Choose Make from the Cropmarks submenu under the Object menu (**Figure 5**). The rectangle will disappear, and crop marks will appear where the corners of the rectangle were (**Figures 6a-b**).

Tips

■ If you don't create a rectangle before choosing the Make Cropmarks command, crop marks will be placed around the current page size.

■ Only one set of crops can be created per illustration using the Cropmarks command. To create more than one set of crop marks in an illustration, apply the Trim Marks filter *(instructions are on the following page).*

Figure 6a. *A rectangle is drawn.*

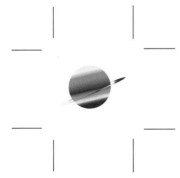

Figure 6b. *After choosing the Make Cropmarks command.*

To remove crop marks created with the Cropmarks command:

Choose Release from the Cropmarks submenu under the Object menu (**Figure 5**). The selected rectangle will reappear, with a Fill and Stroke of None. You can repaint it or delete it.

Tip

■ If the crop marks were created for the entire page, the released rectangle will be the same dimensions as the printable page (and the same size as the Artboard, if the Artboard dimensions match the printable page dimensions).

Crop Marks

The **Trim Marks** filter places eight trim marks around a selected object or objects. You can create more than one set of Trim Marks in an illustration.

To create trim marks:

1. Select the object or objects to be trimmed.

2. Choose Trim Marks from the Create submenu under the Filter menu (**Figure 7**). Trim marks will surround the smallest rectangle that could be drawn around the object or objects (**Figure 8**).

Tips

■ Group the trim marks with the objects they surround so you can move them as a unit.

■ To move or delete trim marks, select them first with the Selection tool.

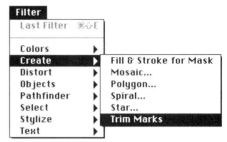

Figure 7. *Choose* **Trim Marks** *from the* **Create** *submenu under the* **Filter** *menu.*

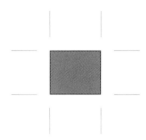

Figure 8. *After applying the* **Trim Marks** *filter.*

To print an illustration that is larger than the paper size:

1. Choose Document Setup from the File menu.

2. Uncheck the Use Page Setup box (**Figure 9**).

3. Click "Tile imageable areas".

4. Click OK or press Return.

5. Double-click the Hand tool to display the entire Artboard.

6. *Optional:* Change the Orientation in the Page Setup dialog box.

7. *Optional:* Choose the Page tool, then press and drag the tile grid so it divides the illustration into better tiling breaks. The grid will redraw (**Figure 10**).

8. Follow steps 1-11 on page 204.

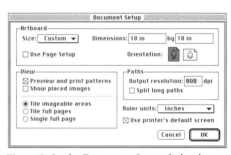

Figure 9. *In the* **Document Setup** *dialog box, uncheck the* **Use Page Setup** *box, enter* **Artboard Dimensions**, *and click* **Tile imageable areas.**

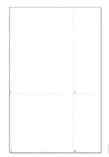

Figure 10. *Tile grid.*

TIP

If you are creating an illustration using complex commands like compounds and masks, print the file in stages as you add complex elements so you will be able to pinpoint where a problem is if one of the versions does not print.

PRINTING GRADIENTS

An Illustrator 5.0 Gradient Fill may not output correctly on a PostScript color printer. To solve this problem, you can try one of the following: check "Use printer's default screen" box in the Document Setup dialog box *(see page 204)*, or save a copy of the file in Adobe Illustrator version 3 (Compatibility pop-up menu in the Save As dialog box), or contact Adobe or your printer manufacturer for upgrade information.

Delete Anchor Point tool

Figure 11.

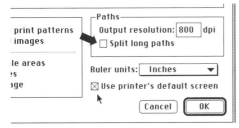

Figure 12. *The Document Setup dialog box.*

How to solve printing problems

Patterns

By default, Illustrator previews and prints patterns. If a document containing patterns does not print, uncheck the "Preview and print patterns box" in the Document Setup dialog box, opened from the File menu (**Figure 9**) and try printing again. If the document prints, the patterns are the likely culprit. Try not to have more than a few pattern-filled shapes in one illustration.

Complex Paths

A file containing long and complex paths with many anchor points may not print — a limitcheck error message may appear in the print progress window.

First, you can manually delete excess anchor points from long paths using the Delete Anchor Point tool (**Figure 11**) and try printing again.

If that doesn't work, check the "Split long paths" box in the Document Setup dialog box (**Figure 12**) and try printing again. Complex paths will be split into two or more separate paths. The outer path shapes will not be changed. The "Split long paths" option does not affect stroked paths, compound paths, or masks. You can also split a Stroke path manually using the Scissors tool. (To preserve a copy of the document with its "non-split" paths, before checking the "Split long paths" box, save the document under a new name using the Save as dialog box. Apply the Unite filter from the Pathfinder submenu under the Filter menu if you want to rejoin split paths.)

Masks may cause printing problems also, particularly those created from compound paths. A document containing multiple masks may not print.

As a last resort you can lower the output resolution of individual objects to facilitate printing *(see the following page)*.

Printing Problems

The degree to which Illustrator renders an object precisely is determined by the object's output resolution. Different objects within an illustration can be rendered at different resolutions. If a complex object doesn't print, lower its output resolution and try printing again.

Note: The Output resolution command replaces the Flatness command found in earlier versions of Illustrator. The higher the Flatness or the lower the output resolution the less precisely a printed curve segment will match the original mathematically defined curve segment.

To lower an object's output resolution to facilitate printing:

1. Choose any selection tool, then click on the object that did not print or you anticipate may not print.

2. Choose Attributes from the Object menu (**Figure 13**).

3. Enter a lower number in the "Output resolution" field (**Figure 14**).

4. Click OK or press Return. Try printing the file again.

Tips

■ If the object prints, but with noticeable jaggedness on its curve segments, its Output resolution is too low. Choose a higher resolution, and try printing again.

■ To reset the Output resolution for all future objects, choose Document Setup from the File menu, then change the number in the Output resolution field. 800 dpi is the default Output resolution.

■ If an object does not print, use the Layers palette to make sure printing is on for the layer that object is on *(see page 118).*

Figure 13. *Choose **Attributes** from the **Object** menu.*

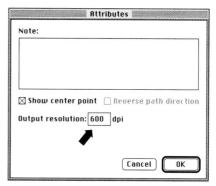

Figure 14. *Change an object's **Output resolution** in the **Attributes** dialog box.*

SEPARATOR/TRAPPING

TO COLOR SEPARATE an Illustrator file, you must use the **Adobe Separator** utility, which is supplied with Illustrator. This chapter contains a brief introduction to Adobe Separator and an introduction to trapping, which helps compensate for color misregistration on press. Trapping and color separations are usually handled by a prepress provider — a service bureau or a print shop. **Talk with your print shop before producing color separations or building traps. They will tell you what settings to use. Don't guess!**

What are color separations?

To print an illustration on press, you need to supply your print shop with paper or film output (color separations) from your Illustrator file — one sheet per process or spot color. If you give your print shop paper, they will have to photograph it to produce film. If you output directly onto film, you will save an intermediary step, and the ultimate print quality will be better. Your print shop will use the film separations to produce plates to use on the press — one plate for each color.

In **process color** printing, four basic ink colors, Cyan (C), Magenta (M), Yellow (Y), and Black (K) are used to produce a wide variety of colors. A document that contains color photographs — whether from Illustrator or from a photo manipulation program or layout program (such as QuarkXPress) — must be output as a four-color process job.

In **spot color** printing, a separate plate is produced for each spot color. Pantone inks are commonly used spot color inks. If your illustration contains more than four or five colors, you will save money if you convert your spot colors into their process color equivalents and run it as a four-color process job — only four sheets of film and only four plates will be required. Pantone colors are usually richer and cleaner looking than process colors, though, and some Pantone colors have no process color equivalents. Using Separator, you can convert spot colors into process colors and you can specify which colors will be output.

To prepare a file for Separator:

1. Calibrate your monitor (*see page 202*).

2. Decide which colors in the illustration will print with the Overprint option (*see the box at right*).

3. Create traps, if needed (*see pages 215-216*).

4. Save the file with a Black & White Macintosh or Color Macintosh Preview (*see page 31*).

WHAT IS OVERPRINTING?

Normally, Illustrator and Separator automatically knock out the background color under an object so the object color won't mix with the background color. If you check the **Overprint Fill** or **Stroke** box on the **Paint Style** palette, the Fill or Stroke color will overprint background colors. Where colors overlap, a combination color will be produced. Turn on the Overprint option if you are building traps. You can simulate the mixing of overlapping colors by applying the Mix Hard filter from the Pathfinder submenu under the Filter menu (*see page 185*).

Colors will overprint on a printing press but not on a PostScript color composite printer.

Separator is automatically installed in the Separator & Utilities folder in the Adobe Illustrator application folder during the Install process (*see the Adobe Illustrator "Getting Started" manual for more information*).

To use Separator:

1. From your Macintosh Desktop, open the Separator & Utilities folder located in the Illustrator application folder.

2. Double-click the Separator icon.

3. Locate and open the EPS illustration you wish to color separate (**Figure 1**).

4. In the PPD (PostScript Printer Description) dialog box, locate and select the PPD file specified by your service bureau for your target printer or imagesetter, then click Open (**Figure 2**). The PPD files should be in the PPD folder, in the Separator & Utilities folder.

5. In the Setup dialog box, you'll see a file preview window on the left and Separator settings on the right (**Figure 3**).

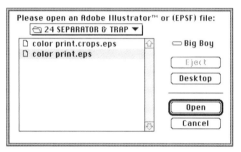

Figure 1. *Locate and **Open** the EPS illustration you wish to color separate.*

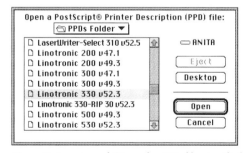

Figure 2. *Locate and **Open** the PPD file specified by your service bureau.*

Separator

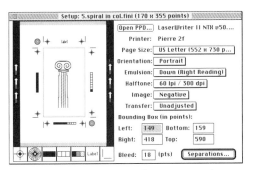

Figure 3. *The illustration will preview on the left side of the Setup dialog box.*

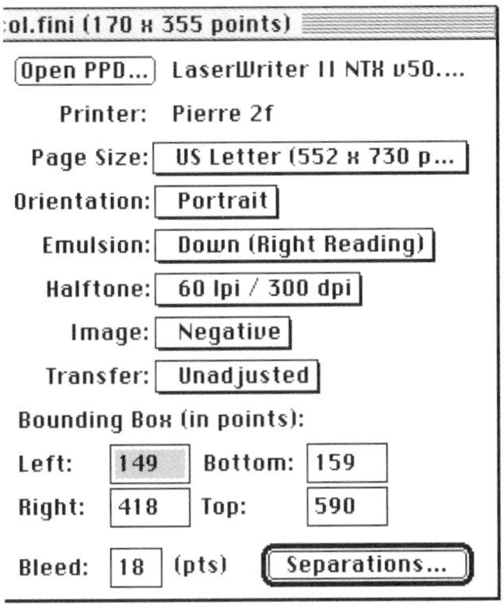

Figure 4. *Choose settings specified by your print shop from the right side of the Setup dialog box.*

6. *Optional:* If you want to change the PPD file, click the Open PPD button at the top of the dialog box, then select a new printer definition.

7. *Optional:* The white area in the preview window represents the page size. Separator will automatically choose the default page size for the chosen printer definition. Choose a new Page Size from the Page Size pop-up menu, if your print shop requests that you do so.

FOR STEPS 8-11, ASK YOUR PRINT SHOP FOR ADVICE.

8. Choose **Portrait** Orientation to position the image vertically within the imageable area of the separation (**Figure 4**).
or
Choose **Landscape** Orientation to position the image horizontally within the imageable area of the separation. The orientation of the image on the page will be affected, not the orientation of the page on the film.

9. Select Up (Right Reading) or Down (Right Reading) from the Emulsion pop-up menu.

10. Select a Halftone screen ruling (lpi).

11. Select Positive or Negative from the Image pop-up menu.

12. *Optional:* Save the document (*see page 214 in this chapter*). The Separator settings will be saved with it. It is now ready to output.

Tip

■ If you open an EPS file for the first time in Separator, the settings last used will appear in the dialog box. To restore the default dialog box settings, choose Use Default Settings from the Settings menu.

Separator

Crop marks in Separator

If you have not created crop marks for your document in Illustrator, Separator will, by default, create crop marks at the edge of the illustration's bounding box, which is the smallest rectangle that can encompass all the objects and direction lines in the illustration. It displays as a gray outlined rectangle in the Separator preview window. Adobe recommends setting crop marks in Illustrator using the Make Cropmarks command rather than using Separator to set crop marks, so you'll know what the exact printing area of the illustration is.

Separator regards crop marks created using the Trim Marks filter as artwork. If your document contains Trim Marks, you'll probably want to delete the Separator crop marks (drag them off the preview window).

The **bounding box** defines the printable area around which Separator places crop marks. You can move the bounding box in the Separator preview window so it surrounds a different part of the illustration, though it usually does not need to be adjusted. If you move or resize the bounding box, Separator crop marks will appear around it, replacing Illustrator's default crop marks. You might need to move the image and/or the bounding box if the illustration contains objects that are outisde the Artboard and there are no Illustrator-generated crop marks, because Separator will include off-the-page objects as part of the image to be printed. Follow these instructions if you wish to move the bounding box (and thus "re-crop" the illustration).

To "re-crop" the illustration in the bounding box:

To move the illustration relative to the bounding box, position the pointer over the image in the preview window (the pointer will turn into a hand icon), then press and drag (**Figure 5**).

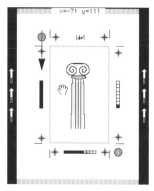

Figure 5. *Moving the image in its bounding box.*

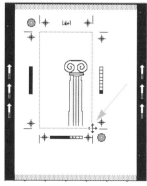

Figure 6. *Hold down Shift and drag a corner to move the bounding box. Note the 4-way arrow pointer.*

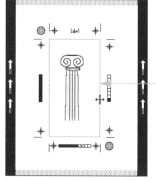

Figure 7. *Moving the side of the bounding box.*

Separator

Settings

Use Default Marks	⌘M
Use Default Settings	⌘T
Use Default Bounding Box	⌘B

Figure 8. *Choose Use Default Bounding Box or Use Default Marks from the Settings menu.*

File

Open...	⌘O
Close	⌘W
Get Info...	⌘I
Separations...	
Save Selected Separations...	
Save All Separations...	⌘S
Print Selected Separations	
Print All Separations	⌘P
Print Composite	
Quit	⌘Q

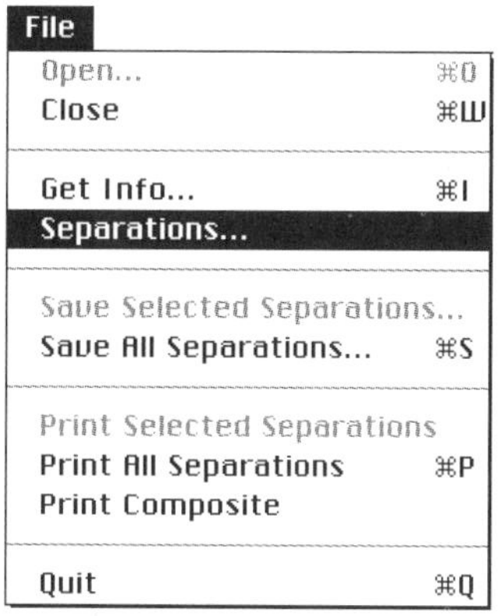

Figure 9. *Choose Separations from the File menu.*

Separation: color print.eps					
Label:	color print.eps				
Color	Print	Convert To Process	Frequency	Angle	
ProcessCyan	Yes	n/a	133.871	18.4349	
ProcessMagenta	Yes	n/a	133.871	71.565	
ProcessYellow	Yes	n/a	127.0	0.0	
ProcessBlack	Yes	n/a	119.737	45.0	
Blue	n/a	Yes	119.737	45.0	
PANTONE 155 CU	Yes	No	133.871	18.4349	
PANTONE 5483 CU	Yes	No	133.871	71.565	

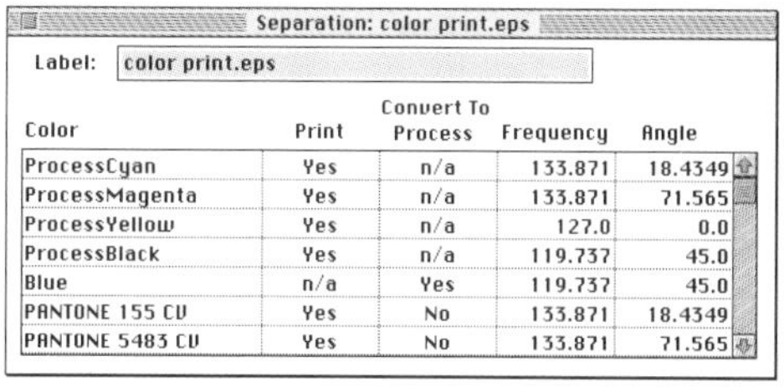

Figure 10. *Click in the **Print** column and/or **Convert to Process** column in the **Separation** dialog box.*

or
To move the gray bounding box itself, position the pointer over a corner of it (the pointer will turn into a four-headed arrow), then hold down Shift and press and drag the box (**Figure 6**).
or
To resize the gray bounding box, press and drag any of its four sides (the pointer will turn into a two-headed arrow) (**Figure 7**).

Tips

■ To restore the default bounding box, choose Use Default Bounding Box from the Settings menu (**Figure 8**).

■ To restore the default printing marks, choose Use Default Marks from the Settings menu.

By default, Separator prints all the process and custom colors in an illustration. Using the Separation dialog box, you can turn printing on or off for individual colors. You can also convert individual custom colors into process colors.

To select colors to print and/or convert to process:

1. With the Setup window still open, choose Separations from the File menu (**Figure 9**).
or
Click the Separations button.

2. When the Separation window opens, you will see a "No" for all colors in the Print column. To print a color, click in the Print column to turn the "No" into a "Yes" (**Figure 10**).

3. Click in the Convert to Process column for each custom color you wish to convert into a process color.

4. Click the window close box.

Tip

■ Do not alter the settings in the Frequency and Angle columns unless advised to do so by your service bureau.

Separator

Printing options

Separator can **Print All Separations** (a separate printout for every color used in the illustration), **Print Selected Separations** (separate printouts of only the colors with a "Yes" under the Print column in the Separation window), or **Print Composite** (all the separations combined in one printout). Choose the appropriate option from the File menu (**Figure 11**).

Note: If you are printing a composite, choose Up (Right Reading) from the Emulsion pop-up menu and Positive from the Image pop-up menu before choosing a printing option *(see steps 9 and 11 on page 211).*

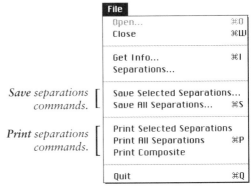

Figure 11. *File menu.*

Save options

Separator saves each separated color as a separate EPS file. The color name is appended to the file name. Choose **Save Selected Separations** from the File menu (**Figure 11**) to save *only* those colors you have selected to print ("Yes" in the Print column in the Separation dialog box). Choose **Save All Separations** to save every color in the illustration, regardless of its Separation window setting.

To get info about an Illustrator EPS file:

Choose Get Info from the File menu.

General: lists the PostScript header code for the EPS file.

Fonts: lists fonts used in the EPS file.

Patterns: lists Pattern Fills used in the EPS file.

(EPSF) Files: lists placed EPS images in the EPS file (**Figure 12**).

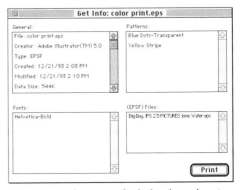

Figure 12. *The* **Get Info** *dialog box showing information about an EPS file.*

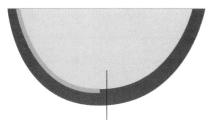

Figure 13. *Spread a lighter color foreground object.*

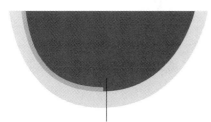

Figure 14. *Choke a darker color foreground object.*

What is trapping?

Trapping is the extension of a color so it overlaps another color. The purpose of trapping is to compensate for gaps that might appear between colors due to misregistration on press.

There are two basic kinds of traps. A **Spread** trap extends a lighter color object over a darker background color (**Figure 13**). A **Choke** trap extends a lighter background color over a darker color object (**Figure 14**). In either case, the extending color overprints the object or background color, creating a combination color where they overlap.

Ask print shop for advice before building traps into your illustration.

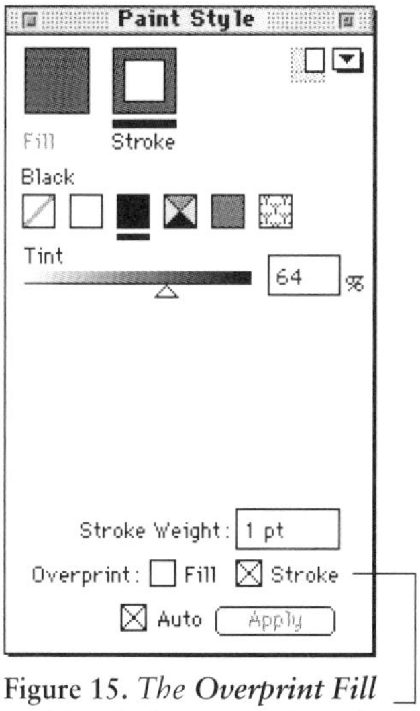

Figure 15. *The **Overprint Fill** and **Stroke** boxes on the right side of the **Paint Style** palette.*

To create a spread trap:

1. Select the lighter color foreground object (**Figure 13**).

2. Apply a Stroke in the same color as the object's Fill. The Stroke Weight should be **twice** the trap width suggested by your print shop for this object.

3. Check the Overprint Stroke box (**Figure 15**).

   The foreground object will overlap the background object by half the thickness of the new Stroke. The new Stroke will blend with the background color via the Overprint option. The Stroke will extend halfway inside and halfway outside the object's edge.

To create a choke trap:

1. Select the darker color foreground object (**Figure 14**).

2. Apply a Stroke in the same color as the lighter background object's Fill. Choose a Stroke Weight that is **twice** the trap width suggested by your print shop for this object.

3. Check the Overprint Stroke box (**Figure 15**).

   The lighter background object will now overlap by half the width of the new Stroke.

Tip

■ A choke trap reduces the area of the darker object by a half the Stroke Weight. Be careful if you choke type!

Figure 16. *Stroke a line.*

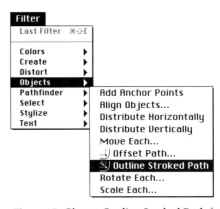

Figure 17. *Choose **Outline Stroked Path** from the **Objects** submenu under the **Filter** menu.*

To trap a line:

1. Apply a Stroke color and Weight (**Figure 16**).

2. Choose Outline Stroked Path from the Objects submenu under the Filter menu (**Figure 17**). The line will become a filled object, the same width as the original Stroke.

3. Apply a Stroke to the modified line. If the line is lighter than the background color, apply the same color as the Fill of the line. Otherwise, apply the lighter background color. Choose a Stroke Weight that is **twice** the trap width suggested by your print shop for this object.

4. Check the Overprint Stroke box (**Figure 15**).

   The line will now overlap the background color by half the width of the new Stroke. The Stroke will blend with the background color when it overprints.

Appendix A: Keyboard Shortcuts

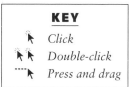

KEY
- Click
- Double-click
- Press and drag

FILES

New dialog box (without template)	⌘ N
New dialog box (with template)	⌘ Option N
Open dialog box	⌘ O
Close	⌘ W
Save	⌘ S
Document Setup dialog box	⌘ Shift D
General Preferences dialog box	⌘ K
Print dialog box	⌘ P
Quit Illustrator	⌘ Q

DIALOG BOXES

Highlight next field/option	Tab
Highlight previous field/option	Shift Tab
Select all characters in field	⌘ A
Delete all characters in field	⌘ A, then Delete
Cancel	⌘ . (Period key)
OK	Return
None	⌘ N

Open/Save dialog boxes (System 7.x)

Desktop	⌘ D
Up one folder level	⌘ Up Arrow
Open file	⭥⭥ file name

PALETTES

Show/Hide Paint Style	⌘ I
Show/Hide Toolbox	⌘ Control T
Reset Toolbox to default setting	⌘ Shift ⭥⭥ any tool
Reset current tool to default setting	Shift ⭥⭥ tool
Show/Hide Layers	⌘ Control L

Show/Hide Info	⌘ Control I
Show/Hide Character	⌘ T
Show/Hide Paragraph	⌘ Shift T

UNDO/REDO

Undo last operation	⌘ Z
Redo last undone operation	⌘ Shift Z

DISPLAY

Artview View	⌘ E
Preview View	⌘ Y
Preview Selection	⌘ Option Y
Display entire Artboard	↖↖ Hand tool
Fit in Window	⌘ M
Actual size (100%)	↖↖ Zoom tool -or- ⌘ H
Zoom out (Zoom tool selected)	Option ↖
Zoom in (any tool selected)	⌘ Spacebar ↖
Zoom out (any tool selected)	⌘ Option Spacebar ↖
Zoom In	⌘]
Zoom Out	⌘ [
Zoom in from center (Zoom tool selected)	Control ····↖
Use Hand tool (any tool selected)	Spacebar
Show/Hide Rulers	⌘ R
Show/Hide Edges	⌘ Shift H
New View dialog box	⌘ Control V
Hide a selected object	⌘ 3
Show All	⌘ 4

CREATE OBJECTS

Create object from center using Rectangle, Rounded Rectangle or Oval tool	Option ····↖
Toggle between Rectangle, Rounded Rectangle and Oval tools and their draw-from-center option	↖↖ tool
Create circle or square using Rectangle, Rounded Rectangle or Oval tool	Shift ····↖

SELECT

Use currently selected selection tool (any non-selection tool selected)	⌘
Toggle between Selection and Direct Selection tool	⌘ Tab

Keyboard Shortcuts

Use Group Selection tool (Direct Selection tool selected)	Option
Selection marquee (any selection tool)	····▸
Select All	⌘ A
Select None	⌘ Shift A

MOVE

Move dialog box	⌘ Shift M -or- ▸▸ Selection tool
Drag a copy of object	Option ····▸
Move selected object in 1-point increments	Direction arrows
Move object along nearest 45° angle	Shift

PATHS

Use Add Anchor Point tool (Pen tool selected)	Control (over segment)
Use Delete Anchor Point tool (Pen tool selected)	Control (over point)
Toggle between Add Anchor Point tool and Delete Anchor Point tool (either selected)	Option
Use Convert Direction Point tool (Pen tool selected)	Control Option
Use Convert Direction Point tool (any selection tool selected)	Control
Use Convert Direction Point tool (any tool selected except Scissors tool, Add/Delete Anchor Point tools)	Control
Use Convert Direction Point tool (Freehand tool selected)	⌘ Option Control
Use Rotate direction line (Pen tool selected)	Option ····▸
Constrain angle of direction line to nearest 45° angle (Direct Selection tool or Convert Direction Point tool selected)	Shift, ····▸
Convert a smooth point into a corner point using Direct Selection tool	Control ····▸
Convert a smooth point into a corner point using Pen tool	Control Option ····▸
Convert a non-continuous curve into a continuous curve using Direct Selection tool	Control ▸ (on direction point)
Use Pen tool (Freehand tool selected)	Control
Use Add Anchor Point tool (Freehand tool selected, over segment)	⌘ Control
Use Delete Anchor Point tool (Freehand tool selected, over point)	⌘ Control

Keyboard Shortcuts

Keyboard Shortcuts

Use Convert Direction Point tool (Freehand tool selected)	⌘ Option Control
Erase while drawing with Freehand tool	⌘ ⤴ (on path)
Use Pen tool (Autotrace tool selected)	Control
Join two selected endpoints	⌘ J
Average two selected points	⌘ L
Average and Join two selected endpoints	⌘ Option J

PAINT

Toggle between Eyedropper tool and Paint Bucket tool (either selected)	Option

RESTACK

Bring To Front	⌘ = (Equal key)
Send To Back	⌘ – (Minus key)
Paste In Front	⌘ F
Paste In Back	⌘ B

TYPE

Use Area Type tool (Type tool selected, over open path)	Option
Use Path Type tool (Type tool selected, over closed path)	Option
Use Type tool (Area Type or Path Type tool selected)	Control Option
Select a word	↖↖
Select a paragraph	↖↖↖
Select all type	⌘ A
Link Blocks	⌘ Shift G
Unlink Blocks	⌘ Shift U
Align left	⌘ Shift L
Align center	⌘ Shift C
Align right	⌘ Shift R
Justify	⌘ Shift J
Justify last line	⌘ Shift B
Increase point size	⌘ Shift >
Decrease point size	⌘ Shift <
Increase leading	Option Down Arrow
Decrease leading	Option Up Arrow
Increase kerning/tracking	Option Right Arrow
Decrease kerning/tracking	Option Left Arrow

Increase kerning/tracking 5x	⌘ Option Right Arrow
Decrease kerning/tracking 5x	⌘ Option Left Arrow
Increase Baseline Shift	Shift Option Up Arrow
Decrease Baseline Shift	Shift Option Down Arrow
Force Hyphenate a word	⌘ Shift – (Hyphen key)

TRANSFORM

Transformation tool dialog box (any transformation tool selected)	Option ⬆
Transform object along nearest 45° angle (Shear or Reflect tool)	Shift ⋯⬆
Rotate object in 45° increments (Rotate tool)	Shift ⋯⬆
Scale object uniformly (Scale tool)	Shift ⋯⬆
Scale object along nearest 45° angle (Scale tool)	Shift ⋯⬆
Repeat transformation	⌘ D
Transform Pattern Fill only (after clicking with transformation tool)	P ⋯⬆
Transform copy of object (after clicking with transformation tool)	Option ⋯⬆

COMPOUNDS

Make Compound Path	⌘ 8
Release Compound Path	⌘ 9

CLIPBOARD

Cut	⌘ X
Copy	⌘ C
Paste	⌘ V

PRECISION TOOLS

Make Guides	⌘ 5
Release Guides	⌘ 6
Lock/Unlock Guides	⌘ 7
Constrain Measure tool to nearest 45° angle	Shift ⬆ or ⬆⬆
Lock (selected object)	⌘ 1
Unlock All	⌘ 2

MISC.

Attributes dialog box	⌘ Control A
Group	⌘ G
Ungroup	⌘ U

Appendix B: Illustrator 5.5

I F IT SEEMS LIKE YOU'VE JUST BARELY CAUGHT YOUR BREATH since the release of Illustrator 5.0, you'll be glad to know you don't have to relearn anything when you upgrade to Illustrator 5.5. Most of the Illustrator 5.5 revision consists of easy-to-use text editing features that you can familiarize yourself with at your leisure.

The new **Text** filters, accessed from a submenu under the Filter menu, change case, check spelling, find and change fonts, arrange text in vertical columns and horizontal rows, and convert keyboard punctuation into professional typesetting marks (smart punctuation). **Tabs** can now be created in Illustrator using a new Tab Ruler.

Other new filters include a **Document Information** filter that displays document specifications or information about a selected object, an **Overprint Black** filter for specifying which Black objects will overprint, a **Custom to Process** filter for converting colors in individual objects, and a **Trap** filter for applying automatic trapping.

A few features from the previous version of Illustrator were improved. Problems printing Gradient Fills can be corrected via a check box in the Document Setup dialog box. The Pathfinder Divide Stroke and Merge Stroke filters were replaced by the **Outline** filter. Multiple pop-up menus in the Save dialog box were combined into one Format pop-up menu. And **object PICTS** can now be opened in Illustrator.

Two features from Illustrator 5.0 that were not covered in the previous edition of this book are covered in this appendix: the **Export** command for exporting text and the **Find** command for finding and replacing characters.

Text filters

The **Change Case** filter changes selected text to all UPPER CASE, all lower case, or Mixed Case (initial capitals).

To change case:

1. Select text with a type tool.

2. Choose Change Case from the Text submenu under the Filter menu (**Figure 1**).

3. Click Upper case, lower case, or Mixed Case (**Figure 2**).

4. Click OK or press Return.

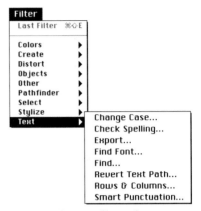

Figure 1. *The* **Text** *filter submenu.*

The **Check Spelling** filter checks spelling in your entire illustration using a built-in dictionary. You can also create your own word list.

To check spelling:

1. Choose Check Spelling from the Text submenu under the Filter menu (**Figure 1**).

2. Leave the currently highlighted Misspelled Word selected or click a different word on the list (**Figure 3**). The word will be highlighted in your illustration.

3. *Optional:* Check the Case Sensitive box to display the Misspelled Word separately if it appears in different cases (such as *Spelle* and *spelle*).

4. **To correct a word with one keystroke:** Press Return to replace the first instance of the word with the currently highlighted Suggested Correction.
or
Double-click a word on the Suggested Corrections scroll list. If no Suggestion Correction appears, there is no similar word in the dictionary.

To correct a word using more than one keystroke:
Click a word on the Suggested Corrections scroll list (**Figure 3**).

Figure 2. *Click an option in the* **Change Case** *dialog box.*

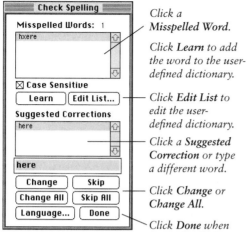

Click a
Misspelled Word.

Click **Learn** to add
the word to the user-
defined dictionary.

Click **Edit List** to
edit the user-
defined dictionary.

Click a **Suggested
Correction** or type
a different word.

Click **Change** or
Change All.

Click **Done** when
you're finished.

Figure 3. *The Check Spelling
dialog box.*

or
Type the correct word in the entry
field. As you type, words starting
with those letters will display on the
Suggested Corrections scroll list.
You can continue to type the whole
word yourself or you can click on any
Suggested Correction.

Then:
Click **Change** to change only the first
occurrence of the Misspelled Word to
the currently highlighted Suggested
Correction.
or
Click **Change All** to change all occurrences of the Misspelled Word.
or
Click **Skip** to leave the Misspelled
Word unchanged.
or
Click **Skip All** to leave all occurrences
of the Misspelled Word unchanged.

5. *Optional:* Click Learn to add the
currently highlighted Misspelled
Word or Words to the Learned Words
list (user-defined dictionary) (**Figure
4**). To add more than one word at a
time, hold down Command (⌘) while
clicking on the words, then click
Learn. Learned Words are added to
the AI User Dictionary file in the Plug-
Ins folder.

6. Click Done.

Tips

■ To modify the Learned Words list
(user-defined dictionary), click Edit
List in the Check Spelling dialog
box, click on a word, retype it, then
click Change; or click on a word,
then click Remove; or type a new
word, then click Add. Hyphenated
words are permitted.

■ There is a bug in this feature: the
corrected word will take on the
styling of the text preceding it, not
the original styling of the Misspelled
Word.

Or highlight a
Learned Word,
then click **Remove.**

Click **Done** when
you're finished.

Highlight a Learned
Word, retype it,
then click **Change.**

Or type a new word,
then click **Add.**

Figure 4. *Create your own word list
using the **Learned Words** dialog box.*

Use the **Export** command to save
Illustrator text in a format that can be
imported into another application.
*(The Export feature was included in the
previous version of Illustrator.)*

To export text:

1. Highlight the text you wish to
export with the Text tool.

2. Choose Export from the Text submenu under the Filter menu.

3. Choose a drive and folder in which
to save the text file (**Figure 5**).

4. Choose a format from the "Export
file" pop-up menu.

5. Enter a name for the new file.

6. Click Export.

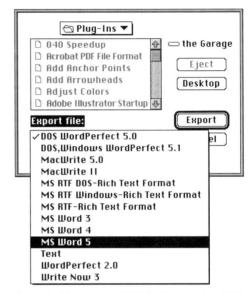

Figure 5. *Choose one of 13 file formats in which
to save your selected text from the Export file
pop-up menu.*

Use the **Find Font** filter to generate a list
of the fonts currently being used in an
illustration, or use it to replace fonts.

To find and replace a font:

1. Choose Find Font from the Text
submenu under the Filter menu.

2. Click a font to search for on the
Find Fonts in Document scroll list
(**Figure 6**).

3. Check one or more of the Multiple
Master, Standard, Type 1 Fonts, or
TrueType boxes to selectively
display only fonts of those types on
the scroll lists.

4. Leave the Document List button
highlighted to display on the Replace
Fonts list only fonts currently being
used in your document of the types
checked in Step 3.

or

Click System List to display on the
Replace Fonts list all the fonts currently available in your system. (To
stop the list from displaying, click the
Document List button.)

Export Text; Find and Replace Fonts

5. Click a replacement font on the Replace Fonts scroll list.

6. Click Change to change only the first occurrence of the "Find Font."

or

Click Change All to change all occurrences of the "Find Font."

7. *Optional:* To create a list of the fonts currently being used in the illustration as a TeachText document, click Save, enter a name, choose a location in which to save the file, then click Save. The TeachText document can later be opened directly from the Finder.

8. Click Done.

Tip

■ To compose a document list before opening the Find Font dialog box, create text in your illustration and apply the desired fonts to it. Or, Copy a text object containing the fonts you wish to add from another document, then Paste it into your document.

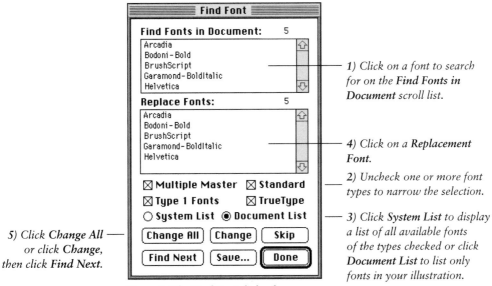

1) *Click on a font to search for on the* **Find Fonts in Document** *scroll list.*

4) *Click on a* **Replacement Font.**

2) *Uncheck one or more font types to narrow the selection.*

3) *Click* **System List** *to display a list of all available fonts of the types checked or click* **Document List** *to list only fonts in your illustration.*

5) *Click* **Change All** *or click* **Change,** *then click* **Find Next.**

Figure 6. *The* **Find Font** *dialog box.*

Use the **Find** dialog box to search for and replace characters.

(The Find feature was included in the previous version of Illustrator.)

To find and replace text:

1. *Optional:* Click with the Type tool to create an insertion point to search from that location. If no text object is selected in your document, the search will begin from the most recently created object.

2. Choose Find from the Text submenu under the Filter menu.

3. Enter a word or phrase to search for in the "Find what" field (**Figure 7**).

4. Enter a replacement word or phrase in the "Replace with" field.

Steps 5-8 are optional:

5. Check the Whole Word box to find the "Find what" letters only if they appear as a complete word — not as part of a larger word.

6. Check the Case Sensitive box to find only those occurrences that match the exact uppercase/lowercase configuration of the "Find what" text.

7. Check the Wrap Around box to

search from the current cursor position to the end of the text object or string of linked objects and then continue the search from the most recently created object.

8. Check the Search Backward box to search backward.

9. Click **Find Next** to search for the first occurrence of the "Find what" word or phrase.

10. Click **Replace** to replace only the first occurrence of the "Find what" text.

or

Click **Replace, then Find** to replace the first occurrence and automatically search for the next occurrence.

or

Click **Replace All** to replace all occurrences at once.

11. Click Done.

Tip

■ There is a bug in this feature: the replacement word will take on the styling of the text preceding it, not the original styling of the "Find what" text.

Figure 7. *In the **Text Find** dialog box, enter text you wish to search for in the **Find what** field and text you wish to change it to in the **Replace with** field. Click **Find Next**, then click **Replace, then Find**, or click **Replace**, or click **Replace All**.*

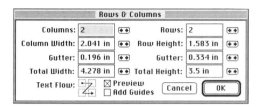

Figure 8. *The Rows & Columns dialog box.*

HERE is some *text* to *arrange* with the Rows & Columns **filter** in the **new** 5.5 illustrator. Notice how **the** text flows from box to box automatically.

Figure 9. *One text object...*

HERE is some *text* to *arrange*

with the Rows & Columns **filter** in the

new 5.5 illustrator. Notice how

the text flows from box to box automatically.

Figure 10. *...converted into two columns and two rows.*

The **Rows & Columns** filter arranges text into columns and/or rows.

To create linked text rows and columns:

1. Select a text object with the Selection tool.

2. Choose Rows & Columns from the Text submenu under the Filter menu.

3. Check the Preview box to apply changes immediately (**Figure 8**).

4. Click the left/right arrows or enter values in the fields to choose:

   The total number of Columns and Rows to be produced.
   and
   The Width of each Column and the Height of each Row.
   and
   The Gutter (space) between each Column and each Row.
   and
   The Total Width and Total Height of the entire block of Columns and Rows.

5. Click the Text Flow icon to have text flow from column to column (vertically) or from row to row (horizontally).

6. Check the Add Guides box to display a grid around the text blocks.

7. Click OK or press Return (**Figures 9-10**).

Tips

■ The Cancel button will not cancel changes if the Preview box is checked. Choose Undo from the Edit menu to undo Rows & Columns changes.

■ If you select the entire block of rows and columns with the Selection tool and then reopen the Rows & Columns dialog box, the current settings for that block will be displayed.

Rows and Columns

To convert a text object into a graphic object:

1. Choose a text tool, select all the text in the object, then press Delete.

2. Choose a selection tool, then click on the object.

3. Choose **Revert Text Path** from the Text submenu under the Filter menu.

4. Check the Delete Text Path box to convert the original text path into a graphic object; uncheck it to convert a copy of the original text path (the graphic object will appear on top of the original text object) (**Figure 11**).

5. Click OK or press Return.

Tip

■ Apply the Revert Text Path filter if you inadvertently click on a graphic object with a type tool, or choose Undo instead. The original Fill and Stroke colors of the object will not be restored if you apply the Revert Text Path filter.

Figure 11. *The **Revert Text Path** dialog box.*

Use the **Smart Punctuation** filter to convert keyboard punctuation into professional typesetting marks.

To create smart punctuation:

1. *Optional:* Select a block of text to change punctuation in that text only.

2. Choose Smart Punctuation from the Text submenu under the Filter menu.

3. Check any of the punctuation option boxes on the left side of the dialog box (**Figure 12**).

4. Click Selected Text Only or Entire Document.

5. *Optional:* Check Report Results to display a dialog box listing the changes you just made.

Tip

■ To access the Ligatures and Expert Fractions options, the Expert font set for the font you are using must be available in your System.

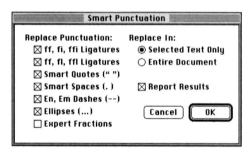

Figure 12. *Check any of the punctuation option boxes on the left side of the **Smart Punctuation** dialog box.*

DIALOG BOX OPTION	KEYBOARD	SMART PUNCTUATION
ff, fi, ffi Ligatures	ff, fi, ffi	ff, fi, ffi
ff, fi, ffl Ligatures	ff, fi, ffl	ff, fi, ffl
Smart Quotes	' "	' " " '
Smart Spaces	. T	. T
En, Em Dashes	--	–
	---	—
Ellipses	...	...
Expert Fractions	1/2	½

Revert Text Path; Smart Punctuation

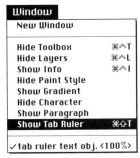

Figure 13. *Choose **Show Tab Ruler** from the **Window** menu.*

Basic Plaid Country Club

	Front 9	Back 9	Total
Arnie	38	44	82
Jack	34	36	70
Lee	42	48	90
Hubie	34	35	69

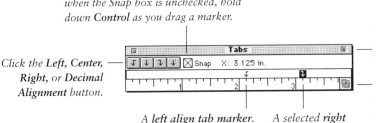

Figure 14. *Text aligned using custom tab stops.*

Default tab stops are half an inch apart. The **Tab Ruler**, displayed as a floating palette, is used to set custom tab stops.

To insert tabs into text:

Press Tab as you input copy before typing each new column. The cursor will jump to the next tab stop.

or

To add a tab to already inputted text, click to the left of the text that is to start a new column, then press Tab.

To set a custom tab stop:

1. Choose the Selection tool and select a text object that contains tab characters.

or

Choose the Text tool and select text containing tab characters.

2. Choose Show Tab Ruler from the Window menu (**Figure 13**).

3. Click in the Tab Ruler where the tab stop is to occur. Text will align to the new stop immediately (**Figure 15**).

4. Click the Left, Center, Right, or Decimal tab alignment button on the left side of the palette (**Figure 14**).

Tip

■ To delete a tab stop, drag the tab marker up and out of the ruler. As you drag it, the word *delete* will display on the palette.

*Check the **Snap** box to have a tab marker snap to the nearest ruler increment as you insert it or drag it. Or, to temporarily turn on the Snap feature when the Snap box is unchecked, hold down **Control** as you drag a marker.*

*Click the **Left, Center, Right,** or **Decimal Alignment** button.*

*Click the **Alignment** box to align the Tab Ruler with the left margin of the selected text.*

*Drag the **Extend Tab ruler** box to the right to widen the ruler.*

*A **left align tab marker.** To move a tab stop, drag the marker left or right.*

*A selected **right align tab marker.***

Figure 15. *The **Tab Ruler**.*

The Document Info filter:

Choose **Document Info** from the Other submenu under the Filter menu (**Figure 16**) to display information about a selected object (or objects) or about the entire illustration.

If an object is selected, the Selection Info dialog box displays information about custom colors, patterns, gradients, fonts and/or placed art in the object (**Figure 17**). To view more detailed information on one of these elements, choose Custom Colors, Patterns, Gradients, Fonts, or Placed Art from the Info pop-up menu. Click Done when you're finished.

If no object is selected and Document is chosen from the Info pop-up menu, the dialog box displays the current Document Setup dialog box settings (**Figure 18**). You can also choose to display information about all Objects, all Custom Colors, etc.

Click Save to save the Document Info as a TeachText document. Choose a folder in which to save the TeachText file, enter a new name for the file, if desired, then click Save. To open the TeachText document, double-click the file icon in the Finder. You can print this file and refer to it when you prepare your document for imagesetting.

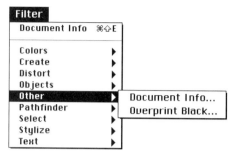

Figure 16. *Choose* **Document Info** *from the* **Other** *submenu under the* **Filter** *menu.*

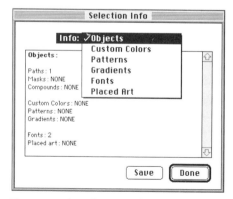

Figure 17. *The* **Selection Info** *dialog box (an object is selected in the illustration).*

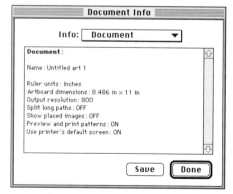

Figure 18. *The* **Document Info** *dialog box (no objects are selected).*

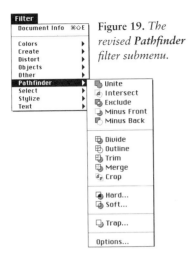

Figure 19. *The revised* **Pathfinder** *filter submenu.*

Figure 20a. *Before applying the Outline filter.*

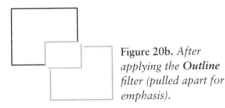

Figure 20b. *After applying the* **Outline** *filter (pulled apart for emphasis).*

Updated Pathfinder filters:

The **Divide** and **Merge** filters function as they did in version 5.0, with one improvement: Gradient Fills are preserved.

The **Outline** filter replaces the Divide Stroke and Merge Stroke filters (**Figure 19**). When this filter is applied, areas where objects overlap become separate objects. All Fill colors are removed, and the objects are Stroked with the removed Fill color, but with a Stroke Weight of zero (**Figures 20a-b**).

The **Trim** filter removes all Stroke colors and removes areas where objects overlap. The frontmost object is not divided; objects behind it are divided. Adjacent or overlapping areas of the same color remain separate (unlike the Merge filter).

The **Hard** and **Soft** filters replace the Mix Hard and Mix Soft filters. Dialog boxes for both filters now include a check box option for converting custom colors to process colors.

The **Crop Stroke** filter was eliminated.

PICT files created in object-oriented drawing programs such as MacDraw, DeltaGraph, and the CAD programs can be opened in Illustrator 5.5.

To open an object PICT in Illustrator:

1. Choose Open from the File menu.
2. Highlight the file you wish to import.
3. Click Open.
4. Click Illustrator Template (PICT) to convert the PICT into a Template (**Figure 21**).
   or
   Click PICT to open it as placed art. *(See page 35 for more information about placed art)* (You cannot open a PICT file that was created in a bitmapped program, such as Photoshop.)

Figure 21. *In the* **Open** *dialog box, click* **Illustrator Template** *to open the PICT as a non-editable image for tracing, or click* **PICT** *to open it as placed art.*

Outline, Trim filters; Open an Object PICT

Normally, in PostScript color separations, objects on top *knock out* the color of objects underneath them so inks don't mix with each other on press. When a color *overprints,* it prints right on top of the color beneath it and mixes with that color. Black is sometimes printed this way to eliminate the need for trapping. Using the **Overprint Black** filter, you can specify which Black areas will overprint. CONSULT WITH YOUR PRINT SHOP BEFORE USING THIS FEATURE.

Note: To access the Overprint Black filter, move its icon from the Optional Plug-Ins folder to the Plug-Ins folder, then restart Illustrator.

To overprint Black:

1. *Optional:* To overprint Black in just one object, select that object.

2. Choose Overprint Black from the Other submenu under the Filter menu.

3. Click Add to turn the Overprint option on for the specified "Percentage black" you enter (**Figure 22**).

4. Enter an amount in the "Percentage black" field. Objects containing this Black percentage will overprint. Ask your print shop what value to use.

5. Click Fill or Stroke to overprint only Black Fills *or* Strokes, or click Both to overprint Fills *and* Strokes.

6. Click Selected to overprint Black in the currently selected object only.
or
Click All to overprint all Blacks of the designated "Percentage black."

7. Check the "Include Blacks with CMY" box to have any CMYK color containing the "Percentage black" overprint.

8. Check the "Include Custom Blacks" box to have any custom color containing the "Percentage black" overprint.

9. Click OK or press Return.

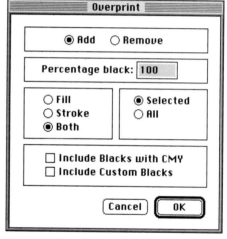

Figure 22. *The Overprint dialog box.*

Overprint Black

The new **Trap** filter creates traps automatically by determining which color object is lighter and then spreading that color into the darker object.

Note: The Trap filter cannot be applied to an object containing a Gradient Fill, a Pattern Fill, or placed art, or an object with a Stroke color but no Fill color.

To create traps automatically:

1. Select two or more objects.

2. Choose Trap from the Pathfinder submenu under the Filter menu.

3. Enter the Thickness amount specified by your print shop for the trap (**Figure 23**).

STEPS 4-6 ARE OPTIONAL. ASK YOUR PRINT SHOP FOR ADVICE.

4. Enter a value in the Height/width field to counter paper stretch on press.

5. Enter a value in the Tint reduction field to prevent the trap area between light colors from being too dark.

6. Check "Convert custom colors to process" to convert custom colors in the selected objects into process colors.

To create a trap on top of a Fill and a Stroke (a workaround):

The Trap filter does not take into account the Stroke color of underlying objects. To overcome this limitation, convert the Stroke into a filled object.

1. Choose the Selection tool, then click on the background object that has a Fill and Stroke.

2. Choose Outline Path from the Objects submenu under the Filter menu.

3. Deselect both objects, then click on the outermost object (the "Stroke").

4. Choose Unite from the Pathfinder submenu under the Filter menu to remove any excess points from the outline path object.

5. Apply the Trap filter *(instructions above)*.

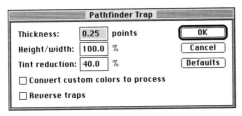

Figure 23. *Enter a trap* **Thickness** *in the* Pathfinder Trap *dialog box.*

TRAPPING TIP

Apply automatic trapping *after* you finalize the size of the objects. If you apply automatic trapping and then change an object's size, the trap width will change.

Automatic Trapping

Multiple pop-up menus in the Save and Save as dialog boxes were replaced by a **Format** pop-up menu. You can choose from seven file formats in which to save your illustration.

To save an illustration as an EPS:

1. For a new, untitled illustration, choose Save from the File menu.
or
For an existing illustration, choose Save as from the File menu.

2. Enter a name in the "Save this document as" field (**Figure 24**).

3. Click Desktop.

4. Highlight a drive, then click Open.

5. *Optional*: Highlight a folder in which to save the file, then click Open.

6. Choose EPS from the Format pop-up menu.

7. Click Save or press Return.

8. Click 1-bit IBM PC or 1-bit Macintosh to create a black & white preview (**Figure 25**).
or
Click 8-bit Macintosh to create a color preview. This option will produce the largest file storage size.

9. Click a Compatibility option. The newest version of Illustrator is the default Compatibility option.

10. Check the Include Placed Images box to save a copy of a placed EPS file with the illustration.

11. Click OK or press Return.

Tips

■ To save a file in the Acrobat (PDF) format, make sure the Acrobat Exchange program is installed.

■ To import an Illustrator file in another application, such as QuarkXPress or PageMaker, save it in an EPS format.

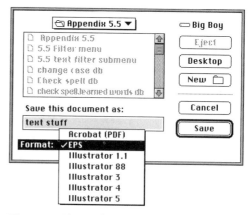

Figure 24. *Choose from the new **Format** pop-up menu in the Save or Save as dialog box.*

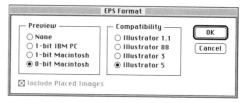

Figure 25. *Choose **Preview** and **Compatibility** options in the **EPS Format** dialog box.*

Save as EPS

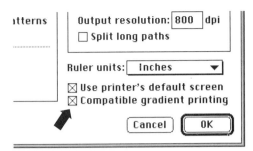

Figure 26. *For improved Gradient Fill printing on a PostScript Level 1 imagesetter, check the* **Compatible gradient printing** *box in the* **Document Setup** *dialog box.*

Improved printing:

1) Many users encountered problems when printing **Gradient Fills** from Illustrator 5.0. To improve Gradient printing on a PostScript Level 1 image-setter, check the new "Compatible gradient printing" box in the Document Setup dialog box, opened from the File menu (**Figure 26**).

Note: Don't check this option if your gradients are printing well — it may slow printing.

2) If you print an Illustrator 5.5 docu-ment from an earlier Illustrator version, you will not be able to take advantage of printing improvements in Illustrator 5.5, and text containing tabs may reflow. Before printing your 5.5 document from an earlier version, save the 5.5 version as an EPS.

You can convert a custom color to a process color in an individual object using the **Custom to Process** filter.

Note: To access the Custom to Process filter, move its icon from the Optional Plug-Ins folder to the Plug-Ins folder, then restart Illustrator.

To convert a custom color to a process color in an object:

1. Select an object with a custom color.

2. Choose Custom to Process from the Colors submenu under the Filter menu.

3. Check the Retain Tint box to make the CMYK color the same tint (lightness) as the original custom color (**Figure 27**).

4. Click OK or press Return.

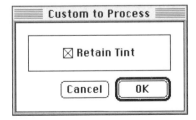

Figure 27. *Check or uncheck the* **Retain Tint** *box in the* **Custom to Process** *dialog box.*

Index

Index

Index

More from Peachpit Press

Camera Ready with QuarkXPress

Cyndie Kopfenstein

A practical guide to creating direct-to-press documents using XPress. Includes a disk full of QuarkXPress templates that you can use to create postcards, brochures and other common documents. $35 *(206 pages)*

Desktop Publisher's Survival Kit

David Blatner

Here is a book that provides insights into desktop publishing on the Macintosh: troubleshooting print jobs, working with color, scanning, and selecting fonts. A disk containing 12 top desktop publishing utilities, 400K of clip art, and two fonts is included in this package. $22.95 *(176 pages)*

DIrector 4 for Macintosh: Visual QuickStart Guide

Helmut Kobler and Andre Persidsky

Learn the basics of Macromedia Director, including the paint window, tools, how to use color, animation techniques, setting the tempo, and more. $18.95 *(248 pages)*

Everyone's Guide to Successful Publications

Elizabeth Adler

This comprehensive reference book pulls together all the information essential to developing and producing printed materials that will get your message across. Packed with ideas, practical advice, examples, and hundreds of photographs and illustrations, it discusses planning the printed piece, writing, design, desktop publishing, preparation for printing, and distribution. $28 *(412 pages)*

Four Colors/One Image

Mattias Nyman

Find step-by-step procedures and detailed explanations on how to reproduce and manipulate color images using Photoshop, QuarkXPress and Cachet. A terrific, invaluable resource for those who need high-quality color output. $18 *(84 pages)*

How to Boss Your Fonts Around

Robin Williams

Ever had a power struggle with your fonts? This book will put *you* in control and answer all your Macintosh font questions. What is a screen font, an outline font, a resident font, a downloadable font? What is ATM? How do you install fonts, use Suitcase or MasterJuggler, avoid font ID conflicts and make sure your fonts print at a service bureau? Written in a friendly style by the author of the bestselling *The Little Mac Book*. $12.95 *(120 pages)*

The Illustrator 5.0/5.5 Book

Deke McClelland

Experienced Illustrator users and novices alike will learn many helpful tips and techniques. Very thorough and comprehensive, *The Illustrator 5.0/5.5 Book* gives in-depth coverage of Illustrator's latest features. $29.95 *(660 pages)*

Illustrator Illuminated, 2nd Edition

Clay Andres

Illustrator Illuminated uses full-color graphics to show how professional artists use Illustrator's tools to create a variety of styles and effects. Each chapter shows the creation of a specific illustration from concept through completion. Additionally, it covers using Illustrator in conjunction with Adobe Streamline and Photoshop. $24.95 *(200 pages)*

Jargon: An Informal Dictionary of Computer Terms

Robin Williams with Steve Cummings

Finally! A book that explains over 1,200 of the most useful computer terms in a way that readers can understand. This book is a straightforward guide that not only defines computer-related terms but also explains how and why they are used. It covers both the Macintosh and PC worlds. No need to ask embarrassing questions: Just look it up in *Jargon!* $22 *(688 pages)*

The Little Mac Book, 4th Edition

Robin Williams

Praised by scores of magazines and user group newsletters, this concise, beautifully written book covers the basics of Macintosh operation. It provides useful reference information, including charts of typefaces, special characters, and keyboard shortcuts. This fourth edition is totally updated and cooler than ever. $17.95 *(408 pages)*

The Macintosh Bible, 5th Edition

Edited by Darcy DiNucci

This classic reference book is now completely updated. *The Macintosh Bible, 5th Edition* is crammed with tips, tricks, and shortcuts that will help you to get the most out of your Mac. $30 *(1,100 pages)*

The Macintosh Bible "What Do I Do Now?" Book, 3rd Edition

Charles Rubin

Completely updated, this bestseller covers just about every sort of basic problem a Mac user can encounter. The book shows the error message exactly as it appears on screen, explains the problem (or problems) that can produce the message, and discusses what to do. This book is geared for beginners and experienced users alike. *$22 (352 pages)*

The Mac is not a typewriter

Robin Williams

This best-selling, elegant guide to typesetting on the Mac has received rave reviews for its clearly presented information, friendly tone, and easy access. Twenty quick and easy chapters cover what you need to know to make your documents look clean and professional. $9.95 *(72 pages)*

PageMaker 5 for Macintosh: Visual QuickStart Guide

Webster and Associates

Here's an ideal book for new users and for those who want to use the latest features of PageMaker 5. Learn about many powerful innovations through an easy, right-brained approach that shows you how to get the most out of PageMaker. $13.95 *(234 pages)*

Photoshop 3 for Macintosh: Visual QuickStart Guide

Elaine Weinmann and Peter Lourekas

Completely revised for Photoshop 3, this indispensable guide is for Mac users who want to get started in Adobe Photoshop but don't like to read long explanations. QuickStart books focus on illustrated, step-by-step examples that cover how to use masks, filters, colors, and more. $19.95 *(264 pages)*

The Photoshop 3 Wow! Book (Mac Edition)

Linnea Dayton and Jack Davis

This book is really two books in one: an easy-to-follow, step-by-step tutorial of Photoshop fundamentals and over 150 pages of tips and techniques for getting the most out of Photoshop version 3. Full color throughout, *The Photoshop Wow! Book* shows how professional artists make the best use of Photoshop. Includes a CD-ROM containing Photoshop filters and utilities. $39.95 *(208 pages, includes CD-ROM, available Fall 1995)*

The QuarkXPress Book, 4th Edition (Mac Edition)

David Blatner and Eric Taub

This is the highest rated, most comprehensive, and best-selling QuarkXPress book ever published. Now totally updated to cover the newest version, this book is made for easy access, including a handy tear-out keystroke shortcut card. You'll find valuable information on XTensions, EfiColor, AppleEvent scripting and more. Winner of the 1991 Benjamin Franklin Award (computer book category). $29.95 *(784 pages)*

QuarkXPress 3.3 for Macintosh: Visual QuickStart Guide

Elaine Weinmann

Winner of the 1992 Benjamin Franklin Award, this book is a terrific way to get introduced to QuarkXPress in just a couple of hours. Lots of illustrations and screen shots make each feature of the program absolutely clear. This book is helpful to both beginners and intermediate QuarkXPress users. $15.95 *(240 pages)*

QuarkXPress Tips & Tricks, 2nd Edition

David Blatner and Eric Taub

The smartest, most useful shortcuts from *The QuarkXPress Book*—plus many more—are packed into this book. You'll find answers to common questions as well as insights on techniques that will show you how to become a QuarkXPress power user. Includes a CD-ROM with useful XTensions and demos. $21.95 *(286 pages, includes CD-ROM)*

Real World Scanning and Halftones

David Blatner and Steve Roth

Master the digital halftone process—from scanning images to tweaking them on your computer to imagesetting them. Learn about optical character recognition, gamma control, sharpening, PostScript halftones, Photo CD and image-manipulating applications like Photoshop and PhotoStyler. $24 *(296 pages)*

ZAP! How your computer can hurt you—and what you can do about it

Don Sellers

This unusual resource book covers everything from eyestrain to pregnancy to carpal tunnel and back problems. *ZAP!* will help you work smarter—and healthier. $12.95 *(150 pages)*

 # Order Form

TOLL-FREE **800-283-9444** • LOCAL **510-548-4393** • FAX **510-548-5991**

Qty	Title	Price	Total
		SUBTOTAL	
		8.25% TAX (CA ONLY)	
Shipping is by UPS ground: $4 for first item, $1 each add'l.		SHIPPING	
		TOTAL	

Customer Information

NAME

COMPANY

STREET ADDRESS

CITY   STATE   ZIP

PHONE (   )   FAX (   )

Payment Method

❏ CHECK ENCLOSED   ❏ VISA   ❏ MASTERCARD

CREDIT CARD #   EXPIRATION DATE

COMPANY PURCHASE ORDER #

Tell Us What You Think

PLEASE TELL US WHAT YOU THOUGHT OF THIS BOOK:

WHAT OTHER BOOKS WOULD YOU LIKE US TO PUBLISH?

MAC   **PEACHPIT PRESS** • **2414 Sixth Street** • Berkeley, CA 94710